ATATÜR

PROFILES IN POWER
General Editor: Keith Robbins

. . . . .

ATATÜRK

A. L. Macfie

LONGMAN
London and New York

Longman Group UK Limited
Longman House, Burnt Mill
Harlow, Essex CM20 2JE, England
and Associated Companies throughout the world.

Published in the United States of America
by Longman Publishing, New York

© Longman Group UK Limited 1994

First published 1994

ISBN 0 582 078628 CSD
ISBN 0 582 078636 PPR

British Library Cataloguing-in-Publication Data

A catalogue record for this book is
available from the British Library

Library of Congress Cataloging-in-Publication Data

Macfie, A. L.
    Atatürk / A. L. Macfie.
    p. cm. — (Profiles in power)
    Includes bibliographical references and index.
    ISBN 0–582–07862–8 (cased). — ISBN 0–582–07863–6 (pbk.)
    1. Atatürk, Kemal, 1881–1938. 2. Presidents—Turkey—Biography.
    3. Turkey—History—1918–1960. I. Title. II. Series:
Profiles in power (London, England)
DR592.K4M3 1994
956.1′024′092—dc20
    [B]
                              93–33763
                                  CIP

Set by 5 in 10½pt Baskerville
Produced by Longman Singapore Publishers (Pte) Ltd.
Printed in Singapore

CONTENTS

CONTENTS

LIST OF MAPS

GLOSSARY

Caliph	Muslim religious leader, successor of Muhammed.
Committee of Union and Progress (CUP)	The secret society which organised the so-called Young Turk revolution of 1908, and later, as a political party, controlled the government of the Ottoman Empire in the period of the Balkan and First World Wars.
devşirme	Christian slave levy.
fedaî	Volunteer, prepared to sacrifice himself for the cause.
Ghazi	Destroyer of Christians.
Grand Vizier	Chief official of the Ottoman state.
imam	Prayer leader.
kadi	judge
Karakol	A secret organisation set up in the Ottoman Empire in 1918.
medrese	Muslim theological school.
millet	A religious community or nation.
Milli Müdafaa (MM)	The intelligence service established by Mustafa Kemal in 1920.
mufti	Muslim priest or expounder of the law.
Padişah	Sultan
People's Party	The political party established by Mustafa Kemal in 1923.
rayah (raâya)	In the wider sense of the word, the productive, tax-paying subjects of the empire. In the narrower, farmers as distinct from urban dwellers and nomads.
sanjak	An administrative unit of the Ottoman Empire.
Sadrazam	The Grand Vizier.

GLOSSARY

Şeriat	Muslim law.
Sheikh-ül-Islâm	Head of the Ulema.
Sultan	Ruler, sovereign.
Tanzimat	A reform movement, instituted in the Ottoman Empire in the nineteenth century.
Ulema	A corps of learned men, trained in the religion of Islam.
vilayet	Province.
Zeybek	A Turkish inhabitant of south-western Anatolia.

INTRODUCTION

. . . .

ACHIEVEMENT

The achievements of Mustafa Kemal Atatürk, the so-called founder of modern Turkey, must be considered by any standards remarkable. In a few short years, from his despatch, as Inspector of the Third Army, to Anatolia in May 1919 to his election as president of the first Turkish republic in October 1923, he succeeded, with the help of a small, select band of like-minded colleagues, in forging a Turkish national movement of exceptional strength and unity, capable of challenging the authority of the Sultan and his government in Istanbul (Constantinople), imposing its authority throughout the greater part of Anatolia, confronting the occupation forces of the western Entente powers (Great Britain, France and Italy), expelling a Greek expeditionary force despatched by those powers to Izmir in May 1919, and finally concluding at Lausanne a treaty of peace with the western Entente Powers and their allies, securing the independence and integrity of a newly created Turkish state, the last of the successor states of the Ottoman Empire. Moreover, in the remaining years of his life he succeeded in carrying through a series of major reforms, radically transforming the traditional, Islamic structure of Ottoman society, and laying the foundations of a modern, westernised, secular nation-state.

When the conditions prevailing in what little remained of the Ottoman Empire in the period immediately following the end of the First World War (1914–18) are taken into account, Atatürk's achievements, and those of the national movement with which he was associated, appear if anything even more impressive. In Istanbul, where a

1

supine government timorously awaited the arrival of the Allied occupation forces, the structure of government, both central and local, had all but broken down, while in Anatolia and eastern Thrace near anarchy prevailed, as more than a quarter of a million deserters, seeking refuge in the hills, raided towns and villages, in search of food and the other necessities of life. As a result, among the Turkish-speaking Muslim inhabitants of those areas (some twelve million or so in number, for the most part small peasant farmers, 90 per cent illiterate) support for the Ottoman Government (widely considered incompetent and corrupt) had all but disappeared, as had the will to further resistance. Indeed, according to one British observer, writing at the time, so great was the despair prevailing, that had the Allies but acted with despatch, they might well have imposed whatever peace terms they wished, virtually unopposed.[1]

Nor would Atatürk's achievements, and those of the national movement with which he was associated, appear in any way diminished, were a comparison to be made with those of other leaders and movements appearing in Europe at the time. Where else among the defeated imperial powers did a movement emerge, capable of challenging the armed might of the enemy and obliging him to conclude a satisfactory peace settlement, securing the independence and integrity of the nation; and where else a leader capable of forging such a movement? In Germany, cowed and humiliated by defeat, the leaders of the recently established Weimar Republic were obliged to accept the harsh terms of the Treaty of Versailles (1919), a fertile source of future conflict. In Russia, the recently installed Bolshevik government, desperate for peace, was obliged by the Central Powers, Germany and Austria–Hungary, to accept the terms of the Treaty of Brest–Litovsk (1918), sacrificing extensive territories in western Russia, the Baltic and Ukraine, while in Austria–Hungary a settlement loosely based on the principle of nationality was simply imposed, willy-nilly, with little or no consideration for the interests of the former imperial powers. Only in the Ottoman Empire, it would seem, did a movement arise capable of building a new, stable order on the foundations of the old; and only in the Ottoman Empire did a leader emerge, capable of forging such a movement. Small wonder that Lloyd George, the British leader, whose career he effectively ruined, was wont to refer to Atatürk as the man of the century,[2] and that others have compared him, in the range and quality of his achievements, with such noted historical figures as Jenghis Khan, Tamburlain and Napoleon, not to mention Alexander the Great, Aristotle and Lenin.[3]

Biographies of Atatürk, such as those by Dagobert von Mikusch (1931), Harold Armstrong (1932), Herbert Melzig (1937), Hanns Froembgen (1937), a commission of Turkish historians (1946), Jacques Benoist–Méchin (1954), and Lord Kinross (1964), drawing heavily on Atatürk's own version of events, as recorded in *Speech* (*Nutuk*), the published version of the great speech he delivered, over a period of six days, before the Congress of the Republican People's Party in Ankara in 1927, and in occasional memoirs and interviews, published about the same time, tend to present what might be described as the heroic version of Atatürk's life and achievement. In this it is taken for granted that Atatürk, a heroic and even at times a semi-legendary figure, played a decisive part in shaping the course of events in the Ottoman Empire in the period of the First World War and its aftermath. Indeed, in some of the more extreme versions, it is even suggested, or at least inferred, that he alone founded the Committee of Union and Progress (CUP) (the secret society which organised the so-called Young Turk revolution of 1908, and later, as a political party, controlled the government of Turkey in the period of the Balkan and First World Wars); conceived the idea of setting up a national resistance movement in Anatolia in 1919; inspired the formation of the national forces, set up to oppose the Greeks in western Anatolia in the summer months of 1919; and convened the Congress of Erzurum, at which the aims and objectives of the national movement were first defined. Moreover, it is even suggested that he foresaw from the beginning the future course of events in what remained of the Ottoman Empire, including the abolition of the Sultanate and the Caliphate, and the creation of a republic.[4] Other works, such as those by Irfan Orga (1958), Şevket Sürreya Aydemir (1969), Jorge Blanco Villalta (1979), and Alexandre Jevakhoff (1989), present a more mundane version of events, though the heroic element is seldom absent. More general histories of the period, on the other

3

hand, such as those by Bernard Lewis (1961), Niyazi Berkes (1964) and Stanford and Ezel Kural Shaw (1977), largely eschewing the cult of personality, tend to emphasise the extent to which the revolution accomplished in the period immediately following the First World War was the product not of individual initiative but of a profound historical process, the economic, political and ideological roots of which must be sought in the history of the Ottoman Empire in the late eighteenth and nineteenth centuries. Finally, Marxist historians, such as Berch Berberoğlu (1982) and Cağlar Keyder (1987), emphasise the social and economic aspects of the war of independence, in which, it is assumed, the petty-bourgeois leadership of the national movement – local bureaucrats, army officers and the professional strata – in alliance with landlords, Islamic clergy and small-holding peasantry, challenged the occupying forces of the imperial powers, and their allies in the Ottoman Palace and the minority, *comprador* bourgeoisie, (for the most part Greek and Armenian merchants, living in Istanbul and Izmir). From the point of view of the student of European and Middle Eastern history, seeking an understanding of the evolution of events in general, and of the impact made by Atatürk on them, neither approach may be considered entirely satisfactory. In this account, therefore, an attempt will be made to set the life and achievements of Atatürk in the context of the general history of the period, paying particular attention to the struggle for power in which throughout the greater part of his life he was engaged, and to the factors that determined its outcome.

It is singularly appropriate that a life of Atatürk should be included in a series entitled Profiles in Power. Throughout his life Atatürk remained totally committed to the acquisition and use of power. In the early stages of his career, until his emergence as a national leader in Anatolia in May 1919, he sought by every means at his disposal to extend the range of his own power and influence, seeking unsuccessfully for the most part, to acquire high office in the Ottoman government and influence policy. In the period of the national struggle and the war of independence, when he acquired great power, he used it ruthlessly both to attain the objectives of the national movement and to extend the power he had acquired. In the period following the final triumph of the national movement, and the creation of the Republic in 1923, when he exercised something approaching absolute power, he again used the power he had acquired ruthlessly, both to suppress opposition and compel change. Thus in 1925, when a number of the Kurdish tribes inhabiting south-eastern Anatolia rose in revolt, he had some hundreds of the rebels hanged; and in the same year he had some hundreds of his own countrymen imprisoned for opposing or infringing the so-called hat law, which demanded the substitution of the European hat for the traditional headgear of the people. Again, in 1926, following the discovery of a plot to assassinate him, he had eighteen of his opponents, including a number of his erstwhile friends and associates, executed. Yet, paradoxically, it was in the exercise of political power, in the employment of the arts of persuasion, rather than in the crude use of force, that he excelled, particularly in the early stages of the national struggle, when he had only limited resources at his command, and throughout his career he displayed a remarkable capacity for the exercise of restraint in the use of power, seeking to achieve merely that which was attainable, thereby avoiding error and excess. Hence, no doubt, his willingness to await the appropriate moment for the abolition of the Sultanate, and later of the Caliphate; and hence too his willingness in the period of the Lausanne peace conference, to compromise with the Allies over the Straits' clauses and Turkey's frontiers in the east. He was, in short, not just a man of power, but a man endowed with an exceptional talent for the exercise of power, employed not only in the military and political, but also in the social sphere.

. . . .

THE MAN

In a recent study of Atatürk, entitled *The Immortal Atatürk* (1984), Vamik Volkan (an eminent Turkish psychologist) and Norman Itzkowitz (an equally eminent historian of the Ottoman Empire) suggest that Atatürk's extraordinary thirst for power derived from his experiences in childhood, when, deprived at an early age of a father and exposed to the unremitting emotional pressure of a grieving mother, he unconsciously developed an inflated concept of his

5

own importance, a 'grandiose self', which would protect him against the everyday hurts of life. As a result of this 'narcissistic personality organisation', he endeavoured, throughout the remaining years of his life, to compel the world to conform to his own expectations; though as Volkan and Itzkowitz themselves remark, it is but seldom indeed that persons with such personality disorders attain to the heights of political power and prestige achieved by Atatürk.

Atatürk was physically handsome, with fair hair, high cheek-bones, regular features and steel-blue or blue-green eyes (Hüsemettin Ertürk, who knew him as a young man, remarked that he had green eyes).[5] He was light in build, and of only medium height – though like many charismatic figures he frequently left his followers with a deceptive impression of height and weight. Atatürk was by no means a typical Turk, and foreigners in particular found him difficult to place. General J. G. Harbord, the head of an American mission, who interviewed Atatürk in 1919, remarked that he appeared to have 'Circassian or other blond blood in his ancestry',[6] while Robert Dunn, an American foreign service officer, who interviewed him in 1921, concluded that every feature showed non-Turkish blood – Hellene, Jewish or Circassian.[7] Turks likewise were frequently uncertain regarding his origins. Sultan Mehmed VI, who in March 1921 referred to him as a 'Macedonian revolutionary of unknown origin', remarked that he might well have passed for a Bulgarian, a Greek or even a Serbian;[8] while Halide Edib, who detected something sinister in his expression, remarked on the faultless shape of his hands, so different from the 'broad hands' of the Anatolian Turk.[9] Many remarked that it was impossible to look him straight in the eye, a fact explained perhaps by the existence of a slight squint, evident in a number of his photographs.

Biographers of Atatürk have frequently portrayed him as a flamboyant 'oriental' figure, an anachronistic throwback to the Tartars of the Steppe, the grey wolf of Turkish legend, a 'fierce, elemental force'.[10] Nor can it be denied that there is some truth in this characterisation. To the end of his life he remained an imposing figure, highly intelligent, shrewd, cynical, at times sarcastic and overbearing, unscrupulous and in his private life dissolute. A heavy drinker, he would frequently consume half a litre of *raki* (the Turkish national drink) a day, and sit up half the night playing poker or carousing with his cronies. Sexually promiscuous, he would openly boast of his prowess. Asked once what quality he most admired in a woman, he is said to have replied 'availability'.[11] At some stage, possibly whilst serving in Bulgaria as military attaché in 1913, he appears to have contracted venereal disease, an experience which, it is said, imbued him for a time with a contempt for life and led him to indulge more frequently in what a British military intelligence report referred to as the 'homosexual vice'.[12] Spectacular and domineering, when need be, on one occasion, when considering the future of the Sultanate in 1922, he threatened to lop off the heads of a joint committee set up to consider the question, should they refuse to adopt the policy he recommended. On another, in the 1930s, when the Italian ambassador in the course of an interview endeavoured to reassert Italy's claims in south-western Anatolia, Atatürk suddenly rose, and excusing himself left the room, only to return some minutes later, wearing the full dress uniform of a Turkish field marshal. He then proceeded with the conversation as if nothing had happened, meanwhile striking rhythmically with a riding whip on one of his outstretched boots, which in profile, as the ambassador could hardly have failed to notice, resembled the characteristic shape of the Italian peninsula. Egocentric, according to Irfan Orga, who served under him, to the point of mania, he could not abide criticism, seeing no reason why a decision once arrived at should be picked to pieces by lesser mortals.[13] Not above sharp practice, when the occasion demanded it, at a critical moment in the national struggle, when discussions with a delegation, despatched by the Istanbul Government, threatened to undermine his position, he simply had the delegation kidnapped and transported to Ankara, where they were held for some months against their will, giving it out in the meantime that they had defected to the nationalist cause. Surprisingly superstitious for a man who prided himself on his western attitudes, according to Halide Edib he believed in omens, and in the early stages of the national struggle hung a green cloth, embroidered with magical inscriptions, written in Arabic, behind the desk in his office.[14]

The characterisation of Atatürk as a flamboyant, oriental figure, much given, in his later years at least, to excess, requires, however, some qualification. To the end he remained what he had always been, a military man, trained to command, albeit with an exceptional talent for politics. Hence no doubt his habit, when faced with a difficult situation, of drawing up a battle plan, carefully researched and based on the most complete and accurate information available, and then, at the appropriate moment, striking with maximum force, if possible catching his opponent off guard, and hence too the brutal sense of reality that inspired his attitude to politics and life, and the complete lack of compassion, pity and sympathy that he is said on occasion to have displayed.[15] An attentive listener, he would generally hear out an argument before intervening in the discussion. Punctilious in dress, even in the worst conditions of war, he would whenever possible insist that the officers on his staff dress for dinner. Hardened by the experience of camp life, he is said to have developed an iron constitution, though paradoxically he was frequently ill, debilitated by a kidney disorder from which he suffered, and malaria, contracted, it is said, in Egypt in 1911, on his way to the Libyan front. Though occasionally indiscreet, swearing like a trooper, in polite society he would invariably exert the greatest self-control; and in his youth he is said to have made strenuous efforts to acquire polish, attending salons, musical soirées and operas. Nor was he completely oblivious of the need for domestic stability. Following his victory over the Greeks in the war of independence, he made an attempt to settle down, marrying Latife Hanım, the daughter of a wealthy Izmir merchant, educated in France; but to no avail. Predictably, when, following a brief honeymoon period, Latife began to exercise the prerogatives of a wife, insisting that her husband cease carousing with his friends and come to bed before midnight, he rebelled, and they were quickly divorced. Thereafter he reverted to his old ways, and later in life took to adopting 'daughters', with one of whom at least he had sexual relations. Nor did he ever fully become adapted to the more civilised conditions prevailing in the presidential palace, during his stay there. In the afternoon, when he had nothing else to do, he would occasionally emerge to watch the soldiers of the presidential guard wrestling on the lawn, and even from time to time join in himself; and to the end of his life he preferred to eat the *pilau* (boiled rice prepared with butter or meat fat), chick-peas and beans to which he had become accustomed in the period of the war of independence. He was, then, a man accustomed to living amongst men, yet in the range and quality of his achievements, an outstanding figure, worthy of further consideration, worthy in short of a profile in power.

. . .

NOTES AND REFERENCES

1. Şimşir B. N., *British Documents on Atatürk (BDA)*, in progress. Türk Tarih Kurumu, Ankara, Vol. 1, No. 22, enclosure.
2. Volkan V., Itzkowitz N. 1984, *The Immortal Atatürk*. University of Chicago Press, p. xxiv. In October 1922, in part as a result of the strains imposed by the Chanak crisis, the coalition government in Britain, led by Lloyd George, collapsed. Lloyd George never secured high office again.
3. Armstrong H. C. 1932, *The Grey Wolf*. Arthur Barker, p. 333; Mikusch, Dagobert von 1931, *Gasi Mustafa Kemal*. P. List, Leipzig, p. ix; Public Records Office, London, Foreign Office (FO) 424 267, No. 48.
4. See for example Seyd Anwarul Haque Haqqi in *Papers and Discussions*. Ankara, 1984, p. 659; Melzig H. 1937, *Kemal Atatürk*. Frankfurt, p. 92; Froembgen H. 1937, *Kemal Atatürk*. Stuttgart, pp. 110–11; Armstrong H. C. 1932, *The Grey Wolf*, p. 135; and Mikusch, Dagobert von 1931, *Gasi Mustafa Kemal*, pp. 183–4.
5. Ertürk H. 1964, *Iki Devrin Perde Arkası*. Pinar Yayınevi, Istanbul, p. 68.
6. Kinross 1964, *Atatürk: The Rebirth of a Nation*. Weidenfeld and Nicolson, p. 189.
7. Robinson R. D. 1963, *The First Turkish Republic*. Harvard University Press, p. 27.
8. Gilbert M. 1973, *Sir Horace Rumbold*. Heinemann, p. 236.
9. Edib H. 1928, *The Turkish Ordeal*. John Murray, p. 127.
10. Armstrong H. C. 1932, *The Grey Wolf*, p. 333.
11. Kinross 1964, *Atatürk*, p. 260.

12. *BDA* Vol. 3, No. 35. Such stories may have been put about by Mustafa Kemal's enemies, in order to discredit him.
13. Orga I. 1958, *Phoenix Ascendant: The Rise of Modern Turkey*. Robert Hale, p. 78.
14. Edib H. 1928, *The Turkish Ordeal*, p. 170.
15. Ibid.

Chapter 1

THE MAKING OF
MUSTAFA KEMAL

. . .

EARLY LIFE

Mustafa Kemal Atatürk, or Mustafa as he was initially known, was born in Salonika in the winter of 1880–81, the fourth of six children born to Ali Riza Efendi, a minor customs official in the Department of Pious Foundations and Excise, and Zübeyde, a handsome, fair-haired peasant girl, possibly of Yürük extraction, from the area west of Salonika near the Albanian border.[1] Little or nothing is known of Ali Riza's father, Ahmed, except that he served for a while in the Salonika Territorial Battalion, and that in May 1876, having become involved in demonstrations in Salonika, against the intervention of the great powers in the internal affairs of the Ottoman Empire (in the course of which the French and German consuls were murdered), he was obliged to flee to the Macedonian mountains, where he was to remain a fugitive for the rest of his life. Shortly before Mustafa's birth, Ali Riza Efendi, unable to make headway in the Department of Pious Foundations and Excise, and tempted no doubt by the fortunes being made in the timber trade in the neighbourhood of Mount Olympus (where he was at the time employed as a customs official), resigned from his post and set up in business with a friend, cutting timber. However, beset by the problems of brigandage, then endemic in the area, his business quickly failed, and in the winter of 1887–88, depressed and unemployed, he died, leaving Zübeyde alone to bring up her three surviving children, the three eldest having died in infancy.[2]

Despite the difficulties created by his father's premature death, Mustafa's early life and education proved surprisingly trouble-free. Following a brief period spent, at his mother's

11

behest, at a local Koranic school, he was eventually enrolled, by his father, in a modern secular school, recently established in Salonika by one Şemsi (Shemsi) Efendi, a courageous and enlightened schoolmaster. Thereafter, following a brief period spent living in a village near Salonika, in the house of his mother's step-brother, and an equally brief period at a State High School in Salonika, he entered, at the age of twelve, the Military Secondary School in Salonika, the first step on an educational ladder that was to lead him, by way of the Military High School in Monastir (1895–99) and the War College in Istanbul (1899–1902), to a prestigious place in the Staff College in Istanbul (1902–05), from which he graduated as a general staff captain in 1905.

What little is known of Mustafa's early life suggests that he frequently displayed the initiative and determination for which he was later to become famous. At the Koranic school, which he attended briefly before entering Şemsi Efendi's academy, he is said to have rebelled against the practice of sitting cross-legged on the floor, writing out extracts from the Koran, in the Arabic script. When he was twelve, his mother, strongly opposed to him taking up a military career, attempted to impose a prohibition on his entry into the Military Secondary School in Salonika. Undaunted, he apparently contrived secretly to have himself enrolled for the entrance exam; and when his mother later remarried, impetuously packed his bags and departed the family home, rather than live with his step-father. At the Military Secondary School at Salonika, where he was given the second name of Kemal (Perfect) by a mathematics teacher, in order to distinguish him from other boys of the same name, or possibly from the teacher himself, he is said to have striven to excel his classmates in their work, particularly in mathematics, a favourite subject; and to have quickly assumed the leadership of the Salonika cadets in their gang fights with the other boys, though he was himself always careful to avoid injury. When in 1897 war broke out between Greece and the Ottoman Empire, he and a friend attempted to run away and join the army at the front, but they were quickly discovered and returned to the school. At the Istanbul War College, from which he passed out twentieth in a class of 460 in his second year, and eighth in a class of 459 in his third, and at the

Staff College, from which he passed out fifth in a class of fifty-seven, he is reputed to have read widely, including the works of banned Ottoman writers, such as Namik Kemal, the 'poet of the Fatherland', Ziya Pasha and Tevfik Fikret; vigorously debated contemporary political affairs with his fellow cadets; and helped publish a hand-written newspaper, containing subversive material.

Later in life Mustafa Kemal frequently recalled the struggle that occurred between his father, Ali Riza, and his mother, Zübeyde, on the occasion of his first entering school:

> The first thing I remember from my childhood is about entering school. There was a deep struggle between my mother and father concerning this. My mother wished that I commence my education by enrolling in the quarter's religious school with chanting of the appropriate religious hymns. But, my father, who was a clerk at the customs office, was in favour of sending me to the newly opened school of Şemsi Efendi and of my getting the new type of education. In the end, my father artfully found a solution. First, with the usual ceremony, I entered the clerical school. Thus, my mother was satisfied. After a few days, I left the clerical school and enrolled in the school of Şemsi Efendi. Soon afterwards, my father died.[3]

. . .

OTTOMAN BACKGROUND

The struggle between Ali Riza, committed to a modern, westernised, secular education for his son, and Zübeyde, committed to a traditional religious upbringing, illustrates all too clearly the deep divisions which existed in Ottoman society in the second half of the nineteenth century between the modernists, who sought radical reform, and the conservatives, who believed that salvation lay in the preservation of traditional Ottoman values. Modernisation and reform in this context implied in the fields of religion and philosophy the acceptance of scientific method and the pursuit of progress; in the field of education the abandonment of the traditional methods of instruction, practised in the Koranic

13

schools, in favour of the progressive approach adopted by such enlightened teachers as Şemsi Efendi; in the fields of industry, commerce and defence, the employment of technology, the fruit of modern science; and in the fields of politics, public administration and law, the abandonment of the principle of autocracy, embodied in the institutions of the Sultanate and the Caliphate, in favour of some kind of parliamentary system, based on the principles of liberty, equality and fraternity, popularised in the period of the French Revolution. The preservation of traditional Ottoman values, on the other hand, implied a vigorous defence of Islam against the assault mounted by the west, and a reversion to the policies pursued so successfully in the reigns of Mehmed the Conqueror and Suleiman the Magnificent, the so-called golden age of the empire. Not that the two approaches were necessarily incompatible. On the contrary, many traditionalists argued that Islam would easily accommodate the new ideas coming from the west, while many modernists aimed not at the demise but at the rejuvenation of the faith.

The government of the Ottoman Empire, both in its formative years and in its golden age, was based on the principles of hierarchy, theocracy and tradition. The ruler, known in the west as the Sultan, and in the empire as the *Padişah*, was according to the traditional view, appointed by God to rule over the body politic. Directly under the Sultan came his vicar, the *Sadrazam*, known in the west as the Grand Vizier, who acted as head of three ruling estates: administrative, military and judicial. Alongside these stood the Ulema, a corps of learned men, trained in the religion of Islam. Members of the Ulema might be appointed to hold the office of *imam* (minister of religion), *mufti* (jurisconsult) and *kadi* (judge). The highest-ranking *mufti*, equal in importance to the *Sadrazam*, was known as the *Sheikh-ül-Islâm*. Beneath the three ruling estates came the common people, the ruled, the tax-paying class of peasants, artisans and traders, known in Turkish as *raâya* and in English as *rayah* (though in English the term is sometimes used to refer merely to Christians living under Turkish rule). The *raâya* were divided into two categories, Muslims and non-Muslims. While the first constituted a politically amorphous community, the second (Jews and Christians) were differentiated according to their ecclesiastical affiliations, in spiritually autonomous religious communities, called *millets*. The function of the Sultan was to hold the various estates of the body politic together. The function of the ruling estates, administrative, military and judicial, was to maintain order, as defined by tradition. The function of the Ulema was to teach religion, interpret the *Şeriat* (Muslim law) and enforce the law. Any deviation from established tradition or departure from the law, as sanctified by the *Şeriat*, was deemed to be unacceptable. It was from the Christian *millets* that the Greek, Bulgarian and Armenian nations, infected by nationalist ideologies, imported for the most part from western and central Europe, were to emerge in the late eighteenth and nineteenth centuries, while it was on the foundation of the Ottoman, Muslim *millet* that Mustafa Kemal and his colleagues in the national movement were to erect a new, Turkish nation-state in the period of national struggle that followed the defeat of the Ottoman Empire in the First World War.[4]

So effective was the Ottoman system of government, and so powerful the ideology of Islam on which it was based, that in the fourteenth, fifteenth and sixteenth centuries the empire grew rapidly, absorbing not only the former territories of the Byzantine Empire, including the greater part of the Balkans and Anatolia, but also Syria, Egypt, Mesopotamia, Arabia and north Africa. At its height it stretched from the Indian Ocean to the gates of Vienna, and from the Crimea to the Barbary coast. But in the seventeenth and early eighteenth centuries, for a complex variety of reasons, including a weakening in the authority of the Sultanate, loss of tax revenue, indiscipline in the army, in particular in the élite Janissary corps, recruited from the *devşirme* (Christian slave levy), and the rise of local chieftains, disaffected military commanders and provincial governors, intent on creating independent dynasties and regimes, the empire fell into a gradual decline, only occasionally halted by the reforming policies of energetic sultans and grand viziers; and in the late eighteenth and nineteenth centuries, infected by the virus of nationalism, it suffered a series of disastrous defeats, resulting in substantial losses of territory. In the last quarter of the eighteenth century, following a series of humiliating defeats, inflicted by the Russians, substantial territories in the neighbourhood of the Black Sea steppe, including the Crimea, were lost; and in 1812 Bessarabia. In 1829, following a Greek insurrection and yet another war against Russia, the Peloponnese was lost; and in 1841, following a series of international crises, provoked by Mehmet Ali, the rebellious viceroy of Egypt, Egypt. Not that victory in war necessarily secured the integrity of the empire. On the contrary, following the Crimean War of 1853–56, in which the Ottomans, with the backing of a coalition of western powers, led by Britain and France, succeeded in defeating the Russians, the empire was nonetheless deprived of what little influence it retained in the Principalities of Moldavia and Wallachia (Romania), though the independence and integrity of the empire was supposedly guaranteed by the great powers in the Treaty of Paris of 1856, which concluded the war. Finally, as a result of the so-called eastern crisis of 1876–78, in the early stages of which Mustafa Kemal's grandfather was obliged to take to the hills, substantial territories were lost to the empire both in the Balkans and the east including Bosnia, Herzegovina, the greater part of Bulgaria, Kars, Ardahan, Batum and Cyprus.[5]

The consequences of Ottoman decline were by no means merely territorial. Throughout the nineteenth century, the increasing importation of manufactured goods brought about a collapse of traditional, mainly domestic, industry; while, in the third quarter, reckless borrowing on the London and Paris money markets, particularly in the reign of Abdul Aziz (1861–76), led to the effective bankruptcy of the empire, with the result that in 1875 the government was obliged to suspend payment on a part of the Ottoman public debt, and in 1881, the approximate year of Mustafa Kemal's birth, to agree to the establishment of a Council of the Public Debt, administered by officers appointed by the foreign, mainly French, bondholders. At the same time foreign, mainly European, financial interests became increasingly engaged in the exploitation of the natural resources of the empire, and in the construction of railways, with the result that parts of the empire, in particular Anatolia and Thrace, were transformed into semi-colonies, dependencies of the European capitalist system.

The initial response of the Ottomans to the decline of their empire, and the loss of territory which this entailed, was a vigorous reassertion of traditional values. Only when this failed were they obliged to adopt a more radical approach, which in due course led to the introduction of a reform programme, based on western concepts of organisation, training and administration. In 1792–93 Sultan Selim III, as part of a series of reforms known collectively as the New Order, created a new corps of regular infantry, trained and equipped along modern, European lines; and in the following years he established military and naval schools, staffed in part by foreign, mainly French, instructors. When Selim's reforms foundered on the opposition of the Janissaries, originally the spearhead of the empire, but now an unruly and indisciplined force, Mahmud II (1808–39), his successor first suppressed the Janissaries, and dissolved the dervish brotherhood of the Bektashis which supported them, and then created a new army, similar to that created by Selim III. This was known as the Victorious Mohammedan Soldiers, a title designed to disguise the radical nature of the reforms introduced. Thereafter, in 1827, a medical school was opened in Istanbul to train doctors for the new army; and in 1834 a School of Military Sciences on the French model; while military and naval personnel were despatched, in increasing numbers, for training in Europe. As a result of these and other substantial reforms, carried out in the 1840s, 1850s and 1860s, Ottoman armies performed creditably, in the war against Russia, which occurred in the period of the eastern crisis (1876–78), holding up the advancing Russian forces for long periods at the sieges of Plevna and Erzurum.

Following the suppression of the Janissaries and the re-organisation of the armed forces which followed, Mahmud II, later known as the Peter the Great of the Ottoman Empire, lost no time in employing the new forces at his disposal to reassert his authority over the rebellious notables, valley lords and army officers, who had for long challenged the authority of the Sultanate; though he never succeeded in imposing his authority on Mehmet Ali, the rebellious viceroy of Egypt. At the same time, in order to raise finance to pay for the new army and reimpose central control, he first subordinated the lands and estates of the numerous pious foundations of the empire to central control, and then reformed the system of land-holding and taxation. In the remaining years of his life he introduced a series of reforms of the system of government and administration, including the reorganisation of a number of the great offices of state along European lines.

In the reign of Abdul Medjid (1839–61), and to a lesser extent in that of his successor, Abdul Aziz (1861–76), the process of centralisation and modernisation, inaugurated by Selim III and Mahmud II, continued unabated. In a series of edicts, orders and regulations, known collectively as the *Tanzimat* (Reform or Reorganisation), inspired for the most part by a desire to secure the loyalty of the Christian *millets* (self-governing religious communities or nations) and, particularly in times of crisis, the support and approval of the great powers, the Ottomans continued their efforts to create a modern, centralised state, based on the principle of equality. In 1839 and 1856 imperial rescripts were issued, promising respect for the life, honour and property of the subject, reform of tax-farming, regular and orderly recruitment to the armed forces, fair and public trial of persons accused and equality before the law, irrespective of religion. In the decades following, a series of edicts and orders were issued designed to achieve these objectives. Thus, in 1840 a new, centralised system of provincial administration was established, based on the French model; and in 1864 a law of *vilayets* (provinces) was promulgated, regulating the government and organisation of the *vilayets, sanjaks* and districts into which the empire was divided. In 1846, following an enquiry, carried out by a specially appointed committee, an ambitious scheme for the provision of a network of primary and secondary schools, and even a university, was instituted; and in the following year a Council of Public Instruction, later transformed into a Ministry of Education, was established, which moved quickly to deprive the Ulema (Muslim clergy) of much of its control of public education. Finally, during the period 1840–80, new Commercial, Penal and Civil Codes, adjudicated by secular courts, were promulgated, along European lines; and special courts set up, manned by both Ottoman and European judges, to try cases involving citizens protected by the system of extra-territorial rights known as the capitulations.[6]

That the reforms of the *Tanzimat* period, based as they were on secular principles, in particular the principle of equality, were incompatible with the basic tenets of Islam, in particular the supremacy of the Muslim *millet*, was evident. Throughout the period of the *Tanzimat*, therefore, Ottoman statesmen were at pains to fashion and promote a new ideology, known as Ottomanism, according to which all Ottoman citizens, irrespective of nationality or faith, would be expected to identify not with their own particular *millet*, but with a new entity, to be known as the Ottoman nation. Thus, in the Imperial Rescript of 1839, Sultan Abdul Medjid, while protesting his loyalty to the faith, expressed the hope that henceforth his subjects would display 'zeal for the dynasty and nation' and 'love of the fatherland', and in the speech he delivered on the occasion of his accession to the throne in 1876, Sultan Murad V promised to preserve the 'fatherland, state and nation'.[7]

In the third quarter of the nineteenth century, liberal ideas of constitutional reform, popular not only in Europe, but also in a number of Muslim countries, including Egypt and Tunisia, spread rapidly among the Ottoman intelligentsia, propagated in particular by a group of Ottoman exiles, based for the most part in Europe, known as the Young Ottomans. As a result, in 1876 Midhat Pasha, a leading reformer, taking advantage of the opportunity for radical reform offered by the outbreak of the so-called eastern crisis, in the course of which the very survival of the empire was once again threatened, was enabled first to appoint a constitutional commission, chaired by himself, and including amongst its members a number of Young Ottomans, and then to have promulgated, on the eve of an international conference, convened in Istanbul to resolve the problems created by the crisis, the so-called First Ottoman Constitution, loosely based on the Belgian and Prussian constitutions of 1831 and 1850. According to the articles of this constitution, while sovereignty would in principle remain with the Sultan, executive power would be placed in the hands of a council of ministers, appointed by the Sultan, and legislative power in the hands of a parliament consisting of a chamber of deputies, elected on a restricted franchise by indirect election, and a senate, whose members would be nominated for life. Subject to such restrictions as might from time to time be imposed by law, Ottoman subjects would henceforth be entitled to enjoy equality before the law, freedom from arbitrary arrest and freedom of the press; but in the event of disturbances occurring in any part of the empire, or a threat of such disturbances arising, the Imperial Government would retain the right to declare a state of siege in the areas affected, while citizens considered a danger to the state might be expelled forthwith.[8]

The promulgation of the First Ottoman Constitution and the election of a chamber of deputies, and appointment of a senate, which followed, proved a short-lived triumph for Midhat Pasha and his supporters. In February 1877, Abdul Hamid, the newly-installed Sultan, bitterly hostile to the aspirations of the liberal constitutionalists, dismissed Midhat Pasha from office and expelled him from the capital; and in February 1878, when the chamber of deputies, sitting in their second session, began to exercise their powers in what he interpreted to be a provocative manner, he simply dissolved the chamber and ordered the deputies to disperse, thereby inaugurating more than three decades of despotism and reaction.

In the prolonged period of despotism and reaction that followed the suspension of the 1876 constitution, Abdul Hamid, determined to preserve the traditional authority of the Sultanate and the Caliphate, and the supremacy of Islam, created an elaborate network of special courts, police informers and spies, both to suppress all forms of opposition to his regime and prevent the spread of western, liberal ideas from Europe. Yet, paradoxically, in the fields of public administration, law, education and transport, he continued to expand and elaborate many of the reforms first instituted in the period of the *Tanzimat*. Thus in the 1880s and 1890s, a considerable increase occurred in the number of students attending the *mülkiye* (civilian) school, first established in 1859, to train civil servants in the arts of government and administration; and in 1879 laws were promulgated, extending the authority of the Ministry of Justice over the system of non-religious courts, earlier established; though Ottoman attempts to limit the extra-territorial rights of foreigners were largely unsuccessful. In the provinces, as in the capital, new elementary and secondary schools were opened, paid for by a special education tax, imposed in 1884; and in 1900, a new university, first mooted in 1845, was opened in the capital.

At the same time the war college, which Mustafa Kemal was later to attend, was extended, as were the military and civil medical schools, in which, to Abdul Hamid's dismay, liberal and progressive ideas were to proliferate. In the field of communications, an area of major importance to a regime intent on extending its authority to the outermost reaches of the empire, the network of railways, first laid down in the 1860s, was further extended, including in 1888 the addition of a line direct from Istanbul to Vienna, and in 1900 the commencement of a line to the Hedjaz. Equally significant in the 1880s and 1890s was the extension of the telegraph system, first installed in the period of the Crimean War, and the training of personnel, so that by the end of the century an efficient network of telegraphic communication existed, that would enable not only Abdul Hamid, but also the conspirators of the CUP who deposed him, and in the period of the war of independence, Mustafa Kemal, himself, to maintain communications with almost every part of the empire.[9]

Effective as Abdul Hamid's system of political repression and censorship was, it failed in the end to prevent the spread of liberal ideas. In 1889, adopting many of the ideas of liberal and constitutional reform, earlier propagated by the Young Ottomans in the 1870s, a group of students at the Military Medical College in Istanbul founded a secret society, the Society of Ottoman Union, seeking an end to the autocratic rule of the Sultan and the reinstatement of the 1876 constitution. In the following years membership of the society expanded rapidly; and in 1896 the society, now renamed the Society of Union and Progress, attempted a *coup d'état*; but the plot was betrayed, and many leading members of the society were arrested, with the result that for some years at least the organisational structure of the opposition movement within the empire was destroyed. But the ideological onslaught could not be so easily contained. Progressive ideas, published in such journals as *Meşveret* (*Consultation*), the *Osmanlı* (*The Ottoman*) and *Mizan* (*Balance of Scales*), continued to spread; while among the Armenian, Greek and Bulgarian communities of the empire, ideas of national liberation, expounded by secret societies such as the Armenian Revolutionary Association, the *Ethniké Hetairia*, the Internal Macedonian Revolutionary Organisation and the Macedonian Supreme Committee, spread rapidly. As a result in 1894–96, following a series of incidents provoked by Armenian nationalists, massacres of Armenians occurred in Istanbul and the eastern provinces; and in 1897 a rebellion against Ottoman rule broke out in Crete, provoking the war between Greece and the Ottoman Empire in which Mustafa Kemal and his friends endeavoured unsuccessfully to enlist, while in Macedonia, following a series of raids by the Supreme Committee designed to provoke an uprising, law and order all but broke down as rival nationalist organisations struggled for supremacy. Finally, in 1903, the Internal Macedonian Revolutionary Organisation organised a revolt in Salonika, aimed at provoking intervention on the part of the great powers.

AN UNDERSTANDABLE RESPONSE

Mustafa Kemal, like other members of his generation, followed these developments with intense interest, though as yet their precise import escaped him. As he later recalled:

> During the years at the War College political ideas emerged. We were still unable to gain real insight into the situation. It was the period of Abdul Hamid. We were reading the books of Namik Kemal. Surveillance was tight. Most of the time we found the chance to read only in the barracks after going to bed. There seemed to be something wrong in the state of affairs if those who read such patriotic works were under surveillance. But, we could not completely grasp the essence of it.[10]

The response of Mustafa Kemal and a number of his friends, including Ali Fuat, the son of an Ottoman general, to the situation they observed was understandable, if somewhat rash. In the War College in Istanbul, as we have seen, they published a hand-written newspaper, containing articles and editorials critical of the government; and at the Staff College they continued vigorously to debate the latest ideas and events. Then in 1905, having but recently graduated from the Staff College, they agreed to rent a room in the house of an Armenian neighbour in Beyazit, in order

22

that they might continue to meet there in private to carry on their discussions. The result was predictable. Betrayed almost immediately by a supposed friend, they were at once arrested, interrogated, and imprisoned; but in the end, in view of their youth and inexperience, they were permitted to resume their duties, on condition that they be posted to one or other of the remoter provinces of the empire, where they might do penance for their sins. In the case of Mustafa Kemal and Ali Fuat this meant a posting to the Fifth Army Corps in Syria. So began, in this unpropitious manner, the career of the future leader of the national movement and the president of the first Turkish republic.

. . .

NOTES AND REFERENCES

1. The precise date of Mustafa Kemal's birth is not known. According to his mother he was born during the winter of 1880–81. See Volkan V., Itzkowitz N. 1984, *The Immortal Atatürk*. University of Chicago Press, p. 12.
2. A fourth child died almost immediately thereafter, leaving Zübeyde with two children to bring up: Mustafa and his sister, Makbule.
3. Volkan V., Itzkowitz N. 1984, *The Immortal Atatürk*, p. 29.
4. For an account of the rise of the Ottoman Empire, and the nature of its institutions, see Inalcik H. 1973, *The Ottoman Empire*. Weidenfeld and Nicolson.
5. For the decline of the Ottoman Empire, see Anderson M.S. 1966, *The Eastern Question*. Macmillan; and Macfie A. L. 1989, *The Eastern Question*. Longman.
6. For reform movements in the Ottoman Empire see Lewis B. 1961, *The Emergence of Modern Turkey*. Oxford University Press.
7. Davison R. H. 1990, *Essays on Ottoman and Turkish History*. Saqi Books, p. 244; Lewis B. 1961, *The Emergence of Modern Turkey*, pp. 329–30.
8. For an account of the history of the Ottoman constitution see *Encyclopaedia of Islam (EI)*, new edition, *Düstur*. The text of parts of the first Ottoman constitution is printed in Hertslet E. 1891, *Map of Europe by Treaty*. Vol. 4, pp. 2531–40.

9. When asked by an American journalist how he had won the war of independence, Mustafa Kemal is said to have replied, with a smile: 'With the telegraph wires'.
10. Volkan V., Itzkowitz N. 1984, *The Immortal Atatürk*, pp. 47–8.

Chapter 2

EARLY CAREER

. . .

THE RISE OF THE COMMITTEE OF UNION
AND PROGRESS

The threat posed to the survival of the Ottoman Empire by
the growing strength of the Greek, Armenian and Bulgarian
nationalist organisations, particularly in Macedonia and the
eastern provinces, and the failure of the government to
respond effectively, provoked a flurry of activity among
the Young Turks. In 1902 the Young Turk organisations
abroad convened a congress in Paris, designed to unite the
movement; but the congress quickly split into two groups:
those who believed that the salvation of the empire lay
in increased centralisation and those who believed it lay
in increased decentralisation and some kind of federal
structure. More significantly, in 1906, a group of army
officers and civil servants, led by Talaat Bey, the chief clerk
in the correspondence division of the Salonika Directorate
of Posts, founded a society in Salonika known initially as
the Ottoman Freedom Society, and later as the Committee
of Union and Progress (CUP), committed to the reform
of the Ottoman Empire and the restoration of the 1876
constitution. Thereafter membership of the society spread
rapidly, particularly among the officers of the Second and
Third Army Corps, based in Edirne and Salonika; and on
4 July 1908 Ahmed Niyazi (a major in the Second Army
Corps), fearful that a military commission despatched from
Istanbul to investigate subversion in the army might discover
his part in the conspiracy, led some 200 or so of his men
and a small band of civilians sympathetic to the cause
into the hills above Monastir, calling at the same time
for the restoration of the constitution. In the following

weeks similar mutinies, inspired for the most part by the agents of the CUP, broke out throughout the area; and on 7 July, Shemsi Pasha, one of the high-ranking officers sent from Istanbul to investigate, was assassinated in the streets of Monastir; while troops despatched from Anatolia to suppress the mutiny were persuaded to refrain from firing on their comrades in arms. As a result, on 24 July Abdul Hamid, thus unexpectedly convinced of the urgent need for reform, was persuaded to announce the restoration of the constitution, the principal rebel demand.[1]

Little is known of the early history of the Ottoman Freedom Society or CUP as it became known. According to a British Intelligence report, it originally employed the 'linked group system', in which groups of five were formed, each group having a leader.[2] The leaders of five adjacent groups then in turn elected a representative, and these representatives another, until the top of the pyramid was reached; though it is unlikely that so rigid a system was ever strictly adhered to. In the early stages the conspirators frequently used membership of a masonic lodge as cover for their activities, thereby persuading the British, in particular, that the movement was largely inspired by 'jews, socialists and freemasons'.[3] Following the Young Turk revolution of 1908 the CUP changed its status to that of a political party, openly arguing its case; and to this end sub-committees or clubs were set up in every quarter of the capital, and in the provinces. Each sub-committee or club was entitled to elect a delegate to attend an annual general council, which together with a central executive committee was responsible for determining policy. Nevertheless, in the years following the revolution power and influence within the committee remained primarily with the army, supported by the police and the gendarmerie, and by a small, select band of *fedaîler* (volunteers, prepared to sacrifice themselves for the cause).

In the period following the Young Turk Revolution of 1908 the CUP rapidly secured a position of considerable power and influence in the Ottoman Government; and in due course one of absolute power. In the elections held immediately after the revolution, in the autumn of 1908, it secured a substantial majority of the seats in the chamber of deputies; and in February 1909 it engineered the resignation of Kiamil Pasha, the liberal Grand Vizier, and his replacement by Hüseyin Hilmi Pasha, considered more acceptable. Following the suppression of a mutiny or counter-revolution in the ranks of the First Army Corps, stationed in Istanbul, inspired by discontented officers and other reactionary elements, opposed to the CUP, possibly including the Sultan, it secured the abdication and exile of Abdul Hamid, a purge of political enemies in the army and the bureaucracy and the suppression of competing groups and parties, including the Mohammedan Union, the Liberal Party and the Ottoman Alliance Association. Finally, in January 1913, following a temporary reverse in its fortunes, brought about by a group of disgruntled army officers, known as the Saviour Officers, who secured the dissolution of the parliament, and the return to power of an anti-CUP government, headed by *Ghazi* Ahmed Muhtar Pasha, and later by Kiamil Pasha, it carried out a *coup d'état*, in the course of which Enver, a young and energetic officer who had played a leading role in the 1908 revolution, and a small group of officers discontented with the way things were going in the war which had broken out in the Balkans, forced their way into the Cabinet room, shot the Minister of War, and sent Kiamil Pasha and his colleagues packing. Thereafter, until the last weeks of the First World War, which broke out in 1914, the CUP ruled in the Ottoman Empire, presided over by a triumvirate of ministers: Enver, Talaat and Djemal.[4]

Of the triumvirate of leaders who ruled over the Ottoman Empire in the First World War, Enver Pasha was undoubtedly the most brilliant, if not always the most responsible. Proud, puritanical (he neither smoked nor drank) brave, daring, vainglorious, devout (he carried a copy of the Koran in his breast pocket when going into battle) and patriotic, he had been amongst the first of the CUP officers to take to the hills around Monastir in 1908; and following the success of the uprising he had become one of the principal leaders of the movement. In Tripolitania, following the Italian occupation, he played a leading part in organising the resistance, mounted by the Senussi Arab tribes, wearing the robes of a sheikh and distributing largesse with the liberality of a sultan; and in the *coup d'état* of January 1913 he led the small group of disgruntled army officers who forced their way into the Cabinet room. Finally, in the second Balkan

War, he entered Edirne (Adrianople), previously lost to the Bulgarians, riding at the head of a cavalry regiment. As a result of these and other achievements, he was appointed Minister of War, an appointment that later enabled him, with the support of only a minority of the ministers in the Ottoman Government, to engineer the entry of the Ottoman Empire into the First World War, on the side of the Central Powers (Germany and Austria–Hungary).

Great as were the problems facing the leaders of the CUP, in the period following the Young Turk revolution of 1908, they did not abandon the programme of secularisation and reform initiated by their predecessors. On the contrary, in the period preceding the First World War, and during the war itself, they continued energetically to implement numerous measures of reform, including a substantial re-organisation of the armed forces, undertaken by Enver, Minister of War, on the eve of the war, a reduction in the powers of the *Sheikh-ül-Islâm*, a further extension of government control over the religious schools, the provision of a number of places in secondary schools and universities for women, the promulgation of a new family code of law, providing a form of secular marriage and monogamous rights for women, the creation of a National Credit Bank, designed to promote local (Muslim) enterprise and investment, and a substantial amendment of the constitution, strengthening the powers of the parliament and weakening those of the Sultan. Henceforth the Sultan would be required, on the occasion of his accession, to swear an oath, promising to respect the constitution, enforce the *Şeriat* and remain loyal to the fatherland and nation. The Grand Vizier and government ministers would be made responsible, not to the Sultan, as hitherto, but to the chamber of deputies, who would acquire the right to cross examine. Were the chamber of deputies to disapprove of the conduct of a minister, then he would be required to resign. Were they to disapprove of the conduct of a Grand Vizier, then the entire Cabinet would be required to resign, and a new one appointed. In the event of the new Cabinet failing to secure the support of the chamber, then the Sultan would be required to dissolve the chamber and hold new elections. Treaties entered into by the Sultan would be made subject to the ultimate approval of the chamber. As for the Sultan's subjects, they would acquire the right to organise themselves in societies, but not to form secret societies, or societies whose purpose was the violation of the constitution, the disturbance of public order, the division of the races of the empire or the destruction of Ottoman territorial integrity; and they would be protected against unlawful search, seizure or imprisonment.[5]

. . .

THE BALKAN AND FIRST WORLD WARS

It was generally believed, at the time of the Young Turk revolution of 1908, that the rebellion was in part motivated by a desire on the part of the CUP leadership to prevent any further erosion of the territorial integrity of the Ottoman Empire, then threatened by events in Macedonia. If such were the case, their efforts, in this direction at least, proved unsuccessful. In October 1908, just a few weeks after the restoration of the constitution, Bulgaria formally announced its independence; and a day or so later Austria–Hungary annexed Bosnia and Herzegovina, the administration of which it had acquired in 1878. Shortly thereafter Crete announced its intention of uniting with Greece; and in 1911 Italy, with the connivance of the other great powers, occupied Tripolitania (Libya). Finally, in October 1912, a league of Balkan states, led by Serbia, seizing the opportunity offered by the Italian occupation of Tripolitania, and the war which it provoked, joined forces to expel the Ottomans from their remaining territories in Europe. This task they very nearly accomplished, but in the end, as a result of their failure to remain united (in the Second Balkan War, which broke out in June 1913, Greece, Serbia and Romania attacked Bulgaria) and Russian determination to prevent a Greek or Bulgarian occupation of the Ottoman capital and the area of the Straits, they succeeded merely in driving the Ottomans out of Macedonia and the greater part of Thrace, including Salonika, Mustafa Kemal's home town.

Threats to the Ottoman Empire in the period of the Tripolitanian and Balkan Wars were by no means confined to Italy and the Balkan powers. In November 1912 the Russians, concerned by the instability provoked by these wars in the area of the Straits, contemplated, not for the first time, a possible seizure of Istanbul and the Straits, possession of which remained a long-standing objective of theirs. Again, in November 1913, believing their interests in the area to be threatened by the despatch of a German military mission to the Ottoman Empire, and by the appointment of its leader, Liman von Sanders, to the command of the First Army Corps, stationed in Istanbul and the area of the Straits, the Russians threatened to occupy a number of Turkish ports or a portion of Ottoman territory, if their demands with regard to the extent of the control exercised by the military mission were not conceded. At the same time, in the area of the Persian Gulf, the Hedjaz and South Arabia, the British were busy extending their influence, as were the French in Syria and the Lebanon. It is not surprising, therefore, that in 1914, when the long-awaited European war broke out between the Central Powers (Germany and Austria–Hungary) and the Triple Entente (Great Britain, France and Russia), the Ottoman Government, or at least elements within it, led by Enver Pasha (the Minister of War), convinced of the supremacy of the German war machine, should have chosen to side not with the Entente but with the Central Powers, thereby bringing about that which they most feared – the complete defeat and destruction of their empire.

Ottoman participation in the First World War, finally accomplished in October 1914, did not bring the immediate victories Enver and his supporters had expected. A campaign against the Russians in the east, organised by Enver Pasha in the winter of 1914, led to a disastrous defeat at Sarıkamış, with the loss of almost 80,000 men, the majority frozen to death as they endeavoured to make their escape in the mountains. On the Egyptian front an expedition commanded by Djemal Pasha was halted by the gunfire of a British fleet defending the Suez Canal, and forced to retire, to take up defensive positions in Palestine. In the area of the Straits, which the western Entente powers tried to force in 1915, a victory was achieved, but at enormous cost. In the course of the fighting, the Ottoman army was decimated, losing over 160,000 men, killed or wounded. In Mesopotamia too the Ottomans succeeded in inflicting a defeat on a British expeditionary force, despatched from India, to hold the head of the Persian

Gulf, at Kut al-Imara; but following reinforcement the British succeeded in capturing Baghdad – a grievous loss to the empire. Nor did the Ottomans succeed in expelling an Allied expeditionary force, which in October 1915 had landed at Salonika; though in conjunction with their allies they did succeed in confining it to a bridgehead. Meanwhile, in the Hedjaz Sherif Husein of Mecca had, with the support of the British, mounted the so-called Arab Revolt, aimed at achieving independence for the Arab provinces. As a result, in the closing stages of the war, the Ottomans found themselves fighting, for the most part against superior forces, on five fronts, unable to make headway on any, except in the east where the collapse of Russia, following the 1917 revolution, had substantially reduced the pressure.

Nor in these years were the Ottomans successful in recovering their independence, a principal war aim; though they did succeed in unilaterally abrogating the capitulations. On the contrary, in 1916, along with Austria–Hungary and Bulgaria, they were obliged to place their armies under the supreme command of the German general staff; and following the loss of Baghdad, to agree to the appointment of a German general, Marshal von Falkenheyn, to the command of a special army group, entitled *Yıldırım* (Lightning), formed to conquer the city. As a result, in the following months, to the consternation of the local Ottoman commanders, the Germans were enabled to take effective control of the area, requisitioning property, occupying churches and mosques, building roads and bridges, establishing banks, printing money, and making contact with the Arab tribes, much as if they intended, in the event of their winning the war, to establish colonies there.

. . .

IDEOLOGICAL DEVELOPMENTS

Until the outbreak of the First World War, at least, Ottoman statesmen and intellectuals remained generally committed to the propagation of Ottomanism, the ideology considered most suited to the needs of the empire. Increasingly, however, in the period of reaction that followed the accession to power of Abdul Hamid, and in the period of the Balkan and First World Wars, in the course of which substantial territories were lost to the empire, both in Europe and Asia, they sought the support of other ideologies, in particular Islamism, or pan-Islamism as it was sometimes known, Turkism and pan-Turkism.

The exploitation of Islam for political purposes was nothing new in the Ottoman Empire. For centuries the Ottoman Sultan, the 'Padişah of Islam', had led his armies, the 'soldiers of Islam', in campaigns designed to expand the 'House of Islam'. In the reign of Abdul Hamid, and to a lesser extent in the reigns of his successors, the power of the faith was once again invoked, both as a means of fostering loyalty and support for the government at home, and as a means of encouraging resistance against the continued advance of the western imperial powers abroad, particularly the advance of Russia in central Asia and the Caucasus, and Britain, France and Italy in the Arab provinces of the Middle East and north Africa. To this end, an increasing emphasis was laid on the Islamic character of the state, and on the importance of the Caliphate, supposedly inherited by the Ottomans from the last Abbasid Caliph, following the Ottoman conquest of Egypt in 1511; though, in the interests of both stability at home and peace abroad, the promotion of Islam as an instrument of home and foreign policy had, in times of peace at least, of necessity to remain muted.[6]

Turkism and pan-Turkism were plants of a more recent cultivation. In earlier times the Turkish peoples of the Ottoman Empire had identified themselves not as Turks but as Ottomans, the followers of Osman, the eponymous founder of the empire, while the word Turk had been reserved for the simple, Turkish-speaking Anatolian peasant, a mere clodhopper or lout. In the second half of the nineteenth century, however, Ottoman scholars and intellectuals, much influenced by nationalist ideologies then popular in central Europe and the Balkans, and by the works of European writers and scholars, such as Léon Cahun (1841–1900) and Arminius Vambéry (1832–1913), who had rediscovered the ethnic identity not only of the Ottoman Turks but also of the Turkic peoples of the world in general, became increasingly convinced of the importance of ethnic identity. Thus in 1869 Mustafa Celâleddin Pasha (a Polish exile, who had converted to Islam), in a work entitled *Les Turcs Anciens et Modernes*, emphasised the ethnic identity of the Turkish peoples, and the contribution they had made to the development of civilisation; and in 1887 Ahmet Midhat Pasha, a leading Ottoman intellectual, in a *History of Modern Times*, emphasised the Turkish ancestry of the Ottomans; while Mehmed Murad, one of the leaders of the Young Turk movement, spoke of the three great nations of Asia: the Chinese, the Indians, and the Turks. Thereafter, the idea that the Turkish peoples of the Ottoman Empire might resolve their political problems by adopting a Turkish identity spread rapidly, vigorously promoted by a number of Turkish intellectuals closely related to the Young Turk movement and the CUP. Thus in 1890, Hüseyinzade Ali Bey, a teacher in the Istanbul medical school, who had studied in St Petersburg, sought to encourage the spread of pan-Turkist ideas among his students; and in 1904 Yüsuf Akçura, a Russian Tartar, educated in France, suggested in the journal *Türk*, published in Cairo, that Turkism, 'Turkish national policy based on the Turkish race', would alone resolve the problems of the empire.[7] In the following years, Ziya Gökalp, a leading Turkish intellectual, in particular, argued strongly in his numerous writings and in the many clubs and societies set up at the time to promote Turkism and pan-Turkism (such as the Turkish Society, 1908, Turkish Homeland, 1911 and Turkish Hearth, 1912), that the Turkish peoples must rediscover their true national identity, based on their common culture (Islam), language and race. Once they had discovered their true identity, he believed, political unification would inevitably follow. So persuasive indeed were such ideas in the decade or so preceding the Balkan and First World Wars, that when in the course of these wars substantial territories, inhabited by many, but by no means all, of the minority peoples, were lost to the empire, leaving merely in the heartlands of the empire, in Anatolia and Thrace, a solid block of Turkish-speaking Muslims, some twelve million or so in number, flanked by small Greek colonies in the coastal regions, and by Armenian and Kurdish communities in the east, Ottoman statesmen and intellectuals had no difficulty in transposing them into a narrower, more specific and more effective ideology: Turkish nationalism.[8]

. . .

OUTLINE OF A CAREER

In the years of revolution and war that followed his departure from Staff College in 1905, Mustafa Kemal, like a number of other young and energetic officers of his generation, rapidly ascended the ladder of promotion in his chosen career – the army. At the same time, he participated fully in the conspiratorial politics of the period. In Syria, to which, as a result of his recent indiscretion, he was first posted, for a period of practical training, he served for a while with a cavalry regiment, attached to the Fifth Army. There he witnessed the depradations practised by units of the Ottoman army on the Druze communities of the area; and joined a secret society, entitled Fatherland, later Fatherland and Freedom, founded by, amongst others, Mustafa (Canteken), a former student of the Military Medical School in Istanbul, exiled to Damascus, following a conviction for revolutionary activities. Moreover, in 1906, in a somewhat premature and ineffective endeavour to make contact with revolutionary elements in Salonika (the epicentre of conspiracy), he secretly travelled, by way of Egypt and Greece, to Salonika, there to found a branch of the Fatherland and Freedom society.

In 1907, his period of practical training completed, Mustafa Kemal was promoted to adjutant-major and posted to the Third Army in Macedonia, where he was attached to the general staff and served for a time as Inspector of the Macedonian Railway. Immediately following the Young Turk revolution of 1908, in which he played a part, appearing with Enver and a group of CUP officers on the balcony of the Olympus Hotel (from which the victory of the revolution was proclaimed), he served for a time in Tripolitania, where he was charged with the task of reasserting Ottoman control, threatened by the events in Salonika, encouraging the foundation of branches of the CUP and explaining the doctrines of the movement. In Benghazi, in particular, he is said to have taken steps to improve the morale of the Ottoman garrison, stationed there, and to have secured the submission of Sheikh Mansur, a rebellious tribal chieftain. Following his return to Macedonia, he served as chief of staff of a division in the so-called Action Army, despatched by the leaders of the CUP from Salonika to suppress the 1909 mutiny or counter-revolution in Istanbul, helping to plan the advance and draw up the proclamation issued by Mahmud Şevket Pasha, the commander of the force. In September 1909, in recognition, no doubt, of the services he had rendered in the suppression of the mutiny, he was appointed Commander of Officer Training in the Third Army, a task in which he is said to have excelled; and in 1911, following active service in Albania, where he assisted in the suppression of a rebellion, and a brief visit to France, as one of three Ottoman army officers, invited to observe French military manoeuvres in Picardy, he was promoted major. Following the Italian occupation of Tripolitania, he volunteered, along with some fifty or so other Ottoman officers, for service there, assuming command for a time of the Senussi Arab guerrilla forces in the neighbourhood of Tobruk and Derna; but following attacks of malaria, contracted in Egypt, and eye trouble, he was obliged to abandon the struggle and return to Istanbul for treatment.

On his return to Istanbul, arriving too late to participate in the greater part of the fighting in the First Balkan War, which had broken out during his absence, Mustafa Kemal was appointed director of operations, and later chief of staff, of a special task force despatched to Bolayir, on the Gallipoli peninsula, to hold the peninsula against the advancing enemy forces. Following the outbreak of the Second Balkan War, Mustafa Kemal was appointed director of operations of the force despatched to retake Edirne; and immediately following the end of the war he was appointed military attaché in Sofia. In March 1914 whilst serving in Sofia, he was promoted to the rank of lieutenant-colonel, a rank he held until June 1915, when in the course of the Gallipoli campaign he was promoted to the rank of colonel. Finally, in April 1916, at the age of thirty-five or thirty-six, he was promoted to the rank of brigadier, which rank he was to hold throughout the remaining years of the war. During these years he served on the eastern front, in command of the Sixteenth Army Corps and the Second Army; and on the Syrian front, in command of a Hedjaz expeditionary force, set up to relieve Medina, and the Seventh Army. Whilst serving on the eastern front, he took vigorous steps to re-establish discipline and root out corruption in the units under his command; and fought a number of successful actions against the Russians, recapturing Bitlis and Muş. In Syria, following his appointment as commander of the Hedjaz expeditionary force, he criticised plans drawn up by Enver for the relief of Medina, arguing that in view of the superiority of the British forces in the area it was imperative that they concentrate on defence; and he likewise criticised plans drawn up by Marshal von Falkenhayn, the German commander, for the recapture of Baghdad by the *Yıldırım* Army Group. So bitter, indeed, did the dispute become that in October 1917, having threatened resignation, and been granted leave of absence, he relinquished his command of the Seventh Army and returned to Istanbul, where he was almost immediately invited by the crown prince, Vahidettin, to accompany him, as a member of his suite, on a state visit to Germany. Whilst in Germany, according to his own account, he made a point of plaguing the German commanders, Hindenburg and Ludendorff, with indiscrete but perceptive enquiries regarding the likely outcome of the campaigns then being undertaken, but to no great avail. On his return, following an attack of the kidney complaint that had troubled him for some years, and a period of treatment and recuperation at a clinic at Karlsbad (the Bohemian spa), he was in August 1918 reappointed commander of the Seventh Army, a post he held until the end of the war when, shortly before its dissolution, he was appointed to the command of the *Yıldırım* Army group. Whilst in command of the Seventh Army in Syria, he played a leading role in organising the retreat that followed the British attack launched in September 1918, and in organising a line of defence in the foothills overlooking Aleppo.[9]

. . .

ASPECTS OF A CAREER

Mustafa Kemal's expedition to Salonika in 1906 proved both risky and unprofitable. Determined to make contact with Şükrü Pasha, an artillery general who had responded sympathetically to appeals for support, he first made arrangements with colleagues to cover his absence, and then travelled secretly, in civilian dress, by way of Egypt and Greece to Salonika. But it quickly transpired that

Şükrü Pasha had no intention of assisting him in his endeavours, while other officers he approached proved equally uncooperative; though he did succeed in persuading a number of his old friends and classmates to form a branch of the Fatherland and Freedom Society in Salonika, swearing allegiance on a revolver and a copy of the Koran. Eventually obliged to return to Syria, where his absence had been detected, he was only saved from arrest by the prompt action of friends and colleagues, who succeeded in persuading the authorities that he had in fact been present in Syria all along, serving in the neighbourhood of Beersheba, on the Egyptian border.[10]

As the rapid growth and extraordinary achievements of the Ottoman Freedom Society (later the CUP) show, Mustafa Kemal's attempts to found branches of the Fatherland and Freedom Society in Macedonia in 1906 might well have proved timely, had he been enabled to remain in the area; but in his absence the society quickly foundered, many of its members joining the new organisation. As a result, when Mustafa Kemal, his period of training in Syria completed, returned to Macedonia in September 1907 he found himself marginalised, obliged to join the new organisation merely as an ordinary member, and unable to play the leading role in events he had envisaged for himself. Yet the position he had attained in the CUP was sufficiently prominent for him to be selected as one amongst a number of young officers despatched to different parts of the empire – in Mustafa Kemal's case to Tripolitania – to assert the authority of the new regime and explain its aims and objectives.

According to the British Vice-Consul in Benghazi, the message that Mustafa Kemal endeavoured to convey to the peoples of Tripolitania was primarily political, a defence of the constitutional changes initiated by the CUP and an explanation of the virtues of Ottomanism. The new regime, he explained on one occasion, speaking to an assembly of Arab notables in Benghazi, believed that the various races of the empire, owing allegiance to the Sultan, should unite to secure the 'consolidation of liberty and the peaceful development of the new constitution'.[11] Only thus would it be possible for them to secure the complete social and cultural regeneration of the empire, newly liberated after more than thirty years of slavery. In order to achieve this end, the existing Young Turk clubs operating in the provinces of Tripoli and Benghazi should be reorganised, and membership opened to all the peoples of the empire, in particular the Arabs.

Unfortunately for Mustafa Kemal, according to the British Vice-Consul, the Arab notables of Benghazi, who 'looked askance upon the proceeding of the Young Turks', and 'shunned participation in the the proceedings of a Club where their very presence might later on be inputed to them as a crime', remained unimpressed:

> As soon as the Major had concluded his preliminary remarks, an elderly Arab rose and requested permission to speak. He said that the Arabs recognised three Authorities, viz. God, the Prophet, and the Sultan or Khalif. And he asked whether the major or his colleagues had any letter of recommendation from the latter, or other credentials to show that his Imperial Majesty recognised and approved of their mission. The answer being in the negative the Arab declared that he and his friends were unable to recognise that mission as a serious one, and the meeting was dissolved.[12]

Not that Mustafa Kemal's endeavours proved entirely wasted. On the contrary, according to the British Consul in Tripoli:

> Since Kemal Bey's arrival (in Tripoli) the two parties of Muttehidyn [sic] and Watania have coalesced and now form one designated El Ittehad El Watany or Patriotic Union. Neither the Progressists or Patriotic Unionists probably come up to the standard required of them by the Liberal Modernism of Salonika, but consideration will doubtless be taken of the fact that political parties of any kind are complete novelties in Tripoli, that politically speaking this country stands on a different footing towards the Empire in comparison with the European and Asiatic dominions of the Sultan and consequently Ottoman national feeling requires development locally.[13]

On his return from Tripolitania, Mustafa Kemal attended the second annual congress of the CUP, held almost immediately following the suppression of the Istanbul mutiny of

1909, as a delegate for Tripoli. At the congress it is said that he argued strongly in favour of the complete disengagement of the army from politics, persuading a number of delegates to support a resolution to that effect; but the resolution was defeated. Thereafter it is said that he forswore political activity for a time, concentrating on his military career; but there is little or no evidence to substantiate this contention either way.

It is frequently asserted that Mustafa Kemal's jealousy and distrust of Enver, later to become notorious, originated in the period of the Tripolitanian war, when Enver, according to some reports, ignoring the realities of the situation, issued exaggerated reports of his own success, thereby misleading the government in Istanbul and placing the lives of his followers at risk.[14] Whatever the truth of this assertion, there is no doubt that an incident in the first Balkan War did seriously damage relations between the two men. The incident occurred shortly after the *coup d'état* of 1913, when the newly-installed government, determined to take the offensive against the victorious Bulgarians, but not yet strong enough to risk a direct assault, decided to execute a plan drawn up by the General Staff for an attack on the enemy forces in the neighbourhood of Kavak, not far from Bolayir, on the Gallipoli peninsula. Following the total failure of the operation, an acrimonious dispute broke out between the officers commanding the Bolayir Corps, to which Mustafa Kemal was attached, as head of operations, and the officers commanding the Tenth Corps, to which Enver was attached, as chief of staff. It had been planned that the Bolayir Corps would engage the Bulgarian forces in front of Bolayir, while the Tenth Corps would land at Şarköy and Ince Burun to take them in the rear; but, so it was alleged, the Bolayir Corps moved prematurely, while the Tenth Corps arrived late and in the wrong place. As a result the Bolayir Corps was badly beaten, and had to be withdrawn, with the loss of half its strength. So bitter did the dispute become that both Izzet Pasha, the Vice-Commander-in-Chief, and Mahmud Şevket Pasha, the Grand Vizier, were obliged to intervene; but to no avail. When Izzet Pasha decided to appoint Hirşit Pasha, the commander of the Tenth Corps, to the command of the whole Dardanelles defence force, Fahri Pasha, the commander of the Bolayir Corps, and a number of his officers, including Mustafa Kemal and Ali Fethi, threatened to resign; and when Mahmud Şevket Pasha declared that he intended to appoint Enver to a post on the General Staff in Istanbul, they repeated their threat. In the end Mahmud Şevket Pasha was only able to resolve the problem by recalling the Tenth Corps, with Hirşit Pasha and Enver, to the Çataldja (Chataldja) front. There Enver, in particular, was once again to distinguish himself, leading a force of some 3,500 volunteers, in a heroic defence of the capital.[15]

* * *

AT GALLIPOLI

While Mustafa Kemal's service in the suppression of the 1909 mutiny, and in the Albanian, Tripolitanian and Balkan campaigns, served to enhance his reputation in military circles, only in the Gallipoli campaign of 1915 did he acquire a national reputation. On 2 February 1915, having applied for active service, he was appointed to the command of the Nineteenth Division, then in the process of formation at Tekirdağ on the Sea of Marmara. On 25 February, preparations being completed, he moved the division to Maydos on the Gallipoli Peninsula, and thence to Boghali. When, therefore, in April 1915 the Allied Powers, having failed in their attempt to force the Dardanelles by naval power alone, landed forces, not as General Liman von Sanders (the German officer commanding the Straits defences) had predicted at Bolayir (Bulair), the narrowest point on the peninsula, but at Ari Burnu, in the neighbourhood of Kaba Tepe, on the Aegean side of the peninsula, Mustafa Kemal's response was immediate. On hearing of the landing of the Allied, mainly Australian and New Zealand forces, at Ari Burnu, he at once ordered up not, as instructed, a mere battalion but the whole division, a decision which in the view of some historians, at least, not only denied the heights overlooking Ari Burnu to the enemy but also proved decisive in determining the outcome of the campaign.[16] Moreover, in the weeks following he launched a series of desperate attacks, designed to drive the enemy forces into the sea, an objective which he very nearly succeeded in accomplishing; and in August, when the Allies, hoping to turn the Ottoman defences, landed substantial forces at Suvla Bay, to the north of Ari Burnu, and advanced across the plain of Anafarta, in the direction of the villages of Büyük and Küçük Anafarta, and the mountain heights beyond, where Mustafa Kemal had been placed in command of the entire front, he again mustered his forces for a series of suicidal attacks on the enemy troops, driving them once more from the high ground. Nor did he relent in the weeks of deadlock that followed. On the contrary, throughout he continued to call for further attacks, designed to drive the enemy into the sea; but for want of reinforcements his requests were turned down. Thus frustrated, on 9 November, a mere week or so before the evacuation of Allied forces from Ari Burnu and Suvla Bay, and a month before the evacuation of all Allied forces from the peninsula, having first threatened resignation, and then, at the suggestion of Liman von Sanders, accepted sick leave instead, he returned in a state of total exhaustion to Istanbul.[17]

Mustafa Kemal's own account of the events leading up to the battle for the control of the Chunuk Bair crest, overlooking Ari Burnu, deserves to be quoted at length:

I spoke on the telephone to . . . Essad Pasha [Commander of the Third Army Corps] at Gallipoli. He said that no clear information about what was going on had yet been obtained. It was at 0630 hours that, from a report which arrived from Halil Sami Bey, it was learnt that a force of enemy had climbed the heights of Ari Burnu and that I was required to send a battalion against them. Both from this report and as a result of the personal observation I had carried out at Mal Tepe, my firm opinion was, just as I had previously judged, that an enemy attempt to land in strength in the neighbourhood of Kaba Tepe was now taking place. Therefore I appreciated that it was impossible to carry out my task with a battalion, but that as I had reckoned before, my whole division would be required to deal with the enemy. . . . The scene which met our eyes was a most interesting one. To my mind it was the most vital moment of the occurrence.

Just then I saw men of a detachment who had been placed on hill Point 261 to the south of Chunuk Bair to observe and cover the shore from there, running back towards, in fact fleeing towards, Chunuk Bair . . . Confronting these men myself, I said 'Why are you running away?' 'Sir, the enemy', they said. 'Where?' 'Over there', they said, pointing out hill 261.

In fact a line of skirmishers of the enemy approached hill 261 and was advancing completely unopposed. Now just consider the situation. I had left my troops, so as to give the men ten minutes' rest. The enemy had come to this hill. It meant that the enemy were nearer to me than my troops were, and if the enemy came to where I was my troops would find themselves in a very difficult position. Then, I still do not know what it was, whether a logical appreciation or an instinctive action, I do not know. I said to the men who were running away, 'You cannot run away from the enemy.' 'We have got no ammunition', they said. 'If you haven't got any ammunition, you have your Bayonets', I said, and shouting to them, I made them fix their bayonets and lie down on the ground. At the same time I sent the orderly officer beside me off to the rear to bring up to where I was at the double those men of the infantry regiment who were advancing on Chunuk Bair who could reach it in time. When the men fixed their bayonets and lay down on the ground the enemy also lay down. The moment of time that we gained was this one. . . . It was about 10.00 hours when the 57th Regiment began its attack.[18]

In his orders Mustafa Kemal, like other commanders at the front, repeatedly called on his men to die in the defence of their country. 'There is no going back', he declared on one occasion. 'It is our duty to save our country, and we must acquit ourselves honourably and nobly. I must remind all of you that to seek rest or comfort now is to deprive the nation of its rest and comfort for ever.' But, as he remarked at the time, it was not for their country, but for Allah that his men, many of them Arabs, died, for the prospect of becoming a *Ghazi* (revered Muslim warrior) or a martyr, destined to ascend direct to heaven.[19]

In recognition of his service in the Gallipoli campaign, Mustafa Kemal was awarded, by the Sultan, Mehmed V, a silver medal for distinguished service and a gold medal for efficiency; by the German Kaiser William II, the iron cross; and by the Bulgarian King Ferdinand the decoration of St Alexander, command rank.[20]

. . .

DEFEAT AND DISAFFECTION

In the period of the First World War, during which Enver and his supporters remained firmly in control, Mustafa Kemal became increasingly critical of the policies pursued by the government. In November 1915, following his return from the Gallipoli front, he made a point of approaching Ahmed Nesimi, the Minister for Foreign Affairs, in order to inform him of his views regarding the military situation and what he saw as the unconstitutional and unacceptable activities of the German military mission.[21] In 1917, in Anatolia, he despatched a circular telegram to the other commanders in the east, urging them to undertake common action. On this occasion Vehip Pasha, the Commander of the Second Army, intercepted the message and passed a copy to Enver, who at once summoned Mustafa Kemal to Istanbul to confront him with the choice of abiding by military discipline, or resigning from the army in order to take up politics. Were he to chose the latter, Enver declared, he would personally see to it that he was provided with a seat in parliament, an offer which Mustafa Kemal, well aware of the impotence of the assembly, politely declined.[22] In the same year, when appointed Commander of the Seventh Army under General Falkenhayn, he despatched, on 20 September, a report to both the High Command and the Cabinet, highly critical of the policies pursued by the government;[23] and in October, according to Rauf Bey (a naval officer in the Ministry of Marine at the time), he initiated a series of manoeuvres, designed to drive a wedge between Enver and Talaat. During his trip to Germany, as a member of the crown prince Vahidettin's suite, he informed the crown prince, several times, of his doubts regarding the policies being pursued by the government; and following his return boldly approached Vahidettin, who

43

in the meantime had succeeded to the Sultanate, suggesting that, as Commander-in-Chief, he take direct control of the army and appoint Mustafa Kemal Chief of Staff.[24] Finally, in October 1918, from his headquarters in Adana, he vigorously supported plans, hatched in Istanbul, for the formation of a new Cabinet, led by Ahmed Izzet Pasha, in which it was suggested Mustafa Kemal might hold the office of Minister of War.[25]

In his report of 20 September 1917 Mustafa Kemal analysed the strategic situation facing the Ottoman Empire as follows. In the west, where fighting had for the moment ceased, a major attack was to be expected at any moment. In the east, thanks to the collapse of Russia, the position was quiet; but Russian forces might at any moment reappear in the Caucasus. In Iraq, the British, having captured Baghdad, were for political, economic and military reasons unlikely to advance further; though they might occupy Mosul. On the Sinai and Hedjaz fronts, on the other hand, the British were preparing for a major campaign, aimed at the conquest of Syria and the consolidation of their control of Egypt, the Red Sea and the heartland of Islam. In these circumstances the Ottoman Empire should concentrate on preparing for the coming attacks in the west and on the Sinai front. Proposals, put forward by Enver and Marshal von Falkenhayn, that the Ottomans might undertake the liberation of Iraq were, in view of the weakness of the Ottoman army and the great distances involved, out of the question. Defeat would only be avoided if steps were taken immediately to strengthen the civil administration, the gendarmerie and the department of justice, where corruption was rife. All political activity in the armed forces must cease forthwith. As for the position of Syria, where the Germans appeared intent on establishing a German Colony, the overall command there must be at once placed in the hands of an Ottoman officer; though Marshal von Falkenhayn might be permitted to remain as military commander, were this deemed necessary. On no account must they, the Ottomans, sacrifice their independence, merely to secure the survival of their empire. Rather they should act as the Bulgarians had done, jealously asserting their independence. Only then would the Germans value them as an ally. Further cooperation would merely encourage them in their plans for the colonisation of Syria and the Hedjaz. Were the Germans to succeed in achieving their ambitions in this direction, it could hardly be expected that the Sultanate and the Caliphate would survive.[26]

In a private conversation with Ahmed Emin Yalman, a Turkish journalist, also held in 1917, Mustafa Kemal expressed his views on the critical situation facing the empire with even greater force. The real enemies of the Ottoman Empire, he declared, were the Young Turk triumvirate of leaders – Enver, Talaat and Djemal – who, convinced that the Ottoman Empire could not stand alone, had committed it to the German alliance, thereby sacrificing its independence and effectively reducing it to the status of a colony. All the active chiefs of the Ottoman General Staff were German, as were the commanders of the Ottoman armies, whose forces were deployed merely to reduce pressure on the German front. 'Our own men in high office are gamblers, staking Turkey's destiny on a single card, final German victory . . . they are not aware that at this moment they have lost the war because Germany has lost the initiative and even the will to succeed.' As for the social and economic fabric of the Ottoman Empire, these were being destroyed by war profiteering, speculation and the breakdown of moral values.[27]

In later years Mustafa Kemal remained convinced that his opposition to, and frequent criticism of, the policies pursued by the leadership of the CUP, in particular Enver, had adversely affected his career, resulting in undesirable postings to Tripolitania, Sofia, eastern Anatolia and Syria, designed to remove him from the centre of power, and expose him to humiliation and defeat. Such a possibility cannot be discounted, but the facts suggest otherwise. Erik Jan Zürcher, the Dutch historian, has shown conclusively that, after graduating from the Istanbul staff college in 1905, as one of the élite group of general staff captains, destined for rapid promotion, his military career was normal enough, though of course he could not compete with such high flyers as Enver and Hafiz Hakki, who, after the 1913 coup and the liberation of Edirne which followed, received exceptionally rapid promotion.[28] Nor is there much evidence to support the contention that the postings he complained of were intended to remove him from the centre of power and expose him to humiliation and defeat. On the contrary, in every case an alternative explanation exists. Conditions in Tripolitania, recently disturbed by the effects of the Young Turk revolution, required the despatch of an able and determined officer, capable of reimposing Ottoman control and persuading the inhabitants of the area of the advantages to be gained from constitutional reform. In the period immediately following the second Balkan War, the exceptional strategic importance of Bulgaria, well understood by both the Central and the Triple Entente Powers, again required the despatch of an able officer, capable of persuading the Bulgarians of the advantages to be gained from an improvement in relations with the Ottoman Empire. The threat posed to the very heart of the empire by the Allied assault on the Dardanelles in 1915, clearly made Mustafa Kemal's appointment to the command of the Nineteenth Division, soon to be posted to the Gallipoli peninsula, one of vital importance; while the conditions prevailing in eastern Anatolia and Syria required the appointment of an officer of exceptional ability. It would seem more reasonable, therefore, to interpret these appointments, not as an attempt to expose Mustafa Kemal to humiliation and defeat, but as a testimony to the high esteem in which, despite his sometimes irascible temper, he was undoubtedly held.

It is evident that by the closing stages of the First World War Mustafa Kemal had acquired a position of considerable power and influence in the Ottoman Empire. Already, in the period of the Young Turk revolution of 1908, and in the period of the Tripolitanian and Balkan Wars which followed, he had carved out for himself an influential place in the CUP, as one of the fifty or so activist officers who formed the backbone of the military wing of the organisation. In the First World War, as a result of his achievements in the Gallipoli campaign, and on the eastern and southern fronts, he advanced further, acquiring high rank and prestige, the necessary preconditions of appointment to high office in the Ottoman Empire. Nor is there any doubt that he was considered a suitable candidate for high office in this period, as a rather curious incident, involving a possible *coup d'état*, supposedly planned by one Yakub Djemil, a well-known *fedaî* (a volunteer prepared to sacrifice himself for the cause), reveals, for in the course of the investigation it was discovered that Mustafa Kemal's name had been mentioned as a possible successor to Enver Pasha as Minister of War; though there is no suggestion that he was himself in any way implicated in the plot.[29] Yet as an opponent of Enver Pasha and his supporters, access to high office remained closed to him. In the closing stages of the First World War, therefore, he must have frequently wondered if he would ever succeed in acquiring real power, the power to determine policy and shape the course of events, the power, in other words, to attempt an answer to the question frequently posed by young men of his generation: *Bu devlet nasıl kurtarılabilir?* (How can this state be saved?)[30]

. . .

NOTES AND REFERENCES

1. For an account of the Young Turk Revolution of 1908 see Ramsaur E. E. 1957, *The Young Turks*. Princeton University Press.
2. Public Record Office, London, Foreign Office (FO) 371 4141, General Staff Intelligence No. 2838, March 1919.
3. Kedourie E. 1971, 'Young Turks, Freemasons and Jews', *Middle Eastern Studies*, Vol. 7.
4. Lewis B. 1961, *The Emergence of Modern Turkey*. Oxford University Press, Chapter 7. Andrew Mango argues convincingly that the events of April 1909 should be seen not as a counter-revolution but as a mutiny, though it is evident that, had the mutiny succeeded, it would quickly have developed into a counter-revolution. See Mango A., 'The Young Turks', *Middle Eastern Studies*, Vol. 8.
5. For an account of the reform of the Ottoman Empire in the Young Turk period see Shaw S. and E. K. 1977, *History of the Ottoman Empire and Modern Turkey*. Cambridge University Press, Chapter 4; and Lewis B. 1961, *The Emergence of Modern Turkey*, Chapter 7.
6. Lewis B. 1961, *The Emergence of Modern Turkey*, Chapter 10.
7. Ibid., pp. 320–1.
8. For an account of the rise of Turkish nationalism see Kushner D. 1977, *The Rise of Turkish Nationalism*. Frank Cass; and Heyd U. 1979, *The Foundations of Turkish Nationalism*. Hyperian Press, Westport, Connecticut.

9. Turkish National Commission 1981, *Atatürk*. Türk Tarih Kurumu, Ankara; Zürcher E. J. 1984, *The Unionist Factor*. E. J. Brill, Leiden; Deny J. 1926, 'Biographie de Moustafa Kemal Pacha', *Revue du Monde Musulman*, Vol. 63; Deny J. 1927, 'Les Souvenirs du Gazi Moustafa Kemal Pacha', *Revue des Etudes Islamiques*, Vol. 1.

10. Volkan V., Itzkowitz N. 1984, *The Immortal Atatürk*. University of Chicago Press, Chapter 5; Zürcher E. J. 1984, *The Unionist Factor*, pp. 32–7; Afet 1937, 'Le Revolver Sacré', *Belleten*, Vol. 1.

11. Simon R. 1984, 'Prelude to Reforms: Mustafa Kemal in Libya', in Landau J. M. 1984, *Atatürk and the Modernisation of Turkey*. Westview Press, Boulder, Colorado.

12. Simon R. 1980, 'Beginnings of Leadership; Mustafa Kemal's First Visit to Libya 1908', *Belleten*, Vol. 44.

13. Simon R. 1984, 'Prelude to Reforms'.

14. Zürcher E. J., 1984, *The Unionist Factor*, p. 54; Mikusch, Dagobert von 1931, *Gasi Mustafa Kemal*. P. List, Leipzig, pp. 115–16. According to one British commentator, the mutual animosity felt by Enver and Mustafa Kemal had, by the end of the First World War, become common knowledge. See *British Documents on Atatürk (BDA)* in progress. Türk Tarih Kurumu, Ankara, Vol. 2, No. 92, Note 5.

15. Zürcher E. J. 1984, *The Unionist Factor*, pp. 56–9.

16. Aspinall-Oglander 1932, *History of the Great War*. Heinemann, Vol. 2, pp. 285–6.

17. James R. R. 1965, *Gallipoli*. Batsford.

18. Ibid., pp. 112–13.

19. Volkan V., Itzkowitz N. 1984, *The Immortal Atatürk*, p. 92.

20. Ibid., p. 91.

21. Deny J. 1927, 'Les Souvenirs', Vol. 1, p. 131.

22. Zürcher E. J. 1984, *The Unionist Factor*, p. 61.

23. Arisoy M. S. 1982, *Mustafa Kemal Atatürk'un Söyleyip Yazdıkları*. Türk Tarih Kurumu, Ankara, pp. 275–81.

24. Zürcher E. J. 1984, *The Unionist Factor*, pp. 62–3; Deny J. 1927, 'Les Souvenirs', pp. 146–59.

25. Deny J. 'Les Souvenirs', p. 162; Zürcher E. J. 1984, *The Unionist Factor*, p. 107; Turkish National Commission 1981, p. 31.

26. Arisoy M. S. 1982, *Mustafa Kemal*, pp. 275–81.

27. Yalman A. E. 1956, *Turkey in my Time*. University of Oklahoma Press, p. 50.
28. Zürcher E. J. 1984, *The Unionist Factor*, pp. 63–7.
29. Deny J. 1927, 'Les Souvenirs', pp. 130–3.
30. Zürcher E. J. 1984, *The Unionist Factor*, p. 22.

Chapter 3

MOMENT OF DECISION

. . .

THE ARMISTICE OF MUDROS:
AN IMMEDIATE RESPONSE

The conclusion, on 30 October 1918, of the Armistice of
Mudros, which ended the participation of the Ottoman
Empire in the First World War, found Mustafa Kemal
at his command post in the hills above Aleppo, busy
trying to regroup his retreating forces. As he surveyed the
terms of the armistice, which included an Allied occupation
of the Bosphorus and Dardanelles forts, the immediate
demobilisation of the Ottoman army (except for such troops
as might be required for the surveillance of frontiers and
the maintenance of internal order), the occupation of the
Taurus tunnel system, the surrender of the remaining
Ottoman garrisons in the Arab provinces, the evacuation
of Cilicia, free use by Allied ships of Turkish ports,
the posting of Allied control officers on the railways,
and the right to occupy strategic points in the event of
a situation arising which threatened Allied security, he
became increasingly concerned. His response was immediate.
Profoundly sceptical regarding the good faith of the Allies,
and convinced that they intended the complete destruction
of the empire, he at once fired off a series of telegrams,
seeking clarification regarding the precise significance of the
terms of the armistice, with particular regard to the area of
his command. He also redoubled his efforts to regroup the
forces under his command, in order to establish a line of
defence stretching from a point just north of Aleppo to a
point on the Mediterranean, to the south of Antakya, and
ordered the transfer of stocks of arms and equipment to
safe places in the interior. Moreover, when the British, in

an apparent infringement of the terms of the armistice, connived at by Izzet Pasha, the newly appointed Grand Vizier, attempted to occupy Alexandretta, supposedly to supply their forces in Aleppo, but in Mustafa Kemal's view in order to outflank the Seventh Army, he gave orders that any attempt on the part of the British to land troops should be resisted, if need be by force:

> The armistice, in the final form in which it has been concluded [he declared in a telegram to Izzet Pasha despatched on 8 November 1918], does not secure the well-being and integrity of the Ottoman Empire. As soon as possible we must discover the precise significance of the terms used. Otherwise, if we continue along the present lines, it is not unlikely that the English, who today wish to advance as far as the Killis–Payas line, will tomorrow want to advance as far as the Taurus, and later the Konya–Smyrna line. Eventually they will seek the right to control our army, and even to choose the ministers of our Cabinet. I know very well just how weak and powerless we are, but I remain convinced that it is necessary for the state to decide the exact limit of the sacrifice that it is prepared to make.[1]

Mustafa Kemal's opposition to what he saw as the pusillanimous policy adopted by the Ottoman Government, and the encroachments of the British forces in the area of his command, proved unavailing. On 7 November Izzet Pasha ordered the liquidation of the *Yıldırım* Army Group, and a few days later, his mission at an end, Mustafa Kemal was obliged to return to Istanbul. There in the following months, until his departure for Samsun in May 1919, he was to remain, ensconced first in the Pera Palace Hotel, and then in a house in Şişli, observing the situation as it developed, consulting with friends and colleagues and, as ever, awaiting an opportunity to play a leading part in the government of his country.

· · ·

THE CHALLENGE FACING THE OTTOMAN TURKS

The situation facing the Ottoman Turks in the period immediately following the end of the First World War

51

was, as numerous commentators have remarked, dire. In Istanbul, in Galata, Pera and Scutari, Allied units, including, in the British contingent, Indian and Singhalese troops, and, in the French, Algerian, were busy establishing garrisons; while in the Golden Horn an Allied fleet lay at anchor, its guns trained on the Yıldız Palace, where the Sultan, Mehmed VI Vahideddin, cowered − terrified of assassination. In the streets of the old city, partially destroyed by fire the previous year, and in the Byzantine ruins, refugees swarmed begging for alms, while in the city centre, in the neighbourhood of the Ministry of War and the great arsenals, hundreds of unemployed officers gathered, seeking employment. Elsewhere, in Anatolia and Thrace, the Allies were at work, implementing the terms of the armistice, occupying strategic points, including Eskişehir, Adana, Mersin, Maraş, Marmaris, Samsun and Trabzon, destroying the Straits' defences and monitoring the disarmament of what remained of the Ottoman army; while minority groups, with substantial support from abroad, were busy preparing the ground for independence or annexation. In northern Anatolia, along the Black Sea coast, Greek organisations, such as Mawrimira (founded by the Greek Orthodox Patriarch of Constantinople), were holding meetings, organising armed bands and spreading propaganda in favour of the creation of an independent Greek state. In Izmir (Smyrna), unofficially promised to the Greeks in the course of the war, Greek agents were active, building up support; and in the eastern provinces, in Kars, Ardahan and Batum, recently recovered from the Russians, Armenian bands, committed to the creation of a greater Armenia, were advancing, wreaking revenge on their enemies for the massacres carried out in the early years of war.

Nor were the Ottomans in any doubt what their enemies intended. In December 1917 the newly installed Bolshevik government in St Petersburg, determined to expose the wicked machinations of the imperial powers, had revealed to the world the contents of the secret treaties and agreements concluded by the Entente powers in the course of the war. These included in particular, the so-called Constantinople Agreement of May 1915, in which the Entente powers had agreed that, in the event of their securing a victorious outcome to the war, Russia might obtain possession of Constantinople and the Straits, including a substantial stretch of territory in north-western Anatolia; the Treaty of London of April 1915, later confirmed in the Agreement of St Jean de Maurienne of August 1917, in which they had agreed that in the event of a total or partial partition of Turkey in Asia, Italy might obtain compensation in the Mediterranean region adjacent to the province of Antalya; and the Sykes–Picot Agreement of May 1916 in which they had agreed that, in the event of victory, Britain might obtain Mesopotamia, France Syria, the Lebanon and Cilicia, and Russia a substantial part of eastern Anatolia, including the *vilayets* of Van, Bitlis, Trabzon and Erzurum.[2]

How far it was the intention of the western Entente powers to implement these treaties and agreements, or at least those of them that remained valid – the Constantinople Agreement of May 1915 had been invalidated by the falling out of Russia, while the St Maurienne Agreement of August 1917 had been made dependent on the consent of Russia, never obtained – remained to be seen. Yet this much was clear. In Mesopotamia, the British, intent on building up a strategic line of defence in the Middle East and securing control of the approaches to India, their greatest imperial possession, were determined to secure control. In Syria, the Lebanon and Cilicia, the French, intent on expanding their imperial interests in the area, were likewise determined to secure control; while the Italians, irrespective of the validity or otherwise of the St Maurienne Agreement, remained determined to secure an appropriate share in any distribution of war spoils undertaken by the Allies. As for the remaining Ottoman territories in Anatolia, it seemed that the British and French, determined to punish the Ottomans for their participation in the First World War, on the side of the Central Powers, and if possible to secure strategic control of the area, intended to impose a settlement, based on the principle of partition, which might include the creation of an independent Armenia and an independent or autonomous Kurdistan; while with regard to the Straits, freed now from the need to consider the interests of Russia, they intended to impose a new regime, based on the principles of internationalisation, neutralisation and demilitarisation, securing freedom of passage not only for ships-of-commerce, as heretofore, but also for ships-of-war. In this way they hoped to secure not only the freedom to exercise naval power in the area of the Black Sea, but also effective control of the Ottoman capital, which would, they believed (mistakenly as it turned out), carry with it control of the interior.

. . .

THE OTTOMAN RESPONSE

Faced with this formidable challenge to its existence, the Ottoman political and military élite responded in a variety of ways. In Istanbul the Sultan, Mehmed VI Vahideddin, convinced of the hopelessness of his position, and determined at all costs to secure the survival of his house, sought to ingratiate himself with the Allies, in particular the British, with whom he hoped to re-establish the relationship that had prevailed throughout the greater part of the nineteenth century, when the British had sought to preserve the independence and integrity of the Ottoman Empire as a bulwark against Russia. To this end, in November 1918 he succeeded in bringing about the resignation of Izzet Pasha's government and the installation of a new, more accommodating one, led by Ahmet Tevfik Pasha, an aged diplomat, committed to cooperation with the Allies and the extinction of the CUP. In the Ministry of War, on the other hand, and in the army in general, many high-ranking officers, including Mustafa Kemal himself until his return to Istanbul, convinced that the Allies had no intention of respecting the terms of the armistice and sceptical regarding the effectiveness of a policy of cooperation, were already active, laying the foundations for further resistance, delaying the demobilisation of the army, building up secret stocks of arms and equipment, and organising and equipping the militia and local resistance groups, particularly in areas threatened by Greek and Armenian armed bands. Thus in November 1918, Ali Fuat, following his appointment to the command of the Second and Seventh Army Corps in Syria (later reformed as the Twentieth Army Corps), took steps to bring the gendarmerie, permitted under the terms of the armistice, up to full strength and set up resistance groups in the area; and later to transfer his troops and their supplies first to Ereğli, in the province of Konya, and thence to Ankara, far removed from the controlling hand of the Allied forces; while Kiazim Karabekir, on taking command of the Fourteenth Army Corps, at Tekirdağ, transferred his troops to the Anatolian side of the Straits, lest they be overtaken by a Greek occupation of eastern Thrace. In Kars, Yakup Şevki Pasha, commander of the Ninth Army, was at pains to delay the evacuation of Kars, Ardahan and Batum, ordered by the Allies; and when finally obliged to comply, endeavoured to set up an independent Muslim government there, before departing, while in south-western Anatolia *Mersinli* Djemal Pasha, appointed Inspector of the Second Army, organised resistance, as did Djafar Tayar in eastern Thrace and Kiazim Bey, commander of the Sixty-First Division, in the Balikesir Bandırma region.[3]

In the weeks immediately following the conclusion of the Mudros Armistice, the possibility of continued armed struggle against the victorious Entente powers was, as Mustafa Kemal and the other military commanders knew, by no means remote. In western Anatolia and the Straits, units of the First, Third and Fifth Armies, numbering some 35,000 men, remained in place, as did units of the Second and Seventh Armies (the *Yıldırım* Army Group), later reformed as the Twentieth Army Corps, numbering some 18,000 men, in northern Syria and Cilicia, and units of the Sixth Army Corps – the Sixth Army Corps surrendered immediately following the conclusion of the Mudros Armistice, but a number of units remained in place – numbering some 8,000 men in the neighbourhood of Mosul. More significantly, in the eastern provinces and the Caucasus, a new army, the Ninth – that commanded by Yakup Şevki Pasha – numbering some 30,000 men, supplemented by 20,000 militia and gendarmerie, well equipped and supplied, had been created by Enver Pasha in the closing stages of the war, from units transferred from the Galician and Moldavian fronts, in the expectation that it might be used to fill the vacuum created by the collapse of Russia and if need be, in case of defeat in the west, carry on the struggle in the east. In the period immediately following the conclusion of the armistice, therefore, the Ottoman army, despite the losses inflicted on it in the course of the war and the effects of desertion, remained a formidable force, numbering some

110,000 men, enjoying an effective structure of command and an efficient system of communication; though in the following months the demobilisation measures, enforced by the Allies, and further desertions substantially reduced its numbers, possibly by as much as a half.[4]

In their preparations for an armed struggle the army leadership received active support from a number of secret organisations, set up in the course of the Balkan and First World Wars, including *Teşkilati Mahsusa* (Special Organisation), a secret organisation, officially founded by Enver Pasha on the eve of the First World War, but in fact established earlier, in order to strengthen the authority of the CUP government and promote the cause of Pan-Islamism and Pan-Turkism in the east; and *Karakol* (Guard), a secret organisation, founded at the instigation of Talaat Pasha, by Kara Kemal, the CUP chief in Istanbul, Halil Bey, Enver's uncle, Kara Vasif, an army officer, and others, in 1918, in order to prepare for post-war resistance and protect CUP officials wanted by the Allies for war crimes, particularly the Armenian massacres, committed in the course of the war. According to Hüsamettin Ertürk, a staff officer of the organisation in Istanbul, *Teşkilati Mahsusa* was officially dissolved in October 1918, but its agents continued to function under a new name, the General Revolutionary Organisation of the Islamic World, in the period immediately following the end of the First World War, preparing on Enver's instructions, for the 'second phase of the war', which it was expected would take place in Azerbaijan and the Caucasus. Not that its activities were confined to those areas. In the following months it assembled substantial stocks of arms and equipment at numerous places in Anatolia, including Erzurum, Kayseri, Kastamonu, Salihli, Ankara and Bozdagi, and organised guerrilla bands there. Following its foundation, *Karakol* likewise set up a network of agents, many recruited from *Teşkilati Mahsusa*, capable of organising resistance; while numerous individuals and groups formed secret organisations, particularly in Istanbul, to prepare for the coming struggle. So effective were these groups and organisations, in the weeks immediately following the end of the First World War, that by the spring of 1919 they had succeeded in laying the foundations of a formidable movement of national resistance, capable of challenging the authority of the Allied Powers and their surrogates amongst the minorities.[5]

Preparations to deal with the crisis generated by defeat in the First World War were by no means confined to the army and the secret services. In the months immediately following the end of the war a host of new political parties and societies were established, and old ones reactivated, organised and inspired for the most part either by supporters of the CUP, supposedly dissolved in November 1918, or by those opposed to it. Parties organised by the supporters of the CUP included *Teceddüt Fırkası* (The Renovation Party), founded in November by Yunus Nadi, the deputy for Aydin, and others, and *Osmanlı Hürriyetperver Avam Fırkası* (The Ottoman Liberal People's Party), founded by Ali Fethi, an old friend and colleague of Mustafa Kemal. Parties organised by those opposed to the CUP, descended for the most part from the parties of the Liberal Union of 1911, included the *Hürriyet ve Itilâf* (Party of Freedom and Understanding) sometimes known as the Liberal Union, supported by, amongst others, Damad Ferid Pasha; *Osmanlı Sulh ve Selâmet* (Ottoman Peace and Safety), supported by army officers opposed to the CUP, and *Ingiliz Muhipler* (Friends of England), supported by Said Molla, a leading reactionary. At the same time, in Istanbul and the provinces, a number of societies and associations were established, at the instigation for the most part, it would appear, of the CUP leadership, for the defence of national rights in the regions. Thus in November, at the instigation of Talaat Pasha, an Ottoman Society for the Defence of Thrace-Paşaeli was set up by amongst others Faik Bey, a Unionist deputy, which in the following months convened congresses, collected evidence proving that the population of the area was in the majority Turkish, and prepared for resistance against a possible Greek occupation. In December a Society for the Defence of the National Rights of the Eastern Provinces was set up by Süleyman Nazif (a leading Unionist) which opened a newspaper to propagate its views in Erzurum and other towns in the area, and convened a series of congresses, including the Congress of Erzurum, later attended by Mustafa Kemal. Again in December a Society for the Defence of Ottoman Rights in Izmir was set up, by Mahmut Djelal, the secretary of the CUP branch in the town, which convened congresses and organised demonstrations; and in February 1919 a Society for the Preservation of the National Rights of Trabzon was established by Faik Ahmet, the Unionist mayor, which convened congresses, despatched emissaries to Paris, to inform the Supreme Council of the true situation (as they saw it) prevailing in the eastern provinces, and organised resistance against the Greek and Armenian armed bands, operating in the area. Also active at the time were *Türk Ocaği* (Turkish Hearth) founded in 1911 by students of the Military Medical Academy, to promote Turkish nationalist ideas; *Milli Talim ve Terbiye Cemiyeti* (National Society for Instruction and Education), founded in 1916 by a group of leading judges and academics, again to encourage the spread of Turkish nationalist ideas, and *Wilson Prinsipleri Osmanlı Fırkası* (Society of Ottomans professing the Principles of President Wilson), established by a group of journalists and intellectuals, including Halide Edib Hanım, the noted Turkish writer and academic, to promote a peace settlement in the Near and Middle East, based on the principles of nationality and justice, enshrined in the so-called Fourteen Points, a peace initiative undertaken by Woodrow Wilson, the American president, in January 1918. In December the Turkish Hearth and the National Society for Instruction and Education joined together to organise a congress in Istanbul, attended by no less than sixty-three political, cultural and professional groups.[6]

. . .

MUSTAFA KEMAL AND THE ANATOLIAN SOLUTION

In the weeks following his return to Istanbul, Mustafa Kemal, like many others in the army and the political élite, remained initially uncertain how to respond to the crisis facing the empire, though throughout he remained convinced of the need for strong leadership, which alone he believed would secure the survival of an independent Ottoman state. To this end he made contact with the *Osmanlı Hürriyetperver Avam Fırkası*, formed by his friend Ali Fethi; and in November when the recently installed government, led by Ahmed Tevfik Pasha, sought a vote of confidence in the chamber of deputies, he argued strongly that the chamber should reject the motion, hoping thereby to bring about the reinstatement of a government led by Izzet Pasha, with himself as Minister of War. Later, when these and other efforts to influence government policy failed – Tevfik Pasha's new government received a resounding vote of confidence, and on 21 December the chamber of deputies was dissolved – he considered a number of alternative responses, including a proposal, discussed with a number of his friends and colleagues, that they attempt a *coup d'état*; a proposal put forward, according to Hüseyin Rauf, the Minister of Marine, by Kara Kemal, the CUP party chief in Istanbul, and founding member of *Karakol*, that they kidnap Ahmed Tevfik Pasha, the newly installed Grand Vizier, in order to delay the implementation of an anti-Unionist policy; and finally a proposal, later adopted, of despatching officers, loyal to the nationalist cause to Anatolia, there to take effective control of the army, and establish a movement capable of defending the interests of the Turkish-speaking Muslim peoples of what remained of the empire.[7]

The idea of creating a centre of national resistance in Anatolia, in the event of defeat in war and an enemy occupation of the capital, was nothing new. Twice in the preceding decade, in the course of the Balkan and First World Wars the Ottoman Government had made plans, in part actually executed, to move the seat of government to the interior, to Bursa, Eskişehir or Konya; and when defeat appeared imminent, Enver had moved substantial forces to eastern Anatolia and the Caucasus in order to prepare for further struggle; while individual commanders, including Mustafa Kemal himself, had built up stocks of arms and equipment at strategic points, strengthened the gendarmerie and organised armed bands to oppose the occupation forces of the Allies and their surrogates. It is scarcely surprising, therefore, that, in the period of acute crisis that followed the defeat of the Ottoman Empire in the First World War, and the occupation of its capital, Mustafa Kemal, like other leading military commanders and officials, should have eventually opted for the so-called 'Anatolian solution'; though the precise timing of the decision, and the manner in which it was arrived at – in *Speech* Mustafa Kemal chose to begin his account of the national movement, and his part in it, in May 1919 – remains a mystery. What is clear is that in the winter months of 1918–19 a plot was hatched by a group of senior army officers, or as Erik Jan Zürcher would have it, a 'closely knit group of Unionist colonels and brigadiers' in the War Office,[8] including amongst others, Mustafa Kemal, Ali Fuat, later commander of the Twentieth Army Corps, Kiazim Karabekir, later commander of the Fifteenth Army Corps, Djevad Pasha, Minister of War, and Fevzi Pasha, Chief of the General Staff, to set up a national resistance movement in the interior, capable of organising resistance against the occupation forces, suppressing the armed bands of the minorities and countering the defeatist attitudes of the government. Thus in December 1918 and March 1919 Mustafa Kemal and Ali Fuat discussed the possibility on several occasions, agreeing on a possible programme of action, involving a halt to the process of demobilisation and disarmament, the appointment of able and energetic officers to the command of army units stationed in the interior, a take-over of the administration there, and the implementation of positive steps to improve morale and prevent internecine strife; though on both occasions Mustafa Kemal made it clear that for the moment at least he would prefer to seek a ministerial appointment, in the capital, still considered a possibility. In March–April, Kiazim Karabekir, recently appointed commander of the Fifteenth Army Corps based in Erzurum, likewise twice discussed the possibility with Mustafa Kemal in Istanbul, shortly before his departure for the east, on the second occasion specifically inviting him to join him in Erzurum, in order to organise the forces of national resistance and found a 'national government' there. Finally, according to Fevzi Pasha, shortly before Mustafa Kemal's actual departure for Anatolia, he and Djevad Pasha, drew up a programme of action, to be taken by Mustafa Kemal, following his arrival in Samsun, including the organisation of national forces in the interior and the setting up of a national administration there. In all probability, therefore, Mustafa Kemal's decision to opt for the 'Anatolian solution' was the product of a conspiracy, organised by senior elements within the War Office.[9] Alternative explanations, however, abound. One, supposedly attributed by Reşid Pasha, a leading Unionist, to the Sivas leader of the Freedom and Understanding Party, is that Mustafa Kemal was despatched to Anatolia by the leadership of the CUP as part of the general plan drawn up by Enver and Talaat Pashas in the closing stages of the war to carry on the struggle there.[10] A second, suggested by Şeref Çavuşoğlu, a member of *Karakol*, is that Mustafa Kemal was invited to head the national forces in the interior by the leaders of *Karakol* who, having built up their organisation there, felt the need to place a respected military figure at its head.[11] A third, unlikely, but by no means impossible, widely believed in Anatolia at the time, is that Mustafa Kemal was despatched to Anatolia to organise national resistance by the Sultan, Mehmed VI Vahideddin and the palace clique which surrounded him; though if such were the case they can hardly have envisaged the type of movement eventually created.[12]

However Mustafa Kemal's decision to opt for the 'Anatolian solution' was arrived at, his appointment as Inspector of the Ninth Army, later designated the Third Army, which greatly facilitated his departure, would appear to have been fortuitous. In March 1919 the representatives of the Entente powers demanded that the Ottoman Government take immediate steps to put an end to the harassment of Christian villagers in the neighbourhood of Samsun; and on 9 March they landed 200 troops at Samsun. Shortly afterwards, Mehmet Ali Bey, the Acting Minister of the Interior, fearful lest the Allies occupy the *vilayet* of Samsun – (in conjunction with the French forces occupying Cilicia, they might well have occupied the whole of central Anatolia, thereby cutting off the eastern provinces from the western parts of the empire) – suggested that the government send a senior officer to the area to suppress the unrest and disarm the Turkish and Greek bands operating there. Mehmet Şakir Pasha, the Minister of War, suggested Mustafa Kemal as a suitable candidate for the post; and on 5 May, with orders carefully formulated by his friends in the War Office, to give him the maximum possible authority, not merely over the army corps in Anatolia but also the civil authorities, he was appointed.[13] At a stroke, it would seem, the problem he faced, of deciding whether to adopt the 'Anatolian solution' was resolved. As he himself remarked: 'What a wonderful thing! Fortune smiled on me, and when I found myself basking in her smile it is hard to describe how happy I was. I recall biting my lips with excitement as I left the office. The cage had opened, the whole universe lay before me. I was like a bird about to soar with the first movement of its wings.'[14]

In the weeks preceding his departure, Mustafa Kemal expected that the Ottoman Government, at the instigation of the occupying powers, would arrest him. Already in January a new series of arrests of officers associated with the CUP had begun; and Mustafa Kemal's name was on a list of unreliable officers, drawn up by British Intelligence.[15] Yet surprisingly nothing was done; and on 16 May, accompanied by a hand-picked staff of twenty officers, he sailed on the *Bandırma*, a clapped-out Turkish cargo boat, for Samsun, on the Black Sea coast of Anatolia, there to initiate the organisation of a national resistance movement, designed, not only to oppose the forces of the occupying powers and bring pressure to bear on the Istanbul Government to strengthen its policy, but also, according to his own later account, to lay the foundations of a new Turkish state, the 'sovereignty and independence' of which would be unreservedly recognised throughout the world.[16]

On the day preceding his departure, in a move guaranteed to provoke outrage amongst the Turkish-speaking Muslim peoples of the empire, a Greek expeditionary force, despatched at the instigation of the British and the French by Eleutherios Venizelos (the Greek prime minister) – Lloyd George (the British prime minister) and Clemenceau (the French premier) wished to pre-empt a possible Italian occupation of the area – landed at Izmir, on the Aegean coast of Anatolia, thereby sparking off a conflagration that was to last for almost three years.

. . .

NOTES AND REFERENCES

1. Deny J. 1927, 'Les Souvenirs du Gazi Moustafa Kemal Pacha', *Revue des Etudes Islamiques*, Vol. 1, pp. 200–1.
2. Woodward E. L., Butler R. (eds), *Documents on British Foreign Policy 1919–1939* (*DBFP*). HMSO first series Vol. 4, Chapter 2; Shaw S. and E. K. 1977, *History of the Ottoman Empire and Modern Turkey*. Cambridge University Press, pp. 320–2.

3. Cebescy A. F. 1953, *Milli Mücadele Hatıraları*. Istanbul, p. 31; Zürcher E. J. 1984, *The Unionist Factor*. E. J. Brill, Leiden, pp. 90–101; Selek S. 1966, *Anadolu Ihtilali*. Burçak Yayınevi, Istanbul, Part 1, pp. 179–83.

4. Ibid., Part I, p. 163; Zürcher E. J. 1984, *The Unionist Factor*, pp. 94–5; Sarihan Z. 1982, *Kurtuluş Savaşı Günlügü*. Öğretmen Dünyası Yayınları, Ankara, Vol. 1, pp. 73, 93, 110.

5. Ertürk H. 1964, *Iki Devrin Perde Arkası*. Pinar Yayinevi, Istanbul, pp. 217–37; Zürcher E. J. 1984, *The Unionist Factor*, pp. 80–5; *Encyclopaedia of Islam (EI)*, new edition, *Karakol Djemiyyeti*.

6. Zürcher E. J. 1984, *The Unionist Factor*, Chapter 3; Jäschke G. 1957–8, 'Beiträge zur Geschichte des Kampfes der Türkei um ihre Unabhängigkeit', *Welt des Islams*, new series, Vol. 5, Part 3; Foreign Office 371 4141 Intelligence Report No. 2538, Part 3.

7. Zürcher E. J. 1984, *The Unionist Factor*, Chapter 3; Selek S. 1966, *Anadolu Ihtilali*, Part 1, pp. 195–203; Kinross 1964, *Atatürk: The Rebirth of a Nation*. Weidenfeld and Nicolson, Chapter 17.

8. Zürcher E. J. 1984, *The Unionist Factor*, p. 96.

9. Jäschke G. 1957–58, 'Beiträge zur Geschichte des Kampfes der Türkei', pp. 30–1; Zürcher E. J. 1984, *The Unionist Factor*, pp. 110–11.

10. Rustow D. A. 1958–59, 'The Army and the Founding of the Turkish Republic', *World Politics*, Vol. 2, p. 543 note.

11. Zürcher E. J. 1984, *The Unionist Factor*, pp. 112–13. That *Karakol* conspired to take over control of the army in Anatolia is not in doubt. In August 1919 they sent a directive to all army units announcing the existence of an organisation, with its own officers, General Staff and Commander-in-Chief. The following is Mustafa Kemal's own account of this extraordinary episode:

> While we were trying to find a way at Erzurum to make the meaning of the decisions that were passed by the congress intelligible to everybody and secure their unanimous acceptance, we received the news that certain circulars, called the 'Regulations of the Organisation of the Karakol Society' and 'Instructions concerning the General Authority of the Karakol

Society', had been distributed among the soldiers and officers. In fact, they were circulated everywhere.

All who read them – even the commanding officers who were closely associated with me – were perplexed, because they thought that I was the author of them. On the one hand, they thought that all through the congress I had displayed open and systematic endeavours in a national sense; but, on the other, that I was trying to form a committee of some mysterious and formidable character.

In reality, this propaganda emanated from certain men in Constantinople who, apparently, were acting in my name.

According to the regulations of this 'Karakol Society', the names of the members of the committee, their number, the place and manner of their meeting, as well as their election and their objects, were kept absolutely secret.

Moreover, the circulation, even in part, of anything concerning it or any intimation that it was in any way dangerous – or was considered to be so – was punishable with instant death.

In the instructions relating to its general powers a 'National Army' is mentioned, and it is clearly expressed that the 'Commander-in-Chief' of this Army, the officers on his Staff, the officers commanding the troops, the Army Corps and the Divisions, with their Staff officers, had been selected and appointed. Their names were not divulged. In the same way, their duties were carried out secretly.

I enlightened the commanding officers immediately by instructing them that they were on no account to obey such orders and instructions. I added that an inquiry had been instituted for the purpose of discovering the origin of this enterprise.

After I had arrived at Sivas I learned from Kara Vasif, who had come there, that he and his companions were the authors of these circulars.

In any case, they had been acting without authority. It was a dangerous thing to try to make people obey the orders of an anonymous committee, with an unknown chief in command and a host of unknown commanding officers, by threatening them with the penalty of death if they dared to disobey. Signs of mutual distrust and fear began, indeed, to make their appearance among the military forces. For instance, it was not improbable that the commanders of some of the Army Corps might ask with perfect right, 'Who is in command of my Army Corps? When and how will he take over the command? What will my position be then?'

When I asked Kara Vasif who constituted the committee and who were the superior officers and anonymous high persons on the General Staff, he replied:

'You and your comrades, of course!'

His answer took me completely by surprise. It had neither reason nor logic in it, because I had never been spoken to about such an enterprise or such an organisation, nor had I given my assent to it in any form.

When we know that this Society tried subsequently to carry on its work, particularly in Constantinople, without altering its name, surely we cannot be favourably impressed with its honesty.

See Mustafa Kemal 1929, *A Speech delivered by Ghazi Mustafa Kemal (Speech)*. Koehler, Leipzig, pp. 63–4.

12. Selek S. 1966, *Anadolu Ihtilali. Burçak Yayinevi*, Part I, pp. 201–2; *British Documents on Atatürk (BDA)*, Vol. 1, No. 22 and Vol. 3, No. 266.
13. Jäschke G. 1957–8, 'Beiträge zur Geschichte des Kampfes der Türkei', Section 4.
14. Volkan V., Itzkowitz N. 1984, *The Immortal Atatürk*. University of Chicago Press, p. 123.
15. *BDA*, Vol I, No. 1.
16. Mustafa Kemal 1929, *Speech*, p. 17.

Chapter 4

FOUNDATION OF THE NATIONAL MOVEMENT

. . . .

OPENING MOVES

Mustafa Kemal arrived in Samsun on 19 May 1919. Following his arrival he lost no time in implementing the plans, drawn up (or at least discussed) in the Ministry of War and elsewhere, to secure control of the Ottoman army and create in Anatolia, far removed from the 'narrow and dependent environment of the metropolis'[1], a national movement capable of uniting the national forces, suppressing the minority guerrilla movements and securing the formation of a government able and willing to confront the occupation forces of the victorious Entente powers and negotiate a satisfactory peace settlement. During the first week or so, in Samsun, he made immediate contact with the army commanders, in particular Kiazim Karabekir, commander of the Fifteenth Army Corps, at Erzurum, Ali Fuat, commander of the Twentieth Army Corps, at Ankara, and Djemal Pasha, Inspector of the Second Army at Konya, expressing concern about the situation in which the country found itself and seeking information regarding the precise disposition of their forces. On 28 May, from Havza (a watering place some twenty-five miles inland, to which he moved on 25 May to escape the watchful eyes of the British garrison in Samsun, and possibly also to take the waters – his health at the time was not good) he despatched a secret circular telegram to the provincial governors and army commanders, instructing them to organise a series of meetings in the major towns, protesting against the Greek occupation of Izmir and calling on the great powers and other 'civilised' nations to intervene to put a stop to the 'intolerable state of affairs' created by the Greek invasion.

At the same time he emphasised that on no account should hostile demonstrations against the minorities be permitted, as these might damage the national cause.[2] On 3 June he instructed the army commanders and provincial governors to encourage the Defence of Rights associations in their areas to seek assurances from the Sultan and the Grand Vizier that, in any talks undertaken by the recently despatched Ottoman delegation, at the Paris peace conference, the delegation would seek to secure the 'complete independence in every way of the (Ottoman) State and the Nation', and the preservation of the national rights of the Muslim majority. Public unease would, it should be made clear, remain until such time as the guiding principles of Ottoman policy with regard to a peace settlement had been laid before the nation.[3] At the same time he secretly instructed Kiazim Karabekir and Refet Bey (recently appointed commander of the Third Army Corps based in Sivas) to take immediate action in the event of a Greek uprising in the Pontus region. Should the Greeks attempt to land an expeditionary force in the area, then it should be expelled. Were Allied troops to be involved, they should be confronted and prevented from advancing, but conflict should if possible be avoided. Armenian and Georgian units accompanying them might be resisted by guerrilla action. Villages inhabited by Muslim Turks should be everywhere encouraged to defend themselves.[4] On 18 June, following his departure from Havza and arrival in Amasya (a small town on the edge of the Anatolian plateau), he informed the Thrace–Paşaeli Defence of Rights Association that it was his intention to convene a general assembly, composed of the national associations of Anatolia and Rumelia, in Sivas, in order to scrutinise the policy pursued by the government with regard to the peace settlement.[5] On 22 June, following consultations with Hüseyin Rauf, Ali Fuat, Refet and others, assembled at his invitation at Amasya (Hüseyin Rauf had resigned from the navy shortly before Mustafa's departure from Istanbul and travelled to western Anatolia to make contact with the national forces in the area). He issued, in conjunction with his colleagues, a circular telegram, seen by some as the founding document of the national movement. In this telegram he invited the provinces and districts to send delegates to a congress to be held at Sivas in the near future, in order that the situation they faced might be there examined and the rights of the nation asserted before the world. Delegates attending the congress, shortly to be convened by the Erzurum and Trabzon Defence of Rights Associations, in Erzurum, would, it was made clear, be invited to attend. Those travelling through districts controlled by elements loyal to the government might, if they wished, travel incognito.[6] Finally, in a letter, despatched to a number of leading figures in Istanbul, including Ferid Pasha (the leader of the Peace and Salvation Party), Abdul Rahman Şerif (the historian and secretary-general of the national congress convened in the capital in November 1918), Kara Vasif and Halide Edib, he pointed out that meetings and demonstrations, organised by the various opposition groups, could not alone be expected to achieve their aims. They must now draw on the 'spiritual power emanating from the soul of the nation'. As for Istanbul, as it was no longer capable of governing Anatolia it must henceforth take a subordinate position.[7]

Not all of Mustafa Kemal's colleagues were convinced of the wisdom of convening a national congress in Sivas. Refet, for one, remained sceptical, believing that the holding of a congress in the town, noted for its hostility to the CUP, might merely provoke disturbances, and even an Allied occupation of the area; while Kiazim Karabekir, consulted regarding the prospect in the period immediately preceding the issuing of the Amasya declaration, pointed out that it would be difficult if not impossible to organise such a congress quickly, as many provinces lacked a national organisation, and time would be needed to organise the election of suitable candidates. In the meantime, might it not be more sensible to proceed with the congress organised by the Erzurum and Trabzon association, due to open in Erzurum on 10 July?[8]

Initially Mustafa Kemal remained unconvinced by these arguments; but following his arrival in Erzurum, and after some further discussion, he was persuaded of the advantages to be gained from his attendance at the Erzurum congress, preparations for which were already well advanced. On 10 July, therefore, having first enrolled as a member of the Erzurum branch of the Defence of Rights Association, he was elected chairman of the executive committee set up to organise the congress, with Rauf as deputy chairman. Not that it proved easy to overcome the numerous constitutional difficulties posed by his participation. On the contrary, many delegates objected on the grounds that he had not been elected a delegate, while others remained deeply suspicious regarding his ultimate intentions, fearing that he intended to hijack the movement for his own purposes. Only following the energetic intervention of Kiazim Karabekir – two delegates were persuaded to resign to make way for the appointment of Mustafa Kemal and Rauf as delegates – were these and other difficulties overcome.[9]

The reaction of the Ottoman Government to Mustafa Kemal's apparent dereliction of duty was both immediate and uncompromising. On 8 June, at the behest of the British High Commissioner, the Minister of War despatched a telegram ordering his recall;[10] and on 23 June, when this order was ignored, Ali Kemal (the newly appointed Minister of the Interior) again ordered his recall, at the same time giving instructions that no government servant should be permitted to enter into communication with him. Although a prominent leader, known for his 'ardent patriotism',[11] his orders must not on any account be obeyed. On 2 July the Sultan's Chief Secretary despatched a telegram, requesting his resignation; and on 8 July the Sultan issued a decree revoking his commission. Finally, on 7 August, following his departure from Erzurum, he was declared a rebel and stripped of his rank and decorations.[12] At the same time posters were issued declaring him to be a rebel and a traitor, and steps taken to secure his arrest. In Sivas, in particular, a plot was hatched by Ali Galib (a colonel on the General Staff) and others to seize him – a plot which Mustafa Kemal, forewarned and forearmed, successfully countered by sweeping into the town some hours ahead of his scheduled arrival, thereby catching the plotters unprepared.[13]

The repeated attempts of the Ottoman authorities to secure either his resignation or his recall, clearly placed Mustafa Kemal in an invidious position. On the evening of 8 July, therefore, the day that the Sultan finally revoked his commission, he resigned not only from his post as Inspector of the Third Army, but also from the army itself, thereby freeing himself to provide the political leadership which he believed essential were the movement he and his colleagues had initiated to succeed; though prior to his resignation it was agreed by his colleagues that he would in practice retain command of the armed forces loyal to the movement. Shortly before his resignation, in order to prepare the ground for the forthcoming struggle he took the precaution of issuing a circular telegram, ordering the army commanders to take immediate control of all centres of communication lying within the areas of their command.[14] On 7 July, disturbed by reports that Djemal Pasha (Inspector of the Second Army in Konya, and supposedly loyal to the movement) had returned to Istanbul, Mustafa Kemal despatched a telegram to the army commanders, ordering that in the event of their being removed from their posts, they should remain in the area of their command and continue to carry out their national duties as before; but on no account should they accept the appointment of men unable or unwilling to defend the nation. In that event they should declare that they had entirely lost confidence in their successors and refuse to obey their orders. Nor should they cooperate in the demobilisation of any part of the army, or disbandment of any national organisation, ordered by the government, with a view to facilitating an Allied occupation of the country. As for the civil administration, it should likewise resist any move likely to undermine the independence of the state and nation. If any district in the country were attacked, then it should at once communicate with the other districts in order to secure cooperation and joint action.[15]

Mustafa Kemal's assumption of the command of the army, and control of the civil administration, or at least the greater part of it, was not accomplished without difficulty. Colonel Kiazim Dirik, an officer on his staff, at once made it clear that he could no longer serve under him, thereby justifying for a time Mustafa Kemal's worst fears that, once deprived of office, his followers would desert him; while rumours that he was finished and that he would be arrested and transported to Istanbul spread rapidly throughout Anatolia; but in the end, thanks largely to the backing of the principal army commanders, in particular Kiazim Karabekir and Ali Fuat, his support remained firm and he retained the leadership of the movement.[16]

THE CONGRESS OF ERZURUM

At the Congress of Erzurum, which opened on 23 July, in one of the classrooms of an Armenian school in the town, Mustafa Kemal and his colleagues, despite considerable opposition from the delegates, quickly secured effective control of the proceedings. On the first day of the congress, the fifty-six or so delegates, the majority merchants, professional men, farmers and men of religion, were persuaded to elect him president; and on the second day to elect him chairman of a representative committee, set up, with wide-ranging powers, to execute the policy agreed on by the congress.[17] Thereafter, following lengthy discussions, it was agreed that a new association, to be entitled the Association for the Defence of the Rights of the Eastern Provinces, should be set up, amalgamating the Erzurum and Trabzon associations; that the new association should be governed by a series of regulations, in effect a constitution; and that, at the conclusion of the congress, a manifesto should be issued, setting out the aims and objectives of the association. In a speech, delivered following his election as president, Mustafa Kemal analysed the situation prevailing in the country. Only by the election of a national assembly, he suggested, founded on the will of the people, and the appointment of a government capable of reflecting that will, could the country be saved.[18]

In both the regulations of the new association and the manifesto, issued at the close of the congress, Mustafa Kemal and his colleagues were at pains to ensure that the national aims of the movement they were seeking to found, and not merely the regional aims of the Erzurum and Trabzon Defence of Rights Associations, would find expression, and in this they were generally successful, though in both the manifesto and the regulations the regional interests of the associations remain evident. Article 1 of the manifesto, which was issued on 7 August, declared that on no account must Trabzon and the six eastern provinces be separated from the Ottoman motherland: 'All Moslem elements living within this area are filled with a reciprocal sentiment of sacrifice, and have undertaken to aim at the same object as regards the future of their country, and cling to their blood and

71

racial bonds.' Article 2 resolved to marshal the forces of the nation, maintain the integrity of the motherland and preserve the Sultanate and Caliphate. Article 3 resolved to resist all attempts on the part of the Greeks and Armenians to occupy or annex Ottoman territory. On no account must special privileges, likely to undermine the country's equilibrium, be granted. Article 4 declared that, in the event of the Ottoman Government failing to preserve the integrity of the country, measures would be taken to secure the attachment of Trabzon and the eastern provinces to the Sultanate and Caliphate. Article 5 gave assurances that minority rights would be respected. Article 6 hoped that the Allies would give up any idea of partitioning those parts of the empire which lay 'within our frontiers when the Armistice was signed on 30 October 1918, in which, as in the other districts in the Eastern Anatolian Vilayets, the Moslems are obviously in the majority'. Article 7 declared that they would accept aid and assistance from abroad, provided the independence and integrity of the country were respected. Article 8 called on the government to convene the national assembly, and submit its decisions to the will of the nation. Article 10 declared that the Association for the Defence of the Rights of the Eastern Provinces was subject to no 'party' influence; and that all Muslim countrymen were natural members of the association. Finally, Article 10 declared that a representative committee had been elected by the association, and that all 'national formations', from village to *vilayet*, might be associated with it.[19]

In a summary of the manifesto and regulations, given in *Speech*, Mustafa Kemal is inclined to suggest that the two documents are more or less identical; and indeed there are substantial similarities; but significant differences exist. While Article 1 of the regulations is identical to Article 1 of the manifesto, Article 3, which elaborates Article 2 of the manifesto, emphasises the right of the eastern provinces to defend themselves in the event of the Ottoman Empire breaking up. Article 4 of the regulations makes provision for the establishment of a provisional administration in the eastern provinces in the event of the Ottoman Government being obliged to give them up; though Ottoman law would continue to apply. In the remaining articles elaborate provision is made for the setting up of the proposed provisional administration, whose duty it would be to defend the eastern provinces, including the creation of a hierarchical system of representation, commencing in the village and culminating in a general congress and an executive or representative committee, responsible for the execution of policy.[20]

Mustafa Kemal's adoption of the aims and objectives set out in the Erzurum manifesto was, it may be supposed, largely pragmatic. As he himself later suggested, the dismemberment of the Ottoman Empire, which had occurred during the previous decade, combined with the more or less complete alienation of the Greek and Armenian communities, had made the concept of a multi-national empire, and the ideology of Ottomanism, associated with it, irrelevant; while the expectation that pan-Islamism and pan-Turkism might fill the breach had been largely discredited by Enver Pasha's failed policies. Apart from further fragmentation, therefore, the only possibility remaining was the creation of some kind of nation-state, based on the Turkish-speaking Muslim peoples of Anatolia and eastern Thrace; though in this context, as the manifesto shows, the concept of nationality might be interpreted as much in a religious as in an ethnic sense. This ambiguity Mustafa Kemal and his colleagues were, no doubt, happy to leave unresolved, as substantial non-Turkish minorities, Kurd, Circassian and Laz, existed. Moreover, many of the delegates to the Erzurum Congress were Kurds, as were members of the representative committee, including Hadji Musa Bey, Sedallah Efendi and Fevzi Efendi.[21]

The success of the nationalists in publicising the aims and objectives of their movement at the Congress of Erzurum could not, as Mustafa Kemal well knew, be matched by effective executive action. The executive committee never actually met, and few if any steps were taken to implement the provisions for the creation of a hierarchical system of representation, set out in the regulations; though vigorous steps were taken to secure control of the existing systems of military and civil administration in Anatolia and eastern Thrace, including where possible the appointment of officers and officials loyal to the movement and the exclusion of those opposed to it, efforts considerably facilitated, with regard to military appointments at least, by the continued support of officers on the General Staff, including Djevad Pasha, the Chief of the General Staff.

. . .

THE CONGRESS OF SIVAS

However effective Mustafa Kemal's efforts to give the manifesto and resolutions drawn up at the Erzurum Congress a national character may have been, the need to convene a truly national congress remained; and it was to this task that in the following weeks he turned his attention. On 29 August he left Erzurum for Sivas, arriving after a difficult and at times dangerous journey – at one point his party was threatened by Kurdish tribesmen, active in the area (on 2 September). At Sivas, on 4 September, threatened by a possible Allied occupation of the province and by government action designed to secure the suppression of the movement, he hastily convened the congress, securing, despite opposition from a number of delegates who were suspicious of his ultimate intentions, his own election as president. Therefore, in view of the urgency of the situation, he and his colleagues quickly drafted a series of amendments to the Erzurum resolutions and manifesto, which enabled them to be adopted wholesale as the resolutions and manifesto of the new association. Henceforth, it was agreed, the Association for the Defence of the Rights of the Eastern Provinces would become the Association for the Defence of the Rights of Anatolia and Rumelia, while the representative committee, previously representative merely of the eastern provinces, would become the representative committee of the whole country.[22] As for the manifesto, which had previously emphasised the attachment of Trabzon and the eastern provinces to the Ottoman motherland, Article I was amended to read:

> The various parts of the Turkish Territory which re-
> mained within our frontier when, on the 30th of October
> 1918 the armistice concluded between the Entente Powers
> and the Turkish Government was signed, are everywhere
> inhabited by an overwhelming Moslem majority and form
> a whole; this cannot be separated and would not, for any
> reason, detach themselves one from another or from the

74

Ottoman Motherland. All the Moslem elements living in those countries are true brothers filled with sentiments of mutual respect and feelings of sacrifice and are absolutely respectful of the racial and social rights and local conditions.[23]

Article 3, which had declared that action would be taken to resist a Greek or Armenian annexation or occupation of Ottoman territory, was amended to emphasise the fact that action would be taken to resist any such attempt, either by the Entente powers or their surrogates; and Article 4 (Article 5 in the Sivas manifesto), which had declared that in the event of the Ottoman Government failing to preserve the integrity of the country, measures would be taken to secure the attachment of Trabzon and the eastern provinces to the Sultanate and the Caliphate, was amended to ensure that the article would refer, not merely to Trabzon and the eastern provinces, but to the country as a whole.[24]

Mustafa Kemal's success in convening the Congress of Sivas at such short notice was remarkable; but it was achieved at considerable cost. As the representatives of the Istanbul Government were not slow to point out, representation at the congress could hardly be called national. Of the 200 delegates originally invited to attend, only thirty-nine eventually arrived, including a dozen or so members of Mustafa Kemal's own entourage. Only two or three delegates attended from the Izmir region, one from Istanbul, none at all from Konya, Cilicia and eastern Thrace. As for the delegates representing the eastern provinces, they claimed that they were neither mandated to attend, nor in practice able to do so. As a result Mustafa Kemal, determined that the eastern provinces should be represented, was reduced to using his authority as Chairman of the representative committee of the Erzurum Congress, to authorise the transfer of the committee, or at least the five members of it willing to travel, to Sivas.[25]

. . .

THREATS OF GOVERNMENT AND ALLIED ACTION

The threat posed to the nationalists by the agents of the occupying powers and the Istanbul Government in the period of the Sivas Congress was by no means insubstantial. Shortly before the opening of the congress, Reşid Pasha, the Vali of Sivas, informed Mustafa Kemal that Major Brunot, the French Inspector of Gendarmerie, had personally informed him that were the nationalists to convene a congress in Sivas, then the town would be immediately occupied; though he later reported that Major Brunot had retracted his threat, declaring that the congress would be permitted to meet provided only that the delegates refrain from making speeches hostile to the Entente powers. Clearly, Reşid Pasha concluded, it was the intention of the French to lure Mustafa Kemal and his colleagues into a trap. Following the opening of the congress, the town would be occupied and they would all be arrested. On no account should they proceed with their plans.[26]

Mustafa Kemal's response to Reşid Pasha's warning regarding the French threat was both shrewd and robust. Major Brunot's threat of an Allied occupation of Sivas was, he declared, in all probability mere bluff; and in any case such an operation could not be easily carried out. Had not the English already landed a battalion at Samsun, designed to intimidate the nationalists; and had they not, when faced with the fixed determination of the national forces to fight, been obliged to withdraw? Major Brunot should be made aware that were the French to decide to occupy Sivas, then they would have to face a 'new and very expensive war', which would entail the necessity of their bringing up fresh troops and incurring very considerable expense.[27]

The threat posed by the agents of the government was both more immediate and more dangerous. Already in July Mustafa Kemal had received reports that members of the Bedrihani clan, accompanied by Major Edward Noel (a British officer despatched with the backing of the Istanbul Government to investigate the position in the Kurdish provinces) were travelling through south-eastern Anatolia, making propaganda in favour of Kurdish independence, or autonomy. On 6 September, in the midst of the congress, he was informed that this party, now accompanied by a band of armed Kurds, had arrived at Malatya, where they had met up with Ali Galib, the Vali of Elazığ – the same Ali Galib who had endeavoured to secure Mustafa Kemal's arrest in Sivas in June – and Halil Bey, Mutasarrif of Malatya and a leader of the Bedrihani clan; and that orders for their arrest, previously despatched had been ignored. Determined to prevent a disaster, on 7 September Mustafa Kemal, bypassing Djevdet Pasha, commander of the Thirteenth Army Corps, whose loyalty to the movement he had cause to doubt, ordered Halit Bey, chief-of-staff of the Thirteenth Army Corps, and Ilias Bey, commander of the Thirteenth Regiment, stationed at El Aziz, to despatch a force of sixty men on horseback to Malatya to arrest Ali Galib and disperse his forces. When Halit Bey and Ilias Bey, doubtful regarding their authority, procrastinated, he made a personal appeal to them to act on their own initiative. The situation was, he stressed serious, the people concerned traitors, the government in Istanbul implicated. Thus convinced, on 9 September Ilias Bey, departed, arriving at Malatya the following day, only to find that Ali Galib and his supporters, forewarned by the local military commander, had fled, pausing only long enough to break into the cashier's office, open the safe and remove 6,000 lira, the 'necessary expenses', they noted, in a receipt left on the table, 'connected with the suppression of Mustafa Kemal and his followers'.[28]

The flight of Ali Galib and his supporters did not conclude the incident. On the contrary, on 11 September Ilias Bey reported that Ali Galib and Halil Bey were busy seeking to raise the Kurdish tribes in the area, encouraging them to sack Malatya, and march on Sivas, killing or dispersing any Turks they might meet on the way; and that a number of tribes had in fact assembled at Raka, some five hours distant from Malatya. In the following days, therefore, Mustafa Kemal took steps to strengthen the national forces in the area, despatching additional units to Malatya; moving the greater part of the Third Army Corps south to form a defensive shield around Sivas; and instructing the Thirteenth and Fifteenth Army Corps to prepare for action, with the result that the Kurdish tribes concerned, made thus aware of the substantial forces raised against them, eventually withdrew and dispersed. As for Ali Galib, he was forced to flee, first to Urfa and thence to Aleppo.[29]

The attempts made by the government to secure the defeat of the national movement in the period of the Sivas Congress aroused in Mustafa Kemal feelings of great anger. On 10 September, happening to be present in the telegraph office during an exchange of telegrams, he dashed off the following to Aadil Bey, Minister of the Interior:

> You are cowards and criminals to prevent the people from laying their demands before their Padishah. You are conspiring with foreign countries against the nation. I did not think it possible that you are so incapable of estimating the strength and the will of the nation or their value; but I cannot believe that you can play the part of traitors to and executioners of the nation and country. You had better think well what you are doing. Beware lest the day should come when you will be called upon to render account to the nation for the infamous acts you are committing when you put your trust in the deceptive promises of nonentities like Ali Galib and his colleagues, and by selling your conscience to such foreigners as Major Nowill [Noel], who are doing all they can to injure the country and our people. When you will hear some day of the fate of the people and the annihilation of the troops on whom you are leaning for support, you may be sure that you will recognise the fate that is lying in wait for yourselves.[30]

Mustafa Kemal's anger was exacerbated by the fact that, in his view, he and his colleagues were fully entitled by the Law of Associations and other laws enacted in the 1909 version of the constitution, to form associations, such as those set up in Erzurum and Sivas, to convene congresses and to petition the Sultan for a redress of grievances. Indeed, as he later made clear in *Speech*, on 24 August he and his colleagues had formally approached the authorities in Erzurum, seeking legal recognition of their activities.[31]

. . .

A POSSIBLE AMERICAN MANDATE

At the Congress of Sivas the question of an American mandate proved the most contentious issue debated. In the weeks preceding the congress, several influential figures, including Halide Edib, Ahmed Izzet Pasha, Djevad Pasha and Kara Vasif Bey, had argued in favour of acceptance. As Halide Edib pointed out in a letter to Mustafa Kemal, the political situation in the country had reached a critical point. The French, having met with disappointment in Syria, wished to compensate themselves in Cilicia. The Italians, openly imperialistic, sought a share in the Anatolian booty. The British, determined to prevent the emergence of a truly independent Muslim state capable of setting an example to the Muslim subjects of their empire, sought either the complete control of the Ottoman state or its decapitation and dismemberment. Only the Americans had no interest in the empire's subjection or partition; and only they had the political skill and expertise to create a new Turkey, capable of enjoying spiritual and economic independence. Far from being a misfortune, an American mandate, extending over the whole empire, would bring numerous advantages. It would prevent the partition of the empire, otherwise inevitable. It would secure the transformation of the people – the peasantry – into a modern nation, sound in mind and body. It would enable the peoples of the empire to escape from the control of a government, which had, in the recent past, lived only for robbery, profit, adventure and self-glorification; and it would provide protection against the thousandfold methods of oppression practised by the imperial powers.[32]

At the congress too the proposal received substantial support. As Refet Bey pointed out, the Turks were not strong enough to stand alone. In a war fought against the Greeks they would almost certainly be defeated; and the alternative to an American mandate might well be enslavement by the British, resulting in the suffocation of the minds and consciousness of the people. In any case they had no real choice, as in the twentieth century it was impossible for an impoverished nation, with a debt of 500 million Ottoman pounds, and revenues of only 10–15 million, to survive without foreign aid. The American mandate must, he concluded, be accepted.[33]

Mustafa Kemal's attitude to the prospect of an American mandate remains unclear. In *Speech* he was at pains to insist that Article 7 of the Sivas Manifesto made provision merely for foreign help; but at the time of the congress, whilst stressing the need to secure the independence and integrity of the country, he was prepared, it would seem, seriously to consider the possibility.[34] In the end, it was unanimously agreed that the American Congress should be invited to send a delegation to study the question; and an invitation was sent; but to no avail, for, following the collapse of President Woodrow Wilson and the effective withdrawal of America from the peace process the issue became irrelevant.[35]

That in the early stages of the national struggle Mustafa Kemal and his colleagues were generally successful in their efforts to found a national movement, with well-defined aims, capable of securing control of the greater part of the army and the civil administration in Anatolia and eastern Thrace, is not in doubt. The extent of their achievements, however, should not be exaggerated. In Konya, Afyon Karahissar, Ankara, Kayseri, Balikesir, Eskişehir, Alaşehir, and a number of other towns, the military and civil administration remained for the most part loyal to the Istanbul Government; though here and there, in Kastamonu, Sinop, Inebolu and other places, energetic supporters of the movement, for the most part army officers and old CUP men, were active, forming branches of the new association, and organising the local citizenry in preparation for the coming struggle.[36] As for the numerous armed bands formed in the west, following the Greek occupation of Izmir, riven by political disputes and internecine warfare, they remained for the most part indifferent if not actually hostile, to the movement. Nor, unlike the Erzurum Congress, was the Sivas Congress generally considered a success. As the Istanbul Government had frequently pointed out, the limited nature of its attendance precluded any claim it might make to national representation.[37] Even Mustafa Kemal was for a time persuaded that in view of the limited number and provenance of the delegates, it might be necessary to hold a third, truly national congress. In the end, however, convinced that such a move would succeed merely in undermining the momentum of the movement, he decided to opt, not for a third congress, but for an immediate attempt to achieve the principal aim of the movement. This remained the election of a chamber of deputies (national assembly), truly representative of the national will, capable of securing the appointment of a strong government and the negotiation of a satisfactory peace settlement which would ensure the independence and integrity of those parts of the empire that had remained unoccupied at the end of the war.[38]

. . .

NOTES AND REFERENCES

1. Mustafa Kemal 1929, *A Speech delivered by Ghazi Mustafa Kemal*. Koehler, Leipzig, p. 49.
2. Ibid., pp. 24–5.
3. Ibid., pp. 28–30.
4. Gologlu M. 1968, *Milli Mücadele Tarihi, Erzurum Kongresi*. Nüve Matbaası, Ankara, p. 48.
5. Mustafa Kemal 1929, *Speech*, pp. 22–3.
6. Ibid., p. 31. The four principal co-founders of the national movement in Anatolia were, like Mustafa Kemal, himself, men of both high rank and wide-ranging experience. Kiazim Karabekir, described by Colonel A. Rawlinson, who met him in Erzurum, as 'the most genuine example of a first-class Turkish officer that it has ever been my good fortune to meet' (Rawlinson A. 1923, *Adventures in the Near East*. Andrew Melrose, p. 180), was born in Istanbul in 1882, the son of a pasha, descended from an old Selçuk Turkish family. After graduating from the War College in 1902, and from the Staff College, first in his class, in 1905, he served for a time with the Third Army in Macedonia, participating in numerous operations against the Greek and Bulgarian *comitadjis*. An early member of the Ottoman Freedom Society, or CUP as it later became known, he is said to have joined Enver in establishing branches of the organisation in Monastir, and later to have worked for the cause in Istanbul. After playing a small part in the Young Turk revolution of 1908, serving in the Action Army, despatched to put down the counter-revolution of 1909, and taking part in the expedition despatched to Albania in 1910, he was promoted major. In the Balkan Wars he served in Edirne, helping to organise the defence of the area; and in the period immediately following, in Istanbul assisting a German military mission invited to advise on the reform of the Ottoman army. This work led him to spend about six weeks in Europe. In the First World War, he served variously, on the eastern front, where he was severely wounded, at Çanakkale, during the Gallipoli campaign, in Istanbul, attached to the General Staff, in Iraq, at Kut al-Amara, and finally,

once again on the eastern front. Frequently promoted, in 1918 he ended the war as a brigadier, in command of the First Caucasian Army Corps, operating in Azerbaijan and the Caucasus. Rauf, a naval officer, born in 1881, was the son of an Ottoman admiral of Circassian extraction. Educated at the Halki naval college, in 1910 he was appointed the commander of the 'Hamidiye', whose exploits were to become famous in the Balkan wars. According to Sir George Clerk, the British ambassador, the outbreak of the First World War found him in England, supervising the construction of the 'Reshadiye,' a battleship ordered by the Ottoman Government (FO 424 268, No. 7 Enclosure). During the war, the entry of the Ottoman Empire into which he is said to have opposed, he served variously in Istanbul, attached to the Naval Staff, Switzerland, Berlin and Persia (Foreign Office 424 268, No. 7 Enclosure, Zürcher E.J. 1984, *The Unionist Factor*. E. J. Brill, Leiden, p. 45). As a member of the Ottoman delegation, he attended the Brest-Litovsk peace conference, and as Minister of Marine he signed the Mudros armistice. Following the war, he served for a time in the Ahmet Izzet Pasha government, before departing for Anatolia. Ali Fuat, a childhood friend of Mustafa Kemal, was born in Istanbul in 1882, the son of an Ottoman general, of Slav and Hungarian extraction (Javakhoff A. 1989, *Kemal Atatürk*. Tallandier, Paris, p. 17). After graduating from Staff College in 1905, and serving a period of 'exile' in Syria, he served for a time as military attaché in Rome. During the First World War he served, under Mustafa Kemal, on the eastern front, and again on the Syrian front. Shortly before the end of the war he was appointed brigadier. Refet, an officer of exceptional courage and ability, was born in 1881. In 1909 he served with the Action Army, despatched to suppress the counter-revolution in Istanbul; and in the First World War he served with distinction on a number of fronts, in particular in Palestine, where he became famous as the defender of Gaza.

7. Mustafa Kemal 1929, *Speech* p. 34.
8. Gologğlu M. 1968, *Milli Mücadele Tarihi, Erzurum Kongresi*, p. 61; Mustafa Kemal 1929, *Speech*, pp. 52–4.

9. Goloğlu M. 1968, *Milli Mücadele Tarihi, Erzurum Kongresi*, p. 65.
10. Turkish National Commission 1981, p. 48.
11. Mustafa Kemal 1929, *Speech*, pp. 34–5.
12. Aktepe M. 1968, 'Atatürk'e Dair Bazi Belgeler', *Belleten*, Vol. 32, pp. 449–51.
13. Mustafa Kemal 1929, *Speech*, pp. 37–40; Jäschke G. 1957–58, 'Beiträge zur Geschichte des Kampfes der Türkei um ihre Unabhängigkeit', *Welt des Islams*, new series, Vol. 5, Part 5.
14. Aktepe M. 1968, 'Atatürk'e Dair Bazi Belgeler', p. 449.
15. Mustafa Kemal 1929, *Speech*, p. 45.
16. Ibid., p. 44.
17. Selek S. 1966, *Anadolu Ihtilali*, Part I, pp. 270–2.
18. Mustafa Kemal 1929, *Speech*, pp. 57–9.
19. Public Record Office (London), War Office (WO) 32 5733, appendix.
20. Goloğlu M. 1968, *Milli Mücadele Tarihi, Erzurum Kongresi*, pp. 187–94.
21. Olson R. 1989, *The Emergence of Kurdish Nationalism and the Sheikh Said Rebellion*. University of Texas Press, p. 36.
22. Goloğlu M. 1969, *Milli Mücadele Tarihi, Sivas Kongresi*. Başnur Matbaası, Ankara, Part 2; Mustafa Kemal 1929, *Speech*, pp. 75–7.
24. WO 32 5733, appendix.
25. Mustafa Kemal 1929, *Speech*, pp. 72–3; Kinross 1964, *Atatürk: The Rebirth of a Nation*. Weidenfeld and Nicolson, p. 185.
26. Mustafa Kemal 1929, *Speech*, pp. 67–9.
27. Ibid., pp. 69–71.
28. Selek S. 1966, *Anadolu Ihtilali*, Part I, pp. 285–7; Mustafa Kemal 1929, *Speech*, pp. 101–8. For a somewhat different account of these events see Olson R. 1989, *The Emergence of Kurdish Nationalism and the Sheikh Said Rebellion*, Chapter 2; *British Documents on Atatürk (BDA)*, Vol. I, Nos 47–9 and Jäschke G. 1957–58, 'Beiträge zur Geschichte des Kampfes der Türkei', Part 5.
29. Mustafa Kemal 1929, *Speech*, pp. 108–9.
30. Ibid., p. 114.
31. Ibid., p. 59.
32. Ibid., pp. 77–87.

33. Ibid., pp. 92–100.
34. Ibid., pp. 98–99.
35. Ibid., p. 100.
36. Goloğlu M. 1969, *Milli Mücadele Tarihi, Sivas Kongresi*, Section E.
37. Mustafa Kemal 1929, *Speech*, pp. 110–11.
38. Volkan V., Itzkowitz N. 1984, *The Immortal Atatürk*. University of Chicago Press, p. 143; Goloğlu M. 1969, *Milli Mücadele Tarihi, Sivas Kongresi*, Section E.

Chapter 5

RELATIONS WITH ISTANBUL

. . .

A CAMPAIGN LAUNCHED

Having successfully persuaded the Sivas Congress to accept
the aims and objectives of the national movement (as set
out in the manifesto issued at the close of the congress),
Mustafa Kemal lost no time in seeking to accomplish the
principal aim of the movement: the election of a chamber
of deputies (national assembly) capable of securing the
appointment of a strong government and the negotiation
of a satisfactory peace settlement. To this end, in the
weeks that followed he launched, with the support of the
principal military commanders loyal to the movement, an
energetic campaign aimed not at the Sultan (the fiction of
whose innocence he was careful to preserve) but at the
government of Damad Ferid Pasha (the recently appointed
Grand Vizier) and his colleagues, who were roundly accused
of treason and criminality. Initially the campaign proved
effective. The Damad Ferid Pasha government was quickly
brought down, and a new one, supposedly committed to the
aims and objectives of the national movement, appointed.
Moreover, in October an agreement was reached between
the government and the representative committee which,
if implemented, might well have enabled the two sides to
present a united front against the occupying powers. In the
end, however, thanks largely to an unexpected change in
policy on the part of the Allies, this possibility was removed;
and Mustafa Kemal and his followers found themselves once
again cut off from the capital, opposed not only by the forces
of the Allies and their surrogates, but also on this occasion by
special forces despatched against them by the Sultan.

Mustafa Kemal's campaign against Damad Ferid Pasha

and his government began on 11 September, with a telegram accusing the government of shedding the blood of loyal Muslims in a fratricidal war, instigating the attack planned by Ali Galib Bey on the Sivas congress and seeking to raise the Kurds in revolt, thereby threatening the integrity of the empire. Until such time as a new Cabinet was appointed, composed of men of honour, all communications between that 'gang of traitors', the government and the national movement in Anatolia would cease. Moreover, when the Grand Vizier refused to accept the telegram, he dispatched a second, signed by the General Assembly of the Congress, warning Damad Ferid Pasha that if he continued in his stubbornness, erecting a wall between the nation and the Padişah, whose 'dignity and honour' he had 'trodden under foot', not only would the nation break off relations with his 'Lawless Cabinet', it would feel free to proceed in 'whatever manner it considered appropriate'.[1]

The threat to break off relations with the government in Istanbul was quickly implemented. On the night of 11 September Mustafa Kemal instructed the commanders of the army corps loyal to the movement to occupy the telegraph offices within the areas of their command; and on (or about) 13 September, in a move which caused considerable concern amongst a number of his colleagues who feared that such action might merely provoke an Allied occupation of the interior (some were also suspicious regarding their leader's ultimate intentions), he ordered that the civil administration be made subject to the authority of the representative committee of the Congress of Sivas and the nation. Henceforth, until such time as a government possessing the confidence of the nation was appointed, the representative committee of the congress would conduct the affairs of the nation. In the meantime, state officials would be expected to continue to exercise their functions, but in a manner conducive to the well-being of the nation. Those who refused to do so would be deemed *ipso facto* to have resigned, and be replaced by others loyal to the movement; while those who worked actively against the aims of the nation and the national movement would be considered to have rendered themselves liable to punishment. At the same time he issued instructions to the provincial governors and Defence of Rights associations, ordering them to prepare for

the election of a new national assembly, which he expected
would be the outcome of his ongoing negotiations with the
government.[2]

The implementation of the proclamation of 13 September
did not prove easy. In the following weeks a fierce struggle
for the control of the civil and military administration of
Anatolia and eastern Thrace occurred, in the course of
which hundreds of officers and officials, including such
prominent figures as Djemal Bey, Vali of Konya, Ali Riza
Bey, Vali of Kastamonu and Hilmi Bey, Vali of Eskişehir,
were removed from office, arrested, and even in a few cases
assassinated; and officers and officials loyal to the movement
appointed. At the same time, at Mustafa Kemal's instigation,
hundreds of telegrams were despatched to the Sultan,
demanding the dismissal of the government. As a result,
Damad Ferid Pasha's government was quickly deprived of
effective control in the interior; and on 2 October, having
failed in an attempt to persuade the occupying powers to
grant permission for the despatch of an army of 2,000 men
to Eskişehir, to hold the nationalists in check, and if possible
suppress them, Damad Ferid Pasha was forced to resign,
handing over the reins of government to Ali Riza Pasha, a
former staff officer, and a so-called 'ministry of conciliation'.[3]

*   *   *

CONCILIATION

In the weeks following the resignation of the Damad Ferid
Pasha government, the new government appeared determined to reach complete agreement with the nationalists.
On 4 October, Ali Riza Pasha, the newly appointed Grand
Vizier, speaking on behalf of a Cabinet which included, as
Minister of War, Djemal Pasha, a supposed 'delegate of the
national forces', assured Mustafa Kemal that the Ottoman
Government was fully committed to the preservation of the
unity and independence of the nation. It was, he declared,
employing the actual terminology of the Sivas manifesto,
their well-defined aim to ensure that all Ottoman territories,
remaining unoccupied at the time of the Mudros armistice
and inhabited by a Muslim majority would remain under the
immediate sovereignty of the Ottoman state; and it was their
aim to secure a just and equitable settlement, safeguarding

the historical, ethnographical, religious and geographical rights of the inhabitants of those territories. No formal agreement of a binding character would be entered into regarding the fate of the nation, until such time as a national assembly had been convened. The government, recognising that the nation must be consulted, would at the earliest possible moment make provision for the holding of elections. Delegates chosen to attend the peace conference would be selected only from such experts as deserved the nation's confidence.[4] On 7 October, following further demands from Mustafa Kemal and the representative committee that the government publish an official declaration recognising the national movement, arrest and try former ministers accused of treason (including Damad Ferid Pasha, Ali Kemal Bey and Aadil Bey), reappoint officials loyal to the national movement and dismiss those opposed to it, Djemal Pasha, the Minister of War, once again declared that the government recognised the will of the nation as sovereign. Henceforth, all actions directed by the government against the national will would cease. Only persons deemed worthy and suitable would be appointed to government office. Those guilty of offences would be punished in the manner prescribed by law; though the government had no wish to be seen as a 'government of revenge'.[5] Finally, at a hastily arranged meeting held between a government delegation, led by Salih Pasha, the Minister of Marine, and a nationalist delegation, led by Mustafa Kemal, at Amasya, on 20–22 October, it was agreed, in the so-called Amasya protocol, that the government would in effect accept all the aims and objectives of the national movement, as set out in the Sivas manifesto, subject to the approval of a newly elected national assembly; while the nationalists for their part gave assurances that, in the event of a national assembly truly representative of the national will being elected, the Anatolian and Rumelian Defence of Rights Association would at once convene a congress to consider its own future, which in effect meant to arrange for its own dissolution.[6]

. . .

CONFRONTATION

The initial optimism generated by the appointment of Ali Riza Pasha's 'ministry of conciliation' and its apparent willingness to reach agreement with the representative committee, was, however, quickly dissipated. On 4 October Ali Riza Pasha dispatched a telegram, calling on the representative committee to evacuate all public buildings occupied by the movement and refrain from further interference in the affairs of government, thereby implying that the activities undertaken by the committee were illegal. On 7 October Mehmed Sherif Pasha (the newly appointed Minister of the Interior) declared that the government had no connection with or partiality for any particular party, and that its chief aim was to see the destiny of the country remain in the hands of the 'real representatives of the nation'. Confident in the 'sense of justice' and 'moderation', exhibited by the great powers, it called on the people to unite in support of the policy it was pursuing.[7] Moreover, in the following weeks, Ali Riza Pasha studiously refrained from issuing the manifesto requested by Mustafa Kemal, declaring that the national movement was both legal and justified, and that peace and order prevailed throughout the areas subject to its control; and he continued to appoint officers and officials opposed to the nationalists and to dismiss those loyal to the movement, while elements within the government, supported by parties and associations opposed to the nationalists, such as the Party of Freedom and Understanding, the Union of the Friends of England, and the Military Society of Protectors, a society established by a group of loyalist officers, continued to organise opposition to the national forces and incite attacks on the Christian minorities designed to provoke Allied intervention.[8] Thus, on the eve of Mustafa Kemal's meeting with Salih Pasha at Amasya, the Party of Freedom and Understanding is reported to have organised the despatch of a telegram bearing the seals of 160 mullahs, notables, merchants and working men resident in the district of Sivas to the Sultan, requesting him to send a commission to investigate the 'criminal activities' of Mustafa Kemal and the nationalists.[9] Shortly afterwards, together with the Union of the Friends of England, it is reported to have made plans to despatch unemployed officers to the Adapazarı region, to organise gangs there; while the Military Society of Protectors is likewise reported to have recruited gangs, led by such notorious bandits as 'Büyük' Arslan, 'Küçük' Arslan, and

'Gumudşineli' Ismail, to create disorder in the Ismit and Gebze region.[10] Finally, in December, Djemal Pasha, the Minister of War supposedly loyal to the nationalists, sought to have Ahmed Fevzi Pasha, the former Under-secretary of State for War (and in Mustafa Kemal's view a man inclined to equate the activities of the nationalists with the promotion of anarchy) appointed to the command of the Twentieth Army Corps at Ankara, and Nureddin Pasha (also an opponent of the nationalist cause) to the command of the Twelfth Army Corps at Konya – a move which if implemented, would, as Mustafa Kemal later remarked, have effectively decapitated the leadership of the movement.[11]

Such activities quickly convinced Mustafa Kemal that no trust could be placed in the government of Ali Riza Pasha and his colleagues and in the Sultan, who he concluded was merely awaiting a favourable opportunity to appoint an even more reactionary Cabinet, capable of upholding autocracy. Nevertheless, on 29 October, in conjunction with the representative committee, he concluded that in the circumstances it would be to the advantage of the country and the nation to keep the Cabinet in power until such time as the national assembly had met and commenced its legislative duties. It would then be possible to form a strong group or party within the assembly, capable of imposing its will upon the government and bringing about a radical change in policy.[12]

In the agreement arrived at in Amasya it had been understood that it would be desirable for the national assembly to meet not in Istanbul, under the guns of an Allied fleet, but in Anatolia. In discussions held during the following weeks, however, it rapidly transpired that majority opinion favoured the holding of the assembly in Istanbul. A meeting in Anatolia, it was argued, would inevitably give rise to problems of communication with the capital, and make it impossible for the Sultan to attend. It might also give rise to a breach with the government, so suggesting to the Allies that the Turks were willing to abandon their capital. Moreover, the Istanbul Government had declared that it would be perfectly safe to hold the assembly in Istanbul, as any attempt on the part of the Allies to interfere in its proceedings would be counter-productive; though it might be wise for Mustafa Kemal and the other leaders of the national movement to stay away, as their safety could not be guaranteed. Against his better judgement, therefore, Mustafa Kemal was obliged to change course; and it was agreed that, notwithstanding the dangers attendant on convening the assembly in Istanbul, the meeting would take place there; but that before going to Istanbul the deputies should first assemble at designated centres in the interior, in order to form parties committed to the defence of the principles laid down in the nationalist programme. At the same time it was agreed that, as Mustafa Kemal and the other members of the representative committee would be prevented by the threat of arrest or assassination from attending, certain deputies, representative of every province and district, should be invited to meet, at a place to be designated, in the neighbourhood of Eskişehir, there to discuss the situation and decide what policy they would wish to pursue in the chamber. In order to facilitate these meetings the representative committee, to which all such designated deputies would be appointed members, would in the near future be transferred to Eskişehir.[13]

In the elections for the national assembly, which took place in November, the opposition parties, convinced that the nationalists would not permit free elections, chose to boycott the ballot. As a result the nationalists, largely unopposed, won an overwhelming victory. During the following weeks, therefore, Mustafa Kemal, was enabled to hold the series of meetings he had arranged with individual deputies and groups of deputies; though not, as originally intended at Eskişehir, but at Ankara, to which, following the reopening of the Ankara–Eskişehir railway and an evacuation of British troops from the area, he had in the meantime transferred his headquarters. In the discussions which then took place he argued that in the forthcoming assembly the nationalist delegates should form a party, to be known perhaps as the Party of the Association for the Defence of the Rights of Anatolia and Rumelia, strong and united enough to enforce its will on the Sultan and his government. At the same time he argued that as he himself would not be able to attend, he should be elected president of the assembly *in absentia*, in order that in the event of an Allied assault on the chamber, the possibility might remain of reconvening the assembly in Ankara and thereby preserving an element of legitimacy in the next phase of the national struggle, which he believed would inevitably follow any such action. The aims and objectives of the new party, it was agreed, would be identical to those of the national movement, as set out in the Erzurum and Sivas manifestos; but in order to clarify these, a new, shorter version would be drafted, later known as the National Pact, specifying the 'maximum sacrifices which can be undertaken to achieve a just and lasting peace'.[14]

In the discussions held in Ankara, Mustafa Kemal was led to believe that the strategy he advocated would be adopted by the nationalist deputies in the assembly. But when on 11 January 1920 the chamber of deputies eventually assembled in Istanbul, it rapidly transpired that a majority of the deputies had no such intention. Though on 28 January they approved the so-called National Pact, they refused to combine to form a single party; and convinced that Mustafa Kemal's election as president *in absentia* would undermine their credibility, they refused to elect him president. Moreover, 'yielding', as Mustafa Kemal put it, 'to local and foreign influences',[15] a number of deputies, including in particular the members of a recently formed party, known as the Party for the Salvation of the Country, argued strongly in support of the policy previously pursued by the government, of seeking to placate the Entente powers. So extensive indeed was the disaffection that when, towards the end of January, Mustafa Kemal, responding to a government decision to accede to an Allied ultimatum demanding the resignation of Djevad Pasha (Chief of General Staff) and Djemal Pasha (Minister of War) – Djevad and Djemal Pasha had been accused of supporting the national forces – called on the chamber to demand the resignation of the government and the appointment of one more capable of protecting the nation's interests, his calls were for the most part ignored. As a result, on 14 February Ali Riza Pasha, thus encouraged, was emboldened to issue a circular, pointing out that henceforth the chamber of deputies must be considered the only body capable of representing the nation. Any such claims made elsewhere, he warned, would be considered illegal. Meanwhile, in the chamber, calls for the dissolution of the Anatolia and Rumelia Defence of Rights Association put forward by elements loyal to the government were, to Mustafa Kemal's consternation, greeted with loud and enthusiastic applause.[16]

Support for the liquidation of the Anatolia and Rumelia Defence of Rights Association was by no means confined to Istanbul. When approached by Mustafa Kemal for his opinion on the issue, Kiazim Karabekir, in a telegram of 23 February, admitted the possibility; and argued that in the event of the chamber of deputies so deciding, the representative committee should at once comply, withdrawing from the affair in a dignified manner and leaving it to the sense of honour and dignity of the chamber to decide what steps should be taken thereafter. In the meantime the national forces, fighting on the Aydin front, might be encouraged to continue, but the campaign would then be considered merely a local one, carried on by local commanders, according to the circumstances prevailing in the areas of their command.[17]

Mustafa Kemal's response to such demands was less than enthusiastic. How, he enquired in a letter to Maşar Mufid (the deputy for Hakkiari) written about this time, could the chamber of deputies be considered free and independent, as long as it met in a city occupied by nearly 80,000 foreign troops – the actual number was in fact much smaller – and dominated by the guns of a foreign fleet? On no account should the representative committee abandon its role until the chamber of deputies were truly free to decide policy and negotiate an acceptable peace settlement. In the meantime the government should be asked to declare definitely whether it supported the maintenance of the national forces; and the chamber of deputies the continued existence of the national organisation.[18]

.   .   .

THE OCCUPATION OF ISTANBUL

The proposal put forward for the dissolution of the national organisation would, if implemented, have placed Mustafa Kemal in a difficult position. At a stroke it would have undermined the foundation on which in the previous months he had so laboriously erected the structure of his personal power. Fortunately for his future career, however, the issue was never put to the test. In February, national forces in Cilicia, aggravated by Armenian attacks on the Muslim peoples of the area, launched an attack on Maraş, driving out the French garrison there and massacring the Armenian inhabitants. Thus provoked, on 19 February the Allies issued a warning to the effect that if such operations, not only on the Adana but also on the western front, did not cease forthwith, then the terms of the peace treaty about to be presented would be substantially altered, to the detriment of the Turkish people; and on 16 March, determined to secure a means of enforcing their will on the Ottoman Government and its people, they ordered an occupation of the Ottoman capital, which in effect meant an occupation of the principal ministries, in particular the Ministries of Posts, Telegraphs and Telephones, Marine and War. Henceforth, the Allied High Commissioners declared, the city would be held by the Allies as a pledge of Turkish good behaviour. At the same time, in order to reduce the effectiveness of the nationalist opposition raised against them, they ordered the arrest of some twenty leading nationalist deputies, including Hüseyin Rauf, Ali Fethi, and Kara Vasif, and more than 150 Ottoman intellectuals, the majority of whom were immediately transported to Malta.[19]

The effects of these ill-advised measures were quickly felt. On 18 March the chamber of deputies, determined to protest against the arrest of its members, voted unanimously for its own prorogation; and on 2 April, Salih Pasha, who had replaced Ali Riza Pasha as Grand Vizier (following the latter's resignation on 3 March), resigned rather than comply with an order issued by the Allies that the government break off all relations with the nationalists in the interior. At this, the Sultan, prepared now to hazard all on a final throw, reappointed Damad Ferid Pasha as Grand Vizier, with instructions to dissolve what remained of the chamber of deputies and initiate a campaign aimed at the complete extinction of the national movement and the forces loyal to it. Meanwhile, in the weeks following the occupation, hundreds of patriotic officers, civil servants, intellectuals and others, including such leading figures as Fevzi Pasha, Ismet Bey and Halide Edib Hanım, finally convinced of the perfidy of the occupying powers, fled to Ankara. As a result the national movement, previously marginalised by its own success in securing the election of a national assembly supposedly committed to the aims of the movement as set out in the National Pact, was enabled to secure a new and unexpected lease of life.[20]

Mustafa Kemal's achievement in the weeks following the conclusion of the Congress of Sivas, in bringing about the resignation of the Damad Ferid Pasha government and its replacement by one supposedly loyal to the nationalist cause, appeared impressive; but appearances proved deceptive. It quickly transpired that the new government, or at least substantial elements within it, remained committed to a policy of cooperation with the Allies, and the extinction of the national movement, while the national assembly, despite Mustafa Kemal's prompting, proved either unwilling, or unable, to initiate change. Moreover, the very success of the nationalists in securing the election of the assembly placed the movement (or at least that part of it represented by Mustafa Kemal and the representative committee in Ankara) in jeopardy, threatening it with dissolution at the hands of its own supporters. Thus, had the Allies not decided on the occupation of the Ottoman capital and on the arrest of many leading nationalists, the movement, deprived of its essential function as the sole effective representative of the national will, might well have withered on the vine. As it was, the Allies, heedless of the advice of many of their agents on the spot, succeeded merely in bringing about that which they had most cause to fear – a resurrection of support for the movement and a revival in the personal fortunes of its leader, Mustafa Kemal. At the same time, in encouraging a further polarisation of Ottoman society, between the forces loyal to the Sultan and the forces loyal to the national movement, they created a situation almost certain to lead, not to the increased stability they supposedly desired, but to disorder, civil strife and war.

· · ·

NOTES AND REFERENCES

1. Mustafa Kemal 1929, *A Speech delivered by Ghazi Mustafa Kemal.* Koehler, Leipzig, pp. 119–21.
2. Ibid., pp. 122–6.
3. Ibid., pp. 142–8; Şimşir B. N., *British Documents on Atatürk (BDA)*, in progress. Türk Tarih Kurumu, Ankara, Vol. 1,

Nos 57 and 66; Kinross 1964, *Atatürk: The Rebirth of a Nation*. Weidenfeld and Nicolson, Chapter 23.

4. Mustafa Kemal 1929, *Speech*, pp. 173–4.
5. Ibid., pp. 185–6.
6. Ibid., pp. 208–13; *BDA*, Vol. I, No. 74.
7. Mustafa Kemal 1929, *Speech*, pp. 174, 196–7.
8. Ibid., pp. 202–3.
9. Ibid., pp. 214–16.
10. Ibid., pp. 213–25, 238, 249–53, 271–6.
11. Ibid., pp. 299–302.
12. Ibid., p. 227.
13. Ibid., pp. 228–38, 287; Kinross 1964, *Atatürk*, Chapter 24.
14. Mustafa Kemal 1929, *Speech*, pp. 308–11; *BDA*, Vol. I, No. 72; Smith E. D. 1959, *Turkey: Origins of the Kemalist Movement*. Judd and Detweiler, pp. 24–5.
15. Mustafa Kemal 1929, *Speech*, p. 323.
16. Ibid., pp. 310–33.
17. Ibid., pp. 335–6.
18. Ibid., pp. 336–7. Allied forces in Istanbul were by no means as numerous as Mustafa Kemal believed. According to a British military report of 23 December 1919 the British occupation force numbered some 4,469 men, and the French a division, divided into six battalions, some stationed in eastern Thrace. See *BDA*, Vol. I, No. 103.
19. Ibid., pp. 352–9; Jäschke G. 1957–58, 'Beiträge zur Geschichte des Kampfes der Türkei um ihre Unabhängigkeit', *Welt des Islams*, new series, Vol. 5, pp. 39–41; Kinross 1964, *Atatürk*, Chapter 25.
20. Smith E. D. 1959, *Turkey: Origins of the Kemalist Movement*, p. 26; Kinross 1964, *Atatürk*, Chapter 26.

Chapter 6

CIVIL WAR

• • •

A FORMIDABLE ASSAULT

In the weeks immediately following the Allied occupation
of Istanbul, and the appointment of a new government
committed to the extinction of the national movement,
Damad Ferid Pasha lost no time in implementing the policy
agreed on. On 11 April 1920 he ordered the dissolution
of the chamber of deputies, previously prorogued; and
on the same day he had the *Sheikh-ül-Islâm* issue a *fetwa*,
declaring the killing of rebels, on the orders of the Caliph,
a religious duty. On 18 April, having first obtained the
permission of the Allied High Commissioners to arm and
equip special gendarmerie units for despatch against the
nationalists, he ordered the formation of the so-called Army
of the Caliphate, recruited, according to one report, for
the most part from the ranks of the criminal classes, and
the unemployed; and on 11 May he had Mustafa Kemal
and a number of his colleagues, including Ali Fuat and
Halide Edib Hanım, now resident in Ankara, convicted
of treason and condemned to death. At the same time he
gave further encouragement and support to anti-nationalist
forces already operating in Anatolia, in particular those of
Ahmed Anzavour. In this way he hoped quickly to defeat the
nationalists and re-establish the authority of the Sultanate;
but in the event he was to succeed merely in sparking off a
civil war that was to end not in victory but in defeat, not in
a strengthening of the authority of the Sultanate but in its
further diminution, and ultimate extinction.[1]

The assault launched on the nationalist forces by the Army
of the Caliphate and the other anti-nationalist forces proved
formidable. In north-western Anatolia, in the districts of

Bursa, Bandırma, Balikesir and Izmit, the Army of the Caliphate launched a series of attacks, defeating the nationalist forces and expelling their garrisons; while in Adapazarı and Geyve the forces of Ahmed Anzavour resumed their activities. Elsewhere, in more than sixty districts, including those of Hendek, Bolu, Düzce, Yenihan, Yozgat, Şile, Konya, Surd, Bersim and Viranşehir, outbreaks of anti-nationalist activity inspired as much by hatred of the nationalists, commonly equated with the CUP, and a simple desire for loot, as by feelings of loyalty to the Sultanate, occurred. In Hendek, Bolu and Düzce Circassian tribes, loyal to the Sultan, rose. In Yenihan an anti-nationalist force captured and disarmed a nationalist unit. In Yozgat the Çapanoğlu valley lords, dominant in the region for centuries, seized control, as did bandit gangs, led by local brigands, such as 'Küçük' Ağa, 'Deli' Hadji and Aynadjı Oğlu, in the Şile region. In Konya where, according to Halide Edib Hanım, almost the whole population rose, a force of some 500 deserters led by 'Deli' Baş, a local brigand, occupied the town; and in south-eastern Anatolia, in the districts of Surd, Bersim and Viranşehir some 4,000 members of the Mylli tribe, mounted for the most part on mules and camels, advanced, driving the nationalist forces before them.[2] As Mustafa Kemal later remarked, throughout Anatolia the clouds of treachery, ignorance, hatred and fanaticism rose, darkening the sky and casting a deep shadow over the country.[3] So great indeed was the loss of nationalist control that at one point anti-nationalist forces advanced to within a few miles of Ankara, threatening the headquarters of the movement and forcing Mustafa Kemal and his colleagues to consider flight.

Mustafa Kemal's response to the assault launched by the Ottoman Government and its supporters was twofold. On the one hand he ordered the immediate suppression of the Army of the Caliphate and the other anti-nationalist forces. On the other, convinced as ever of the need to promote national unity, the essential prerequisite, in his view, of a successful outcome to the war of independence in which they were engaged, he pressed on with preparations already undertaken for the convening of a new national assembly in Ankara.

So ferocious was the attack launched by the Army of the Caliphate and the other anti-nationalist forces, and so complete the breakdown in law and order, that for many months the outcome of the struggle remained in doubt; but in the end, despite immense difficulties, the forces loyal to Mustafa Kemal and the representative committee in Ankara triumphed, and order was restored. In April irregular forces, established in western Anatolia following the Greek occupation, including those of 'Çerkes' Ethem and Ibrahim Bey, renowned guerrilla leaders, were despatched to the Adapazarı and Geyve districts to suppress the forces of Ahmed Anzavour. This they rapidly succeeded in doing, defeating Anzavour's forces in a series of battles and skirmishes, culminating in a decisive battle fought in the neighbourhood of Geyve Pass. In May regular forces, commanded by Ali Fuat Pasha, succeeded in liberating Adapazarı, occupied by the Army of the Caliphate; and in the following weeks, Bolu, Düzdje, Hendek and Izmit were relieved. Following their victory in the north-west, the forces of 'Çerkes' Ethem and Ibrahim Bey were at once transferred to the Yenihan and Şile districts, east of Ankara, there to suppress the Çapanoğlu and the 'Küçük' Ağa, 'Deli' Hadji and Aynadji Oğlu gangs; while in the south the Fifth division, advancing from Diarbakir, gradually succeeded in enforcing a withdrawal of the Mylli tribe from the cultivated areas. In October forces despatched from Kütahya, Afyon Karahissar and Ankara succeeded in relieving Konya, razing many villages in the process; while forces from the Adana front recaptured Karaman, Seydişehir and Beyşehir. Finally, during October–November forces from the western front defeated anti-nationalist forces in the neighbourhood of Ilgin, Kadinhani, Çekil and Yalvaç.[4]

The struggle for supremacy in Anatolia was by no means confined to the battlefield. On the ideological front too an energetic counter-offensive was mounted. In April, in order to counter the effects of the *fetwa* condemning the nationalists, issued by the *Sheikh-ül-Islâm*, 153 Ulema, resident in Anatolia, were persuaded to issue a counter *fetwa*, accusing the Sultan–Caliph of complicity in the suppression of the national assembly and betrayal of the nation; while throughout Anatolia the people were instructed in the aims and objectives of the national movement, as set out in the National Pact, and informed of the harsh peace terms the

Allies intended to impose on what remained of the Ottoman Empire.

. . .

THE TREATY OF SÈVRES

The peace terms the Allies intended to impose on the empire were first revealed, in draft form, to an Ottoman delegation in Paris in May 1920; and they were finally incorporated virtually unchanged, in a treaty, concluded by the Ottoman Government and the Entente powers at Sèvres on 10 August.[5] In this treaty provision was made for the cession of eastern Thrace, up to the Çatalja lines, to Greece; the preservation of a Greek administration in the Izmir region, subject to a proviso that after five years a plebiscite be held to determine the final outcome; the internationalisation and demilitarisation of the Straits; the creation of a Straits' zone, garrisoned by Allied troops; the creation of an independent Armenia; the possible creation of an independent Kurdistan; and the imposition of Allied supervision and control on what remained of the Ottoman state. Small wonder that the Muslim inhabitants of Anatolia and Thrace were enraged when they heard of the contents of the treaty, and that an American commentator writing at the time felt bound to describe it as 'one of the most primitive peace arrangements and one of the most daring and deliberate division of war spoils in modern history'.[6]

The humiliating provisions contained in the Treaty of Sèvres did not complete the catalogue of injuries which the Entente powers intended to inflict on the Ottoman Empire. In a separate agreement, known as the Tripartite Agreement, concluded at Sèvres, it was agreed that Anatolia would be divided into three spheres of interest, British, French and Italian, in which the three powers might each respectively enjoy exclusive rights of commercial exploitation.[7]

Throughout the period of the civil war the Allies remained for the most part content to avoid direct intervention in the struggle, but in June 1920 when, following the defeat of the forces of Ahmed Anzavour and the Army of the Caliphate, nationalist forces advanced on the Straits threatening the Allied position in the area (Allied control of Istanbul was dependent on control of the Straits, the only available access route) the Allies thus threatened responded by calling on the Greek forces in western Anatolia and Thrace to advance and give the nationalists what David Lloyd George (the British prime minister) referred to as a 'knock'.[8] As a result, towards the end of June, the Greek expeditionary forces in western Anatolia advanced rapidly, driving nationalist forces before them and occupying Balikesir, Bursa, Akhissar, Soma and Nasilli; while in eastern Thrace a Greek force advancing from the west quickly overcame the nationalist forces in the area (a nationalist army, commanded by Djafar Tayar, chose to seek sanctuary in Bulgaria rather than risk defeat) and occupied the province.[9]

. . .

THE GRAND NATIONAL ASSEMBLY

The business of convening a national assembly in Ankara, following the Allied occupation of Istanbul and the dissolution of the parliament there, was begun immediately. On 19 March Mustafa Kemal issued a communiqué, calling on the deputies expelled from the Istanbul parliament at once to reassemble in Ankara, there to convene a new national assembly, endowed with extraordinary powers; and he ordered that new elections be held in the existing electoral districts. As a result, a substantial number of deputies, both old and new, were quickly assembled; and on 23 April, following processions, sacrifices and prayers, the new assembly, initially attended by just over a hundred delegates, but ultimately by over 360, was opened in the converted offices of the CUP headquarters in Ankara.[10]

In dealing with the complex constitutional problems raised by the convening of the national assembly in Ankara, Mustafa Kemal would, according to his own later account, have preferred to adopt a radical approach, creating a new system of government based on the principle of the sovereignty of the people and involving some kind of constituent assembly; but in view of the strength of the opposition to so radical a change he was obliged to accept a provisional arrangement, whereby the Grand National Assembly (as it became known), acting as custodian of the national will, would enjoy both executive and legislative powers; though the actual business of government would be carried out by a Council of Ministers, presided over by the president of the assembly, directly elected by the assembly and individually responsible to it. As for the position of the Sultan–Caliph, the principal issue in dispute between the progressives and the conservatives, it was agreed that, once freed from the coercion to which he was at present subjected, he should be provided with a place within the new system, in a manner to be determined by the assembly. In the meantime no regent or other provisional head of state should be appointed.[11]

Having thus agreed on a provisional system of government – in theory the 1876 constitution as amended in 1909 remained in force – the assembly lost no time in electing a president and a Council of Ministers. Mustafa Kemal was, not without considerable difficulty (he received only 110 votes as against 109 votes given to the alternative candidate, Djelalettin Arif, the former president of the Istanbul assembly) elected president, while Bekir Sami Bey (a Circassian diplomat) was elected Minister of Foreign Affairs, Fevzi Pasha (recently defected from Istanbul) Minister of War and Ismet (one of Mustafa Kemal's most loyal supporters) Chief of the General Staff.[12]

From Mustafa Kemal's point of view the provisional system of government set up by the Grand National Assembly in Ankara had a number of advantages. It provided a foundation of legitimacy for the control of the military and civil administration which he and his colleagues already exercised. It obliged the members of the assembly to commit themselves wholeheartedly to the cause of the national struggle, for the direction of which they were now to be made collectively and individually responsible, and it obviated the dangers which a more elaborate system of government, based perhaps on models of constitutional monarchy, involving Cabinet responsibility and a division of powers, much promoted at the time, might have posed to his own control of the regime. But it failed to resolve the contradictions, inherent in the system, between the principle of popular sovereignty, espoused by Mustafa Kemal and a number of his supporters, and the theocratic principle of the sovereignty of the Sultan–Caliph, espoused by the conservatives. In the following months, therefore, a fierce battle was fought, both in the national assembly and in a special constitutional commission, set up to look into the question, in the course of which the progressives, including a number of committed socialists, such as Ziya Gökalp, now deputy for Diarbakir, and Hakki Behiç, the Minister of Finance, argued that all power derived from the people, while the conservatives, led by Djelalettin Arif, the vice-president of the assembly, argued strongly in defence of the old order. Not until January 1921 was the conflict finally resolved, when Mustafa Kemal, concerned lest the legitimacy of the Grand National Assembly be called in question at an international peace conference, shortly to be held in London, finally persuaded the assembly to pass a 'Law of Fundamental Organisation', which declared that sovereignty belonged unconditionally to the nation. Executive and legislative power would henceforth be vested entirely in the Grand National Assembly; while the business of government would be carried on by the 'Government of the Grand National Assembly'. Not that the new law necessarily implied the abolition of the Sultanate and Caliphate – though in Mustafa Kemal's view it did. In the debates preceding the passing of the law, it was agreed that in view of the critical situation facing the country and the impossibility of resolving the question while the Sultan remained a prisoner in Istanbul this contentious issue should for the moment be left in abeyance.[13]

In a speech delivered at the opening of the Grand National Assembly Mustafa Kemal analysed the situation facing the nation in some detail. In the past, he explained, the Ottoman Turks had endeavoured to erect a gigantic empire, incorporating not only the Roman Empire and parts of Germany, but also the Islamic world; and to some extent they had succeeded. But in the end their ambition had proved unrealisable, for in incorporating so many nations and communities, they had undermined the unity of their empire, thereby making both its internal organisation and its external relations unmanageable. Nor was there any prospect that a new state based on the ideologies of pan-Islamism or pan-Turkism, might be created. All such attempts to create 'ideal' states, incorporating the whole of humanity or a particular race, had failed. The only solution remaining was the creation of a state based on the nation. The Ottoman state should, therefore, pursue an exclusively national policy, seeking to maximise the happiness and welfare of the nation.

On no account should they encourage the people to pursue fictitious aims, certain to lead merely to misfortune.[14]

Having thus laid the foundation of an effective system of government in Ankara, Mustafa Kemal and his colleagues set to work to create the instruments of its power. On 29 April they passed a draconian law against high treason, the enforcement of which required the creation of special independence courts with substantial powers (including the power to dispense summary justice), manned not by judges but by deputies. At the same time, they created a series of new agencies for the collection of intelligence, the enforcement of passport controls, the dissemination of propaganda, the purchase of arms and equipment and the transportation of officers and other skilled personnel from Istanbul to Ankara. By far the most important of these agencies was a new intelligence agency, known as the *Milli Müdafaa* (National Defence), or MM for short, manned for the most part by former members of *Karakol*, now disbanded, which was placed under the direct control of the General Staff and charged with the duty of collecting intelligence, both at home and abroad – branches were quickly established in Rome, Zurich, Berlin, Paris and Moscow, and contact made with foreign intelligence agencies, such as the French and the Italian, known to be sympathetic to the nationalist cause – organising counter-intelligence and preventing subversion.[15]

. . .

THE CHALLENGE FROM THE LEFT

The defeat of the Army of the Caliphate and the other anti-nationalist forces and the establishment of the Grand National Assembly in Ankara were not, in themselves, sufficient to secure the national unity, which Mustafa Kemal and his colleagues deemed essential. In western Anatolia irregular forces, such as those led by 'Çerkes' Ethem, continued to assert their independence, resisting all attempts on the part of the government of the Grand National Assembly to integrate them into the regular army; while socialists, Islamic socialists, left-wing intellectuals and other groups loyal to what was known at the time as the 'Eastern Ideal', were busy promoting ideas of class war and revolution, threatening, as a British Intelligence report put it at the time, to overwhelm the moderates of the national movement and involve them in the maelstrom of Bolshevik revolution.[16]

Left-wing ideologies had made little headway in the Ottoman Empire in the nineteenth century; but in the period of the First World War they had made some progress, particularly among the educated classes. In 1910 Hüseyin Hilmi, an early convert, founded an Ottoman Socialist Party; and in 1919, following a period of exile, he set up a Turkish Socialist Party, with branches in Istanbul, Eskişehir and Paris. In the same year a group of Ottoman students, recently returned from Germany where they had witnessed, and in some cases even participated in, the Spartakist (communist) uprising, founded a Turkish Workers' and Peasants' Socialist Party and published a Marxist journal, entitled *Kurtuluş* (Salvation). Meanwhile, in Russia, Mustafa Subhi, a Turkish journalist, recently converted to the cause of international socialism during a period of internment in Kaluga and the Urals, had with the help of the recently established Bolshevik government, endeavoured to establish a Turkish Communist movement, recruiting members from the thousands of Ottoman prisoners of war held in the Crimea and Turkistan. Following his arrival in Baku in May 1920, he succeeded in taking control of a Turkish Communist Party, recently established there; and in the following months he worked energetically to promote the cause, opening a school to train party workers in the principles of socialism, translating Communist classics, such as the *ABCs of Communism*, and publishing a journal, *Yeni Dünya* (*New World*), widely distributed throughout Anatolia. As a result, in the period of the civil war, socialist ideas spread rapidly; and a number of parties and organisations adopting a left-wing or populist stance, were established, including in the national assembly, a People's Group of deputies, committed to the propagation of socialist ideas, or at least the supposedly 'socialist' precepts of Islam; the so-called Green Army, a secret society, established by the People's Group and their supporters, to propagate socialist ideas and fight the forces of reaction; and a People's Communist Party of Turkey. So powerful, indeed, did these groups and organisations become that in September they succeeded in securing the election of Nâzim Bey, a leading Communist, as Minister of the Interior; while on the western front they succeeded in infiltrating the irregular forces, particularly those of 'Çerkes' Ethem, one of whose units was known as the Bolshevik detachment. Moreover, in Eskişehir, they established a Muslim Bolshevik Committee, joined by Ethem, and published a Bolshevik newspaper, known initially as *Arkadaş* (*Friend*), and later as *Seyyarei Yeni Dünya* (*Partisans of the New World*).[17]

The threat posed by the success of the People's Group of deputies and the Green Army in promoting socialist ideas in the national assembly and infiltrating the irregular forces was, from Mustafa Kemal's point of view, exacerbated by the fact that many of the People's Group of deputies and their supporters remained loyal to Enver Pasha, the exiled leader of the CUP. Following his flight to the Crimea in October 1918, Enver Pasha had made contact with the Soviets in Moscow and seemingly adopted the socialist cause. In September 1920 he had attended a Congress of the Peoples of the East, organised by the Bolsheviks in Baku; and at about the same time he had formed a People's Soviet Party, committed to radical reform in the Ottoman Empire. It was becoming increasingly clear, therefore, that he expected to return to his homeland and play an active part in its politics. Indeed, it was even rumoured that he intended to return to Anatolia and supplant Mustafa Kemal as leader of a redirected national movement.[18]

Mustafa's response to the threat posed to his position by the People's Group of deputies and their supporters was devious and cunning. Convinced of the urgent need to secure Soviet support for the national movement in its struggle with the imperial powers, and determined to secure the backing of the People's Group and their supporters, in the war against the anti-nationalist forces, then in progress, he first reacted sympathetically to requests from a number of leading Communists, that they be permitted to organise in Anatolia; and he encouraged the formation of the Green Army. But when the Green Army proved more effective than he had expected, infiltrating the irregular forces (in particular those of 'Çerkes' Ethem), he quickly changed tack. He first requested the voluntary dissolution of the Army and then, in a move designed to secure political control of the situation without sacrificing Soviet aid and support, he persuaded a number of the more moderate members of the People's Group, together with some of his own closest supporters (including Ali Fuat, Refet and Ismet), to found a new, official 'Communist Party of Turkey'. This was ostensibly committed to the principles of international socialism, but was really opposed to them, as secret instructions despatched to the military commanders, ordering them to prevent the spread of such 'illegitimate' ideas, made clear. Having thus effectively isolated the genuine revolutionaries, in particular those with international connections, he then moved quickly to suppress them, launching a campaign in the nationalist press accusing them of acting without the consent of the 'official' party, arresting and expelling their leaders, and closing down their parties and organisations. Most notable was the suppression of the People's Communist Party of Turkey, which had been founded by leading Communists, following the establishment of the 'official' party. As for Enver Pasha and his associates in Central Asia, vigorous steps were taken to prevent their return to Anatolia, and orders issued for their arrest should they succeed in doing so.[19]

· · ·

THE IRREGULARS

The problem of integrating the irregular forces in western Anatolia, some 21,000 in number, many well-equipped and well-supplied, remained. Made up for the most part of troops displaced by the Greek occupation of Izmir, army deserters and *Zeybek* brigands, many of whom had done good service in the civil war, these forces had continued to resist all attempts on the part of the Ankara regime to integrate them into the regular army; and some had even harboured ambitions, fostered by the agents and supporters of the Green Army, to overthrow the regime and replace it with a fully-fledged Bolshevik government. Mustafa Kemal's response was, as usual, cautious. Initially, he sought merely to persuade the irregulars to comply; but in November, more or less secure now in his victory over the Army of the Caliphate and the other anti-nationalist forces, and angered by an irresponsible attack, mounted by 'Çerkes' Ethem, in defiance of a General Staff directive, on Godos, on the Greek front, which resulted merely in a Greek counter-attack and the loss of Yenişehir and Inegöl, he decided to adopt a more forceful approach. Gambling on the fact that the Greeks were unlikely to launch an attack on the western front in winter, he then divided the Izmir front into two sectors, a northern, commanded by Ismet, and a southern, commanded by Refet. Next, he assembled the bulk of the regular forces available, including four infantry divisions and seven cavalry units, in the vicinity of the irregulars. Finally, following further attempts to secure voluntary compliance, he ordered Ismet and Refet to advance. Faced thus with the certain prospect of defeat, the irregular forces in the southern sector for the most part submitted; but in the northern sector the forces of 'Çerkes' Ethem, some 3,000 in number, well-armed and equipped, chose to resist. Moreover, in the following weeks 'Çerkes' Ethem and his followers mounted a vigorous campaign, calling on their supporters in the national assembly and the other irregular forces to oppose the government and reject integration. Only the irregular forces, it was argued, were capable of defeating the enemy. The regular army was of no use to anyone. It should be disbanded. At the same time appeals were issued in *Seyyarei Yeni Dünya*, and the other socialist journals, calling on the railway and other workers to come out on strike, while officials loyal to the Ankara regime were arrested or dismissed. Thus confronted, Mustafa Kemal concluded that he had no choice but to proceed. Issuing an ultimatum demanding the immediate submission of the remaining irregular forces, he had 'Çerkes' Ethem branded a traitor and his brother Reşid expelled from the national assembly; and on 27 December he once again ordered Ismet to advance and compel submission. On this occasion the operation proved a success. The irregular forces were quickly amalgamated or dispersed; and on 5 January 1921, 'Çerkes' Ethem, defeated in a last stand at Gediz, defected, with a handful of his supporters, to the Greeks (with whom in the preceding weeks he had taken the precaution of establishing contact).[20]

Threats to Mustafa Kemal's position at this time did not come merely from the irregular forces and the revolutionaries. In October 1920, following the defeat of the Army of the Caliphate and the other anti-national forces, Damad Ferid Pasha resigned. As a result a new government, led by Tevfik Pasha, was appointed in Istanbul. Determined to reach an accommodation with the nationalists, Tevfik Pasha despatched a delegation led by Izzet Pasha and Salih Pasha (both former grand viziers) to meet a nationalist delegation led by Mustafa Kemal at Bilejik, a station on the line between Istanbul and Eskişehir. From Mustafa Kemal's point of view the arrival of a government delegation in Anatolia, apparently willing to adopt the greater part of the nationalist programme, posed a serious problem. Any expectation that the Istanbul Government and the nationalists might resolve their differences would almost certainly undermine the spirit of resistance in Anatolia, while a refusal to participate in the negotiations might prove unpopular. Placed thus on the horns of a dilemma, Mustafa Kemal resolved the problem with his customary deviousness. Inviting the government delegation to board the train standing in the station, in order that they might discuss the question further, he proceeded to order the train's immediate departure, meanwhile explaining to the surprised delegation that they might continue their talks on the journey, and later in Ankara, where they might remain for a while as the 'honoured guests' of the regime. Moreover, following their arrival in Ankara, he gave it out that they had defected to the nationalist cause; though some five or six weeks later, by which time the danger their initiative posed had subsided, he did permit them to return.[21]

The success of Mustafa Kemal and his colleagues in securing the defeat of the Army of the Caliphate and the other anti-national forces, the suppression of the revolutionaries and the integration of the irregular forces into the regular army enabled them to establish the authority of their regime throughout the greater part of Anatolia; but their position remained fragile. In the east, on the Armenian front, Armenian forces were advancing, seeking to secure control of a substantial part of the eastern provinces, together with the three administrative districts of Kars, Ardahan and Artvin, originally lost to Russia in 1878 but recovered in 1917. In the south, following their defeat at Marash, the French were busy regrouping, preparing to reassert their control. In the west, the Greeks, supremely confident after their victories in the campaigns of June and July, were preparing for a further advance, aimed at the complete extinction of the nationalist forces; while in the area of the Straits, at Bandırma and Mudania, the Allies were busy strengthening their position. It remained to be seen, therefore, whether Mustafa Kemal and his colleagues would succeed in securing the survival of the regime they had established in the previous months with such courage and determination; and whether Mustafa Kemal, the principal beneficiary in terms of power and prestige of the victories achieved, would succeed in further consolidating his position.

. . .

NOTES AND REFERENCES

1. Kinross 1964, *Atatürk: the Rebirth of a Nation*. Weidenfeld and Nicolson, p. 216; Edib H. 1928, *The Turkish Ordeal*. John Murray, pp. 143–4; Şapolyo E. B. 1958, *Türkiye Cumhüriyeti, Tarihi*. Istanbul, pp. 78–9.

2. Selek S., *Anadolu Ihtilali*. Burçak Yayınevi, Part I, pp. 351–9; Şapolyo E.B. 1958, *Türkiye Cumhüriyeti, Tarihi*, pp. 78–9; Mustafa Kemal 1929, *A Speech delivered by Ghazi Mustafa Kemal*. Koehler, Leipzig, pp. 371–88, 399–400, 422–3.

3. Ibid., p. 383.

4. Edib H. 1928, *The Turkish Ordeal*. John Murray, Chapter 5; Selek S. 1966, *Anadolu Ihtilali*, Part I, pp. 351–9; Mustafa Kemal 1929, *Speech*, pp. 371–413; *British Documents on Atatürk (BDA)*, Vol. 1, Nos 93, 102.

5. Hurewitz J. C. 1956, *Diplomacy in the Near and Middle East*. D. van Nostrand, Princeton, No. 31.

6. Grew J. C. 1953, *Turbulent Era*. Hammond Hammond, Vol. I, pp. 476–7.

7. Hurewitz J. C. 1956, *Diplomacy in the Near and Middle East*, No. 32.

8. *Documents on British Foreign Policy*, first series, Vol. 8, No. 26.

9. Mustafa Kemal 1929, *Speech*, pp. 394–7, 419–21.

10. Ibid., pp. 364–5, 373–5.

11. Smith E. D. 1959, *Turkey: Origins of the Kemalist Movement*. Judd and Detweiler, Chapter 3; *Encyclopaedia of Islam (E. I.)*, new edition, *Düstur*; Mustafa Kemal 1929, *Speech*, pp. 379–81; Jäschke G. 1958, 'Auf dem Wege zur Türkischen Republik', *Welt des Islams*, new series, Vol. 5.

CIVIL WAR

The extent to which Mustafa Kemal and his colleagues modelled the Grand National Assembly on the Bolshevik Soviet remains a matter of dispute, but the resemblance is evident.

12. Smith E. D. 1959, *Turkey*, pp. 41–3.
13. Ibid., Chapter 4.
14. Mustafa Kemal 1929, *Speech*, pp. 376–9.
15. *BDA*, Vol. 4, No. 12, enclosure No. 2; Ertürk H. 1964, *Iki Devrin Perde Arkası*. Pinar Yayınevi, Istanbul, pp. 461–85.
16. Harris G. S. 1967, *The Origins of Communism in Turkey*. Stanford University Press, Chapter 4; *BDA*, Vol. 2, No. 92; Mustafa Kemal 1929, *Speech*, pp. 401–4; Tunçay M. 1967, *Türkiye'de Sol Akımlar 1908–1925*. Ankara University Press; Zürcher E. J. 1984, *The Unionist Factor*. E. J. Brill, Leiden, Chapter 5.
17. Harris G. S. 1967, *The Origins of Communism in Turkey*, Chapters 1–3; Dumont P. 1978, 'La Revolution Impossible', *Cahiers du Monde Russe et Soviètique*, Vol. 19.
18. Harris G. S. 1967, *The Origins of Communism in Turkey*, pp. 57, 63, 103; Sonyel S. R. 1989, 'Mustafa Kemal and Enver in Conflict 1919–22', *Middle Eastern Studies*, Vol. 5; Zürcher E. J. 1984, *The Unionist Factor*, p. 129.
19. Ibid., 1984, pp. 123–30; *BDA*, Vol. 2, No. 92 and Vol. 4, No. 115, appendix. When, in December 1920, Mustafa Subhi and a delegation of Communist Party members arrived in Trabzon, they were first prevented from proceeding further and then drowned at sea by Yahya Kahya, the leader of the local boatmen and CUP party boss.
20. Mustafa Kemal 1929, *Speech*, pp. 423–67; Harris G. S. 1967, *The Origins of Communism in Turkey*, pp. 86–9.
21. Kinross 1964, *Atatürk*, pp. 254–6.

Chapter 7

WAR

. . .

THE THREAT POSED

The threat posed to the national forces by the forces of the occupying powers and their surrogates in the period of the civil war and its aftermath appeared formidable. In Istanbul, the area of the Straits and the Caucasus, British forces, numbering some 9,000 men, were stationed; in Istanbul and eastern Thrace, six French battalions, operating as a division; in Cilicia a second French force, again consisting of six battalions, three composed of Armenian units, commanded by French officers; in south-western Anatolia, an Italian force, numbering some 6,000–7,000 men; and finally in western Anatolia a substantial Greek force made up of three army corps, numbering some 150,000 men; while in eastern Anatolia and the Caucasus Armenian partisan units, many well-equipped, were advancing, threatening nationalist control. Against these substantial forces the nationalists, debilitated by the effects of the civil war, were able to muster at best on the western front a force of some 30,000–35,000 men, including 15,000–20,000 irregulars, many badly supplied and ill-equipped, and a similar number on the eastern front, where the Fifteenth Army Corps (commanded by Kiazim Karabekir) remained in place.[1]

In reality, however, the threat posed by the occupying powers and their surrogates was by no means as formidable as it appeared. Throughout the Near and Middle East the British, the principal players in the region, were under extreme pressure. In Egypt, in March 1920, Egyptian nationalists seeking independence had provoked a rebellion. In Mesopotamia, in May, an insurrection, in part provoked by nationalist agents (in the following months it was to cost

112

8,000 Arab and 2,250 British killed and wounded) had broken out; whilst in northern Persia a Russian force landing at Enzeli (on the Caspian Sea) had occupied Resht and forced a British withdrawal from the area. As a result the British, already over-extended (the huge forces built up during the First World War had been rapidly demobilised) had become increasingly convinced of the urgent need to retrench, not only in Anatolia and the Caucasus but throughout the Near and Middle East, and on a wider global scale. As Sir Henry Wilson, Chief of the Imperial General Staff, put it at the time: 'What is essential is *concentration* of forces in the theatres *vital* to us viz: – England, Ireland, Egypt, India, Mesopotamia: in that order.'[2] Likewise the French, preoccupied with the problem of securing control of Syria, were intent on reducing their commitments; while the Italians, preoccupied with problems elsewhere, particularly in the Adriatic, were rapidly losing interest in their latest colonial venture.[3]

The extent of Allied weakness in Anatolia was revealed in April 1920 when the Supreme Council (sitting in Paris) requested a commission of Allied military and naval experts to report on the size of the forces which might be required to execute the proposed peace treaty, then in the process of completion. In their report the commission advised that, in view of the growing strength of the nationalists in the interior, twenty-seven divisions would be required to implement the treaty in full, but that only eighteen were available. As a result it was agreed that in the event of serious opposition arising to the proposed settlement in the interior the Allies might seek to secure merely a partial implementation of the treaty, employing the forces available to occupy strategic points and enforce a trade embargo which, it was hoped, would quickly oblige the nationalists to submit.[4]

Doubts regarding the effectiveness of Allied policy in Anatolia and Thrace were not confined to the question of its implementation. In the British Foreign Office, India Office, War Office and Admiralty it was frequently pointed out at the time that Britian's true interest lay, not in the implementation of the partition clauses of the proposed treaty, but in the resurrection of a strong Turkey, capable of fulfilling her traditional role as a bulwark against the advance of Russia in the area; while in Paris it was likewise

113

argued that France's interests lay, not in the implementation of the treaty, which would bring advantage merely to Britain and her protégé, Greece, but in the resurrection of a strong Turkey. As for the Italians, opposed as they were to further Greek expansion in the eastern Mediterranean, they too had long since concluded that advantage lay in supporting the Turks. By the autumn of 1920, therefore, despite the apparent show of unity and determination displayed by the Allies in Istanbul, only the Greeks remained fully committed to the defeat of the nationalists and the imposition of the peace terms contained in the Sèvres treaty, or at least those parts of it that affected their own people.[5]

For the Greeks the inability and apparent unwillingness of the Allies fully to implement the terms of the Treaty of Sèvres and the Tripartite Agreement in Anatolia and Thrace posed a serious problem. As originally envisaged, it had been expected that the Greek administration in western Anatolia would form part of a complex structure of mutually dependent succession states, mandated territories and spheres of influence, administered or controlled for the most part by the Allies. Any failure on the part of the Allies to create the proposed system would, therefore, leave the Greeks exposed, unable to preserve their position except at the expense of continual conflict with an unremittingly hostile neighbour. Faced with this dire prospect, the Greeks for a time considered withdrawal; but in the end, optimistic regarding their capacity to overcome the Turkish national forces and determined to avoid the national humiliation which they believed withdrawal would entail, they chose to proceed. It was to prove a costly decision.[6]

It was at this critical juncture that Fate, apparently unsympathetic to their cause, chose to strike the Greeks a damaging blow. On 25 October 1920, the King of Greece, Alexander, died unexpectedly of a disease contracted from the bite of a pet monkey. In the dynastic crisis which followed, Eleutherios Venizelos (the architect of Greece's participation on the side of the Allies in the First World War) was removed from office and ex-King Constantine (a friend of the Central Powers) returned to the throne. As a result, in December, the Allies, incensed by what they saw as a Greek betrayal, cut off all financial aid and assistance to the Greeks, and imposed an embargo on the delivery of military supplies; while the French and the Italians, in particular, seizing the opportunity offered to change direction, publicly repudiated whatever debt of gratitude they might have owed to their erstwhile ally. Henceforth it was made clear that if the Greeks wished to fight to preserve their position in Anatolia they would have to do so alone.[7]

. . .

MUSTAFA KEMAL'S RESPONSE

Mustafa Kemal's response to the threat posed to the nationalist position by the Allied powers and their surrogates was nothing if not consistent. Eschewing all suggestions that he revert to the pan-Islamic or pan-Turkic policies of his predecessors, aimed at the recovery of the Arab provinces or the creation of some kind of Turkish super-state in the Caucasus and Central Asia, or that he join forces with the Bolsheviks and other discontented elements to launch an assault on the interests of the imperial powers in Asia, Mustafa Kemal chose rather to seek merely the creation of an independent Turkish state, within secure boundaries, as defined in the National Pact. In the east, in order to obtain Soviet aid and support and establish a secure frontier (deemed essential were the bulk of the nationalist forces to be transported to the west, where it was envisaged the decisive battles would be fought), Mustafa Kemal endeavoured to establish good relations with the Bolsheviks; though Bolshevik attempts to penetrate Anatolia were everywhere resisted. In the south, whilst making it clear that in the event of a French withdrawal from Cilicia, he would be prepared to negotiate an amicable settlement establishing secure frontiers, he continued to encourage the national forces in their resistance, at the same time spreading anti-French propaganda in Syria and the Lebanon and promoting insurrection there. In the south-west he likewise continued to maintain the pressure, whilst seeking to secure an Italian withdrawal. Finally, in the west, in order to avoid conflict with the Allied forces in the area of the Straits and to isolate the Greeks (the principal enemy), Mustafa Kemal endeavoured to establish good relations with the Allies, though as he made clear on a number of occasions he would be prepared to fight any power that remained in possession of Turkish territory, as defined by the National Pact and if need be, in the event of such a war breaking out, to conclude with the Bolsheviks an alliance designed to promote insurrection throughout the east.[8]

. . .

THE EASTERN FRONT

Mustafa Kemal's relations with the Soviets proved tortuous; but in the end an acceptable agreement was arrived at. Having first made contact with the Bolsheviks in Havza in May he quickly concluded that much advantage was to be gained from an association with the new regime established in Moscow. Following the formation of the Grand National Assembly, therefore, he at once despatched a nationalist delegation, led by Bekir Sami Bey, the Foreign Minister, to Moscow; and at the same time he dispatched a letter (drafted for the most part by Kiazim Karabekir) to Lenin, in which it was made clear that the nationalists would welcome Soviet aid and support in their struggle with the imperial powers, provided only that the Soviets agreed to recognise the complete independence of Turkey. Should they agree to act together, the nationalists might abandon Georgia and Azerbaijan to the Soviets, while the Soviets for their part might allow the nationalists to suppress what was referred to as the 'Imperialist Armenian Government'. Moreover, the nationalists might agree to refer the question of the Straits, as ever an issue of major importance to the Russians, to a conference of the Black Sea littoral powers, while the Soviets might support the nationalists in their struggle for independence, by supplying them with arms and equipment.

The Soviet response to Mustafa Kemal's letter, despatched on or about 2 June 1920, proved discouraging. Whilst apparently welcoming the nationalist proposals, and promising support for the aims and objectives set out in the National Pact, the Soviets in their reply gave what Mustafa Kemal and his colleagues considered to be an undue emphasis to nationalist assurances regarding the rights of the minority peoples. Despite all their assurances to the contrary, therefore, they concluded that the Russians intended merely to encourage the establishment of a series of independent states on the borderlands of Russia, in the expectation that in due course they might once more be absorbed into a Russian empire. In this way large parts of eastern Anatolia – greater even than those to which the Tsarist Empire had laid claim – might be lost to Turkey.

Turkish suspicions regarding the intentions of the Soviets were confirmed when talks opened between the nationalist delegation and Russian officials in Moscow. When Bekir Sami and his colleagues insisted on the need to open a route through the 'independent' republics of Armenia and Georgia, in order that supplies might pass freely to Anatolia, the Soviets prevaricated. Not only did they declare that they were too weak to open the road, they also insisted that the Turks should not themselves undertake the task. Later, however, they changed tack, quickly agreeing the main clauses of a draft treaty, promising the nationalists aid and support on a substantial scale. Having thus whetted their appetite, they then informed the nationalist delegation that the actual signature of the treaty, and the despatch of the promised aid, would depend on the nationalists agreeing to the cession of territories in eastern Anatolia to the Armenians. On being informed of this development, Mustafa Kemal decided to act. He accordingly informed the Soviets that on no account would he agree to cede territory in eastern Anatolia. At the same time he ordered the forces of Kiazim Karabekir to advance and occupy the disputed territories. His gamble paid off. In the following weeks the disputed territories, including Sarıkamış and Kars, were quickly occupied; and in December the defeated Armenians were obliged to conclude a peace treaty, establishing agreed frontiers, at Gümrü. As for the Soviets, they made no effort to come to the assistance of the Armenians. Rather, in December, making the best of a bad job, they negotiated an agreement (later confirmed in a treaty signed in Moscow on 16 March 1921) with a second nationalist delegation visiting Moscow, promising aid and support to the nationalists and recognising Turkey's frontiers in the east.[9]

. . .

THE SOUTHERN FRONT

On the southern front too a diplomatic settlement was eventually arrived at. Already in the spring of 1920 the

French authorities, unable to cope with the Arab guerrilla bands operating in Syria and the Lebanon, had despatched a delegation led by Monsieur de Caix (a representative of the French High Commissioner in Syria) to Ankara, to negotiate an armistice. As a result, in May 1920, an armistice lasting twenty days was concluded, which as Mustafa Kemal later remarked, relieved the immediate pressure on the southern front, gave the national forces an opportunity to consolidate their position and provided a useful boost to the prestige of the national regime, now for the first time officially recognised by one of the great powers.[10] Thereafter fighting again broke out, but attempts to resolve the issue were not abandoned. In March 1921 a French delegation attending a peace conference in London concluded a provisional agreement with the nationalist delegation, promising an immediate evacuation of Cilicia in return for economic concessions; and in September, following a nationalist repudiation of the London agreement (inspired by Mustafa Kemal) on the grounds that it contravened the National Pact, the French once again made approaches, despatching Monsieur Franklin-Bouillon (a French diplomat) to discuss the question. As a result, on 20 October, following lengthy negotiations, carried on in part by Mustafa Kemal himself – at one point he went through the National Pact clause by clause with Monsieur Franklin-Bouillon explaining its significance – an agreement, known as the Franklin-Bouillon Agreement, was concluded. This made provision for a rapid French withdrawal from Cilicia and the establishment of agreed borders; though with regard to the province of Alexandretta, known as Hatay (an area of mixed race) it was agreed that a special regime should be established.[11]

In south-western Anatolia the Italians caused Mustafa Kemal and his colleagues few problems. Already in May 1919, before Mustafa Kemal's departure for Samsun, Count Sforza, the Italian High Commissioner, deeply suspicious of the intentions of the British and of their surrogates, the Greeks, had assured him that in the event of a Turkish national movement arising in the interior it might count on Italian support, only provided that Italy were rewarded with economic concessions. Following the Greek occupation of Izmir they gave immediate support to the irregular forces, supplying them with arms and equipment; and in March

1921 they concluded at the Conference of London an agreement similar to that concluded by the French with the nationalist delegation, promising an immediate evacuation of south-eastern Anatolia in return for economic concessions. Thereafter, despite a nationalist repudiation of the proposed agreement, they continued with their withdrawal of forces from south-western Anatolia, finally completed in June.[12]

· · ·

THE WESTERN FRONT

On the western front, in view of the evident intransigence of the Greeks, no alternative existed to a military resolution of the conflict; though the western Entente powers did make repeated efforts to resolve the question by diplomatic means. Here Mustafa Kemal's strategy was first to avoid defeat, and then, when the position had improved, to avoid a confrontation until such time as he would be enabled to muster forces sufficient to inflict a decisive defeat on the enemy. His approach proved surprisingly contentious, provoking opposition in the Grand National Assembly; however, he held to it, and in the end it proved successful. Following a series of desperate battles fought in the most difficult circumstances, defeat was avoided, and in 1922, after a substantial build-up of forces on the western front, the nationalist forces were enabled to turn defence to attack and launch a short, sharp campaign which in the brief space of a fortnight led to the complete defeat of the Greek expeditionary forces and their expulsion from Anatolia.

That in the early stages of the war the Turkish nationalist forces frequently faced the prospect of defeat is not in doubt; but despite the odds against them they held on with dogged determination. In January 1921, following a Greek advance in the direction of Eskişehir, the Greeks were checked at Inönü – the so-called first battle of Inönü – and forced to retire. In March, following the breakdown of a peace conference convened by the Allies in London, when the Greeks once again advanced in both the Bursa and Uşak sectors, they were once again checked (in the so-called second battle of Inönü) and forced to retire. Thus thwarted in July the Greek forces, now under the personal leadership of King Constantine, changed tack and advanced on Afyon

Karahissar, in the southern sector, hoping to capture the railhead there and then march north along the railway to capture Kutahya and converge with the northern forces on Eskişehir. On this occasion the plan proved effective. Afyon Karahissar and Kutahya were quickly captured and the nationalist forces in the neighbourhood of Eskişehir threatened with encirclement. As a result the nationalist forces were forced to withdraw, halting on the River Sakarya (some fifty miles west of Ankara) where they endeavoured as best as they could to establish a new front. Some four weeks or so later (in August), the Greeks, now confident of victory, resumed their advance, hoping once again to outflank the nationalist forces, capture Ankara and extinguish the national movement in western Anatolia. In the so-called battle of Sakarya which followed – the battle lasted for twenty-two days, one of the longest pitched battles in history – they very nearly succeeded, but in the end the Turkish front held, and the Greek forces, bled white (Greek losses in the battle were some 20,000 dead and wounded, Turkish losses 30,000) were forced to retire to their original position in the neighbourhood of Eskişehir. Following their withdrawal the Greeks claimed victory; but in reality they had suffered a major defeat. As Winston Churchill later remarked: 'The Greeks had involved themselves in a politico-strategic situation where anything short of decisive victory was defeat: and the Turks were in a position where anything short of overwhelming defeat was victory.'[13] There followed a period of stalemate, in the course of which the Greeks, still confident of victory, or at least of a victory achieved in the negotiating chamber, continued to manoeuvre for position; but their efforts, which included an attempted occupation of Istanbul, frustrated by the Allies, proved unavailing. Finally, in August 1922 the Turks, having in the meantime mustered substantial forces on the western front, launched a sudden and unexpected attack on the Greek forces in the neighbourhood of Afyon Karahissar. As a result, after a fierce battle, the Greek front collapsed; and in the course of the following fortnight the Greek expeditionary forces were expelled, first from Afyon Karahissar and Eskişehir, and finally from the whole of Anatolia.[14]

In the early stages of the war against the Greeks, Mustafa Kemal remained for the most part in Ankara, where as president of the Council he was primarily concerned with establishing the principles of military policy rather than with its execution; but in the later stages, particularly following his appointment on 5 August 1921 as Commander-in-Chief, he did become increasingly involved. On three occasions in particular he was to be called on to accept ultimate responsibility: for the decision to withdraw from the Eskişehir front, for the conduct of the battle of Sakarya, and for the planning of the final campaign. On each occasion he was to find himself the subject of fierce criticism, particularly in the national assembly, but in the end he was to emerge victorious, his power and prestige greatly enhanced.

The decision to withdraw from Eskişehir proved by far the most onerous. A decision to stand and fight might well have resulted in encirclement and defeat; but a withdrawal of forces, always a hazardous operation, would in all probability have resulted in a complete collapse. Following a hastily arranged visit to the front to investigate the position on the spot, Mustafa Kemal quickly concluded that the risks of defeat outweighed those of withdrawal. On 18 July, therefore, he ordered Ismet Pasha, the army commander, to withdraw his forces to new positions on the River Sakarya, some seventy miles to the east, where it was expected they might meet the enemy under more favourable circumstances. In the ensuing retreat, the army (according to some reports) all but disintegrated; however, thanks to the skill and enterprise of the officer corps the operation was successfully accomplished.[15]

In the national assembly the withdrawal of the national forces from the Eskişehir front was greeted with something approaching hysteria. As a result calls, motivated (according to Mustafa Kemal's own later account) as much by rancour and resentment as by any positive expectation of improved leadership – it was frequently suggested that the burden of responsibility for the coming defeat should be placed squarely on the shoulders of Mustafa Kemal, the man responsible for leading the nation into its present impasse – were made for the appointment of Mustafa Kemal to the post of Deputy Commander-in-Chief – the Sultan traditionally held the post of Commander-in-Chief. To these calls Mustafa Kemal, determined as ever to secure maximum advantage from the opportunity offered, responded with his usual mixture of shrewdness and cunning. Initially he kept his own council, refusing to respond. Then, at the appropriate moment, he informed the assembly, in secret session, that he would accept the appointment, on condition that he be appointed, not Deputy Commander, as custom demanded, but Commander-in-Chief, exercising the full authority of the Grand National Assembly; though in order to propitiate his opponents he suggested that the appointment be limited to three months. Many of his opponents (particularly those loyal to the Sultan) objected, but their objections were overruled, and on 5 August he was appointed to the post. Thereafter, at regular intervals, despite substantial opposition (on one occasion the assembly refused for some days to vote for his reappointment) Mustafa Kemal was reappointed to the post; and on 20 July 1922, shortly before the final battle with the Greeks, the appointment was made indefinite.[16]

Following his appointment as Commander-in-Chief, Mustafa Kemal at once employed the extraordinary powers he now enjoyed to implement a policy of total mobilisation. A national commission for requisitions was established in every district with the following powers: to confiscate, on the promise of future compensation, 40 per cent of all goods in store, including cloth, linen, cambric, cotton, wool, mohair, leather, corn, straw, flour, beans and oats; to enforce the provision of military transport, free of charge; and to confiscate arms and ammunition, suitable for military purposes. At the same time reinforcements were drafted in from the Black Sea area, the eastern provinces and the southern front; and independence courts were despatched to round up deserters and enforce the new measures. As a result on 23 August when the Greeks, supremely confident of victory, recommenced their advance, the nationalists were able to confront them with an army of some 78,000 men, for the most part well-armed and well-equipped.[17]

In the orders, issued by Mustafa Kemal on the eve of the battle, it was made clear that on this occasion there would be no retreat: 'You will no longer have a line of defence, but a surface of defence. Retiring groups will halt where they can, but the whole line will not retire to form a new front. All of Turkey will be our surface of defence, upon which our units will resist everywhere and all the time.'[18]

In the course of the battle Mustafa Kemal remained for the most part, at the headquarters at Alagöz, where Halide Edib observed him fuming, swearing, walking up and down, talking loudly, and occasionally summing up the situation with the 'rare lucidity of a delirium'[19]: but in the later stages of the battle he fought for a time at the front, commanding an artillery unit. Following the victory, greeted with intense relief both in the Grand National Assembly and the country, he was appointed Marshal and granted the title of 'Ghazi': 'Destroyer of the Christians'.

In the final battle for the control of Anatolia, fought during August–September 1922, Mustafa Kemal chose to adopt the strategy of concentration and surprise, employed by General Allenby against the Turkish forces in Syria in the closing stages of the First World War. Secretly assembling the bulk of his forces on the Aydin front, in the south, and feigning an attack in the north, he proceeded to launch an all-out attack on the Greek lines at Afyon Karahissar and Dumlupinar, aimed at smashing a hole in the Greek defences, cutting the Greek lines of supply and opening the road to Izmir and the sea. In the weeks preceding the campaign, units from the northern front were marched south by night, whilst by day a pretended reinforcement of the northern sector was maintained. In the meantime rumours that the nationalist forces were not yet ready to mount a campaign were assiduously spread; and the absence of Mustafa Kemal and the other army commanders from Ankara concealed. As a result, on 26 August, when the nationalists launched their attack, surprise was all but complete. Nevertheless, resistance proved stiff, and for a time the issue remained in doubt; but after some hours the Greek front broke, and a road was opened for nationalist cavalry units, stationed in the rear, to sweep through and attack the Greek supply lines. In response, General Hajianestis (the Greek Commander) ordered a withdrawal of his forces, but in the ensuing chaos retreat turned to rout. By 30 August half of the Greek forces had been either captured or destroyed. By 10 September the remainder had gone.[20]

Throughout the period of the war against the Greeks in Anatolia, particularly following the return to power of Constantine, Mustafa Kemal, determined to secure the isolation of the Greeks and an enhancement of the prestige of his own regime, was at pains to respond positively to the numerous attempts of the Entente powers to resolve the conflict by diplomatic means. Thus an invitation to attend a peace conference held in London in March 1921 was accepted, despite the presence there of a delegation representing the Istanbul Government, as was an Allied proposal, put forward in March 1922, for the implementation of an armistice (though rigorous conditions, regarding an evacuation of Greek forces from Anatolia, were attached). But with regard to the terms of peace outlined in the National Pact Mustafa Kemal remained obdurate. Concessions offered by the Allies in June 1921, September 1921 and March 1922 regarding Turkish sovereignty in the Izmir zone, Turkey's frontiers in Europe and eastern Anatolia, the extent of the proposed Straits zone and the financial controls, were invariably rejected. On no account, it was made clear, would any settlement be accepted which did not secure the complete independence, political, juridical, economic and financial, of the Turkish state; though with regard to the Straits some international supervision, as outlined in the National Pact, might be accepted.[21]

THE CHANAK AFFAIR

Following their victories on the western front the nationalist forces at once turned their attention northwards to threaten the Allies and the Greeks in their possession of Istanbul, the Straits and eastern Thrace. Here the nationalists faced a peculiar dilemma. Conflict with the meagre Allied forces defending the Straits – a single British battalion, supported by a small Italian force at Çanakkale and an Allied, mainly British, force of some 8,000 men defending an eighteen-mile front at Izmir – might well provoke a powerful Allied response; but a failure to press home the advantage the nationalist forces had gained would leave them in a weak negotiating position in any peace conference likely to be convened. In the following weeks, therefore, Mustafa Kemal responded by adopting a high-risk strategy of threatening war but at the same time seeking peace. It was to prove a hazardous approach; but in the end, thanks largely to a breakdown of Allied unity, it was effective.

Initially, in the early stages of the crisis, sometimes known as the Chanak affair, Mustafa Kemal was at pains to emphasise the belligerent aspects of his approach. When, following the nationalist occupation of Izmir, General Pelle (the French High Commissioner) enquired regarding his intentions, advising him to avoid the neutral zone on the Straits, or area of Allied occupation (as the nationalists preferred to call it), he responded merely by insisting that the nationalist forces approaching the Straits would not – indeed, could not – be stopped until the liberation of eastern Thrace were completed; and when Monsieur Franklin-Bouillon (who had arrived at Izmir on board a French warship) enquired, he replied in a similar vein, adding, however, that hostilities might yet be avoided, if the Greeks were to evacuate eastern Thrace. Later, however, when the British in particular, provoked beyond endurance, threatened war (on 29 September the British Cabinet, concerned as to the security of the British forces defending Çanakkale, instructed General Harington, the commander of the British forces in the area, to issue an ultimatum demanding an immediate withdrawal of Turkish forces) he was at pains to avoid a conflict; and when, following prolonged negotiations, the Allies, conceding an immediate Greek evacuation of eastern Thrace and the eventual return of the area to the Turks, invited the nationalists to attend a peace conference to conclude a final peace treaty, he quickly accepted. As a result, on 11 October 1922 an armistice guaranteeing the return of eastern Thrace to the Turks was signed by the representatives of the Allied powers and a nationalist delegation, led by Ismet Pasha, at Mudania.[22]

. . .

ABOLITION OF THE SULTANATE

As Tevfik Pasha (the Grand Vizier) and others were quick to point out, the victories achieved by the nationalist forces in Anatolia and the conclusion of the Armistice of Mudania made the dual system of government operating in the empire superfluous. At the same time it raised once again the contentious question of the future of the Sultanate, which in the period of the civil war and the war of independence Mustafa Kemal and his colleagues had preferred to ignore. With regard to both issues, Mustafa Kemal, confident now in the immense power and prestige which he had acquired as a result of his victories, concluded that the time for decisive action had come. Ignoring proposals put forward by Tevfik Pasha, that the Istanbul Government be permitted to resume complete control of the administration in Anatolia and eastern Thrace, he moved quickly to impose nationalist control on the apparatus of government in the capital, despatching Refet Pasha (appointed governor of eastern Thrace) to accomplish the task. He also took immediate steps to secure the abolition of the Sultanate. On 30 October he arranged for a motion to be put forward in the national assembly, declaring that the Ottoman Empire was dead, and that a new Turkish nation, enjoying absolute sovereignty, had taken its place; and on 1 November he proposed a separation of the Sultanate and the Caliphate, with the immediate abolition of the former. As a result the assembly was persuaded to refer the issue to a joint committee made up of members drawn from the Constitutional, Judicial and *Şeriat* Committees; but it quickly became evident that majority opinion was opposed to abolition. Thus thwarted, Mustafa Kemal, who had observed the proceedings of the committee from a corner of the room, concluded that the time had come to take decisive action. Casting aside all pretence of constitutional propriety, he climbed onto a bench and declared in a loud voice:

> Gentlemen, neither the sovereignty nor the right to govern can be transferred by one person to anybody else by an academic debate. Sovereignty is acquired by force, by power and by violence. It was by violence that the sons of Osman acquired the power to rule over the Turkish nation and to maintain their rule for more than six centuries. It is now the nation that revolts against these usurpers, puts them in their right place and actually carries on their sovereignty. This is an actual fact. It is no longer a question of knowing whether we want to leave this sovereignty in the hands of the nation or not. It is simply a question of stating an actuality, something which is already an accomplished

fact and which must be accepted unconditionally as such. And this must be done at any price. If those who are assembled here, the Assembly and everybody else, would find this quite natural, it would be very appropriate from my point of view. Conversely, the reality will nevertheless be manifested in the necessary form, but in that event it is possible that some heads will be cut off.[23]

The impact of his intervention was, as he later remarked, considerable. 'Pardon me', responded Hodja Mustafa Efendi, deputy of Angora, 'we had regarded the question in another light. Now we are informed.' What happened then is, perhaps, best described in Mustafa Kemal's own words:

The draft Act was quickly drawn up and was read on the same day in the second sitting of the Assembly.

Following a motion to proceed to nominal voting, I mounted the tribune and declared: 'This procedure is useless. I believe that the High Assembly will unanimously adopt the principles which are destined to preserve the independence of the nation and the country for all time.'

Shouts were raised: 'Vote!' 'Vote!' Finally, the chairman put the motion to the vote and declared: 'It is unanimously agreed to.' One single voice was heard declaring: 'I am against it,' but this was drowned in cries of 'Silence!'

In this way, Gentlemen, the curtain fell on the last act of the overthrow and breakdown of the Ottoman Monarchy.[24]

Some two weeks or so later a bill was passed in the national assembly appointing Abdul Medjid Efendi, the Sultan's cousin, Caliph. At the same time, action was taken to prevent the escape of the Sultan; but on 17 November, Mehmed VI Vahideddin, having accepted an offer of protection from the British, secretly boarded a British warship in Istanbul, and escaped from the capital, accompanied by his doctor, valet, bandmaster, two secretaries, two eunuchs, and a choice selection of items from the Ottoman treasury, sufficient to keep himself and his staff in modest comfort for the rest of their lives.

Mustafa Kemal's decision to abolish the Istanbul Government

caused little surprise; but his decision to abolish the Sultanate was not widely expected, though in correspondence with Tevfik Pasha (provoked by Allied invitations to the Istanbul Government and the Ankara regime to attend the London peace conference, issued in January 1921) he had made his position abundantly clear. In telegrams to Tevfik Pasha, dated 28 January 1921 he had pointed out that, as the Grand National Assembly had been established by the Law of Fundamental Organisation as the only independent and sovereign power, it alone was entitled to negotiate the terms of a peace settlement with the Allies; and he had suggested that the Sultan issue a public declaration, recognising the authority of the assembly as the only institution capable of expressing the national will. In the event of the Sultan agreeing, the assembly would at once take over full responsibility for the administration of the country, while any such institution functioning in Istanbul would cease to exist. Provision would however, be made in the budget of the Grand National Assembly for all such expenditures as might be connected with the civil list. Were the Sultan to refuse to agree, on the other hand, then 'the position of His Majesty, the occupant of the Throne of the Sultans, and the dignity of the Caliphate would run the risk of being shaken'.[25]

Mustafa Kemal later sought to justify his decision to abolish the Sultanate on the grounds that it was made necessary by the need to present a united front at the forthcoming peace conference; but such an argument cannot be sustained, for it is evident that a united representation at the peace conference could have been achieved equally well by the preservation of the Sultanate in the form of a constitutional monarchy, the solution to the problem advocated not only by a number of Mustafa Kemal's closest colleagues, including Rauf and Refet, but also by majority opinion in the national assembly. The true explanation for Mustafa Kemal's precipitate action must be sought elsewhere, in his profound conviction that the institution would, if permitted to survive, prove incompatible with the constitutional system based on the principle of popular sovereignty which he and his colleagues had created, remain a focal point of reaction, and impose a significant restraint on his own exercise of power.

In the peace treaty finally concluded after lengthy
negotiations and further threats of war at Lausanne on
24 July 1923, Mustafa Kemal and his colleagues secured
virtually all of the demands set out in the Erzurum and
Sivas manifestos and the National Pact. These included the
repossession of eastern Thrace; the recovery of Karaağaç
(ceded by Greece in return for the cancellation of a Turkish
claim for reparations); a recognition of Turkey's frontiers
in the east and south; an end to the capitulations; and
an arrangement for a mutual exchange of Greek and
Turkish populations. With regard to the Straits, an issue
of major importance for the great powers, it was agreed
that they would henceforth remain open not only to ships-
of-commerce but also to ships-of-war – from Turkey's point
of view a major concession. Moreover, passage of the Straits
would be administered by an international commission, while
an area adjacent to the Straits would be demilitarised. As for
Mosul, claimed by the Turks, it was agreed that this question
should be set aside for later adjudication by the League of
Nations.[26]

Mustafa Kemal's high-handed action in abolishing the
Sultanate provoked outrage not only amongst his enemies
but also amongst a number of his closest supporters who
remained loyal to the institution. As a result, during the
following weeks opposition to his leadership both within and
without the national assembly grew, exacerbated by fears
regarding his ultimate intentions, particularly with regard
to the Caliphate, criticism of his protégé Ismet Pasha's
handling of the negotiations at Lausanne (the members
of the assembly were particularly unwilling to contemplate
the loss of Mosul, being as they were committed to its
preservation by the National Pact) and personal rivalry.
So profound indeed was the disillusion, that in December
1922 a group of opposition deputies endeavoured to enact
a new law, restricting membership of the national assembly
to those persons born within the frontiers of the Turkish
state, or to those who had for at least five years remained
resident in the same electoral district, which if passed
would have made Mustafa Kemal ineligible for election.[27]
Not that opposition to Mustafa Kemal in the national
assembly was anything new. On the contrary, from the
beginning conservative elements loyal to the Sultanate and

the Caliphate had remained profoundly sceptical regarding
his ultimate intentions; while a number of committed
Unionists, loyal to the former leadership, had remained
hostile. In October 1921, following their return from Malta,
Rauf and Kara Vasif, in particular, had formed an opposition
group within the assembly, known as the Second Group; and
in May 1922 members of this group, determined if possible
to curb their leader's already excessive powers, had mounted
a campaign to prevent his reappointment as Commander-
in-Chief. In this they had proved unsuccessful; however,
they had succeeded in persuading the assembly to enact
an amendment to the Law of Fundamental Organisation,
providing for a separation of the offices of president
of the assembly and president of the council (previously
combined) – a change which deprived Mustafa Kemal of
the power he had acquired to select candidates for ministerial
office. Moreover, following the amendment of the Law of
Fundamental Organisation, they had succeeded in having
Rauf, a popular candidate, elected to the office of prime
minister – a position he was to hold until August 1923.[28]

Mustafa Kemal's response to the opposition mounted by
the Second Group and others in the national assembly was
two-fold. On the one hand he continued to strengthen
his control of the army and the intelligence services, the
real instruments of power. On the other he mounted a
major offensive, aimed at securing complete control of the
assembly. Already in May 1921 he had formed a political
group within the assembly, known as the First Defence of
Rights Group, made up for the most part of members
representing the Anatolia and Rumelia Defence of Rights
Associations. In April 1923, concerned as he was regarding
the increasing strength of the opposition, he took steps to
transform this group into a political party, known initially
as the Party for the Defence of the Rights of Anatolia
and Rumelia, and later as the People's Party or Republican
People's Party. Then, having carefully prepared the ground,
with a series of personal appearances, a well-orchestrated
press campaign and the publication of a manifesto promising
support for the principles of popular sovereignty and
representative government, he had the assembly dissolved
and an election called. As a result, in the ensuing ballot
(held in June 1923) candidates loyal to Mustafa Kemal and

personally vetted by him won a resounding victory, securing a substantial majority of the seats.[29]

One of the first acts of the new assembly, convened on 11 August, was the ratification of the Treaty of Lausanne. Another, quickly pushed through by Mustafa Kemal, was the transfer of the capital from Istanbul (a centre of reaction) to Ankara, the new seat of government.[30]

CREATION OF A REPUBLIC

After the abolition of the Sultanate it quickly became evident that further constitutional reform would be required if the vacuum in the constitutional system thus created were to be filled. Numerous solutions were considered, including the appointment of the Caliph as head of state, president and even constitutional monarch or sovereign; but for Mustafa Kemal only one option appeared viable: the creation of a republic, on the western model. Initially, however, particularly in the period leading up to the election of June 1923, he was at pains to avoid any reference to the question, lest it provoke a hostile reaction; though among his friends and associates the possibility was discussed at some length. Only in October, following the victory of his party in the June election and the opening of the new assembly, did he decide to act. Confident then of majority support in the assembly, and of the backing of the army (the ultimate weapon in his arsenal), he proceeded to initiate a carefully-thought-out plan, designed to secure not only the creation of a republic but also a substantial diminution in the powers of the assembly. Instructing Fethi Bey (the new prime minister) and the other members of the government to resign, and to refuse posts in any new Cabinet, he carefully engineered a political crisis, which for some days left the country without a government – the assembly proved incapable of agreeing on a new list of ministers – and then, supposedly responding to a call, issued by Fethi Bey, to arbitrate, he came to the chamber and proposed that it adopt a draft amendment (prepared by Mustafa Kemal himself the previous night) to the effect that henceforth the form of government of the Turkish state would be a republic, with the president as head of state. Moreover, the president, who was to be

elected by the assembly, would have the right to appoint
the prime minister, who in turn would appoint the other
ministers, subject to the final approval of the assembly. This
proposal (earlier approved by a caucus of the People's Party)
was, after a short debate, carried by 158 votes – more than
a hundred deputies abstained – and that evening Mustafa
Kemal was elected president.[31]

In securing his own election as president of the republic
Mustafa Kemal succeeded in putting in place the last brick
in the elaborate structure of power he had so successfully
erected in the years of national struggle. As president of
the republic, he controlled the appointment of the prime
minister and, by implication, the members of the council
of ministers and the executive. As Commander-in-Chief,
he controlled the army and the intelligence services, the
essential instruments of power; and as president of the
People's Party, the legislature. Not that the power he
exercised could be considered absolute. On the contrary,
his dependence on the support of the national assembly
imposed a significant restraint on his freedom of action;
though the fact that, as president of the People's Party he
was enabled to select not only the members of the party but
also the candidates for election to the assembly substantially
reduced the effectiveness of this restraint.

Following his acquisition of something approaching
absolute power, Mustafa Kemal was in no doubt what he
intended to do with it. As he had once remarked in an entry
in a private diary, made in Karlsbad in June 1918:

> If I obtain great authority and power, I think I will bring
> about by a coup – suddenly in one moment – the desired
> revolution in our social life. Because, unlike others, I
> don't believe that this deed can be achieved by raising the
> intelligence of others slowly to the level of my own. My
> soul rebels against such a course. Why, after my years of
> education, after studying civilization and the socialization
> processes, after spending my life and my time to gain
> pleasure from freedom, should I descend to the level of
> the common people? I will make them rise to my level.
> Let me not resemble them: they should resemble me.[32]

What Mustafa Kemal meant by the 'desired revolution in
our social life' was the completion of the reform process,

begun by Mahmud II, in the early years of the nineteenth century, continued by Abdul Medjid, in the period of the *Tanzimat*, and further advanced by the CUP governments of the Young Turk period. What he intended, in other words, was the complete secularisation, modernisation and westernisation of the Turkish state.

. . . .

NOTES AND REFERENCES

1. *British Documents on Atatürk (BDA)*, Vol. 3, No. 65, appendix 2.
2. Jeffrey K. 1977, 'Sir Henry Wilson and the Defence of the British Empire', *Journal of Imperial and Commonwealth History*, Vol. 5, p. 276.
3. Nicolson H. 1937, *Curzon: The Last Phase*. Constable, Chapters 3, 5, 6.
4. Cabinet [papers] 24 103, General Staff Comments on the Report from Marshal Foch, 7 April 1920; CAB 29 86, ICP 99 1.
5. Nicolson 1937, *Curzon*, Chapters 3 and 4; Macfie A. L. 1975, 'The British Decision regarding the Future of Constantinople', *Historical Journal*, Vol. 18; *Documents on British Foreign Policy*, first series, Vol. 18, appendix 2. The extent to which British and Turkish interests converged was made clear in a series of private conversations held by Refet Pasha and Major J. Douglas Henry, a British officer, in November–December 1921. See *British Documents on Atatürk (BDA)*, Vol. 4, No. 47. In these conversations Refet Pasha pointed out that Britain's long-term objectives in the Near and Middle East might be best secured by reverting to the traditional nineteenth-century policy of preserving a strong Turkish state, capable of acting as a bulwark against the expansion of Russia in the area. At the same time British control of Mesopotamia might be secured by the creation of an Arab state, controlled by the Turks, which in conjunction with a strong Turkish state might form some kind of dual state or federation.
6. Dakin D. 1972, *The Unification of Greece*. Ernest Benn, Chapter 6.
7. Nicolson 1937, *Curzon*, Chapter 9.

8. Öke M. K. 1988, *The Armenian Question*. Rustem and Brother, Sections 6, 7 and 8; Mustafa Kemal 1929, *A Speech delivered by Ghazi Mustafa Kemal*. Koehler, Leipzig, pp. 360, 393.

9. Selek S. 1966, *Anadolu Ihtilâli*. Burçak Yayınevi, Part 2, pp. 43–58; Bayur H. 1966, 'Genel Savaştan Sonra Antlaşmalarımız', *Belleten*, Vol. 30; Degras J. (ed.) 1951, *Soviet Documents on Foreign Policy*. Oxford University Press, Vol. I; Karabekir K. 1933–51, *Istiklâl Harbımızın Esasları*. Sinan Matbaası and Neşrujat Evi, Istanbul, p. 784; Öke M. K. 1988, *The Armenian Question*, pp. 184–93.

10. Mustafa Kemal 1929, *Speech*, pp. 390–1.

11. Ibid., pp. 498, 523–24; *BDA*, Vol. 4, p. 109; Kinross 1964, *Atatürk: The Rebirth of a Nation*. Weidenfeld and Nicolson, Chapter 36.

12. Mustafa Kemal 1929, *Speech*, pp. 498–9; Kinross 1964, *Atatürk*, pp. 142–3; *BDA*, Vol. 3, No. 41.

13. Churchill W. S. 1929, *The World Crisis, the Aftermath*. Thornton Butterworth, pp. 400–2.

14. Kinross 1964, *Atatürk*, Chapters 32–9; Jensen P. K. 1979, 'The Greco-Turkish War', *International Journal of Middle Eastern Studies*, Vol. 10; *BDA*, Vol. 4, No. 9.

15. *BDA*, Vol. 3, No. 220, enclosure; Orga I, 1958, *Pheonix Ascendant: The Rise of Modern Turkey*. R. Hale, p. 106; Mustafa Kemal 1929, *Speech*, pp. 513–14.

16. Ibid., 1929, pp. 518, 549–58; Kinross 1964, *Atatürk*, pp. 271–2.

17. Smith E. D. 1959, *Turkey: Origins of the Kemalist Movement*. Judd and Detweiler, p. 68; Mustafa Kemal 1929, *Speech*, pp. 519–22.

18. Kinross 1964, *Atatürk*, p. 278.

19. Edib H. 1928, *The Turkish Ordeal*. John Murray, p. 297; Mustafa Kemal 1929, *Speech*, pp. 522–3.

20. Kinross 1964, *Atatürk*, Chapters 38, 39.

21. *BDA*, Vol. 3, Nos. 46, 74, 126, 149; Nicolson 1937, *Curzon*, Chapter 9; Macfie A. L. 1983, 'The Revision of the Treaty of Sèvres: the First Phase', *Balkan Studies*, Vol. 24; Mustafa Kemal 1929, *Speech*, pp. 490–1.

22. Macfie A. L. 1979, 'The Chanak Affair', *Balkan Studies*, Vol. 20; Nicolson 1937, *Curzon*, Chapter 9.

23. Mustafa Kemal 1929, *Speech*, p. 578.

24. Ibid., p. 578.

25. Ibid., pp. 470–4.
26. Nicolson 1937, *Curzon*, Chapters 10 and 11; Macfie A. L. 1979 'The Straits Question: The Conference of Lausanne', *Middle Eastern Studies*, Vol. 15; Mustafa Kemal 1929, *Speech*, pp. 585–7, 608–42.
27. Volkan V., Itzkowitz N. 1984, *The Immortal Atatürk*. University of Chicago Press, pp. 213–14.
28. Mustafa Kemal 1929, *Speech*, pp. 534–58; Frey F. W. 1965, *The Turkish Political Elite*. MIT Press, Cambridge, Mass., Chapter 11; *BDA*, Vol. 3, No. 135.
29. Smith E. D. 1959, *Turkey: Origins of the Kemalist Movement*, Chapter 6; Mustafa Kemal 1929, *Speech*, pp. 598–9.
30. Ibid., p. 644.
31. Smith E. D. 1959, *Turkey: Origins of the Kemalist Movement*, Chapter 6; Mustafa Kemal 1929, *Speech*, pp. 644–57; Jäschke G. 1958, 'Auf dem Wege zur Türkischen Republik', *Welt des Islams*, new series, Vol. 5.
32. Volkan V., Itzkowitz N. 1984, *The Immortal Atatürk*, p. 104.

Chapter 8

MODERNISATION, WESTERNISATION AND REFORM

REFORM

In the decade or so following his election as president of the first Turkish Republic, Mustafa Kemal, true to his word, used the considerable power he had acquired to force through a wide-ranging series of reforms, designed to transform Turkey into a modern, westernised, secular nation state. In March 1924, determined to strike at the heart of the old order, he had the Caliphate and the office of the *Sheikh-ül-Islâm* abolished, and the Ministries of *Şeriat* (Religious Law) and *Evkaf* (Pious Foundations) replaced by a Directorate of Religious Affairs, under the direct control of the prime minister. At the same time, in a move designed to secure public control of the *medreses* (religious schools), he had a Law for the Unification of Public Instruction enacted, which placed all educational institutions under the control of the Ministry of Education. In April he had the *Şeriat* courts abolished, and he had a new constitution promulgated, which in confirming the new order, based on the principle of the sovereignty of the nation, effectively secularised all legal processes. In September 1925, following a revolt among the Kurdish tribes, inspired in part by supporters of the Caliphate, he had the numerous dervish orders, brotherhoods and sects operating in Turkey dissolved, and the wearing of religious vestments or insignia by a person not holding a recognised religious office banned. In November he had the famous Hat Law enacted, forbidding the wearing of the fez, the primary outward manifestation of religious affiliation; and in December he had the Gregorian calendar officially adopted. In 1926–30 he had new codes of law, based for the most part on the Swiss civil code, the Italian penal code and the German commercial code, enacted; and in 1928 he had the Arabic script replaced by a suitably adapted version of the Latin script. In 1934 he had a law enacted obliging every Turkish citizen to adopt a surname – it was at this time that Mustafa Kemal was given the name Atatürk (Father of the Turks) by the Grand National Assembly – and another abolishing all non-military titles. Finally, in 1935 he had the day of rest transferred from Friday to Sunday, in order that it might coincide with the day adopted in the west.[1]

Opinions differ on whether Mustafa Kemal had elaborated a master-plan for the series of reforms he carried out in the decade or so following the foundation of the republic. Kinross (1964, pp. 378–9) suggests that he had, while Dumont (in Landau J. M. 1984, p. 25), Akural (in Landau J. M. 1984, p. 126) and Yapp (1991, p. 155) conclude that his approach was largely pragmatic, dictated by the pressure of events. One way or another, there is no doubt regarding the motivation that inspired the changes he introduced – a desire to secure the complete secularisation of the Turkish state. Only thus, he believed, would it be possible for the Turkish people to free themselves from the deleterious influence exercised by the religious classes, the *hocas*, *imams* and *khatibs*, who had for centuries encouraged them to sacrifice themselves in the pursuit of the unattainable ideal of a universal Islamic state; and only thus would it be possible for them to construct a 'state of society entirely modern and completely civilised in spirit and form'.[2] Not that Mustafa Kemal was necessarily irreligious. On the contrary, he frequently asserted his belief in the validity of the fundamental principles of the Islamic faith, which he believed to be both rational and natural; and in the Faculty of Divinity, which he established in 1924, he made courses available in the history of Islam, Muslim philosophy, world religions, the psychology of religion and the sociology of religion; but he harboured a profound contempt for the great tribe of *sheikhs*, *dedes*, *seyyids*, *çelebis*, *babas* and *emirs*, the play-actors of religion, who had for centuries, as he once put it, led the people by the nose.[3]

Conservatives and reactionaries frequently argued that modernisation did not necessarily imply westernisation, that Islamic civilisation was capable of generating its own version of an advanced society; but for Mustafa Kemal no doubt existed, for, as he once remarked in the course of a speech delivered at the opening of a faculty of law in Ankara in 1925, only by means of westernisation was the nation likely to secure its survival:

> The Turkish Revolution signifies a transformation far broader than the word revolution suggests . . . It means replacing an age-old political unity based on religion with one based on another tie, that of nationality. This nation has now accepted the principle that the only means of survival for nations in the international struggle for existence lies in the acceptance of the contemporary Western civilization.[4]

What precisely westernisation and civilisation meant to Mustafa Kemal remains unclear, but it would seem that he tended to equate these concepts with the application of modern science and technology. As he remarked in a speech given in 1924, in commemoration of the anniversary of the ending of the war of independence:

> Surviving in the world of modern civilisation depends upon changing ourselves. This is the sole law of any progress in the social, economic and scientific spheres of life. Changing the rules of life in accordance with the times is an absolute necessity. In an age when inventions and the wonders of science are bringing change after change in the conditions of life, nations cannot maintain their existence by age-old rotten mentalities and by tradition-worshipping . . . Superstitions and nonsense have to be thrown out of our heads.[5]

To the orthodox jurisconsult of the Ulema, Mustafa Kemal's reforms constituted, with few exceptions, *bid'at* (unacceptable innovation or heresy). For the most part, however, such opinions caused Mustafa Kemal little concern. Already in the *Tanzimat* and the Young Turk periods, Ottoman statesmen had introduced substantial reforms, secularising parts of the government system; and throughout Ottoman history sultans, such as Suleiman the Magnificent, known to his people as Suleiman the Law-Giver, had enacted *kanun* (statute) law, derived not from divine revelation but from the will of the ruler – though they had generally been at pains to secure the approval of the jurisconsults of the Ulema for their actions. With regard to the separation of the Sultanate and the Caliphate, and the abolition of the Caliphate, however, it is evident that these actions constituted, as the Ulema of Egypt and India were not slow to point out, innovation of an unprecedented kind. Indeed, according to Mustafa Sabri, the ex-*Sheikh-ül-Islâm* who, following the separation of the Sultanate and the Caliphate, fled to Egypt, they showed that the Turkish Government had committed 'apostasy from its religion'. Throughout the remaining years of his life, therefore, Mustafa Kemal, fully aware of the strong feelings provoked by the issue, remained deeply concerned lest popular support for the Caliphate, inspired by agents of the Ulema operating at home and abroad, provoke an Islamic reaction of unpredictable proportions.

. . . .

ASPECTS OF REFORM

According to his own later account, Mustafa Kemal would have preferred to abolish the Caliphate along with the Sultanate in November 1922; but, fearful of the hostile reaction which he believed so revolutionary a step would provoke, he procrastinated. Within a matter of months, however, convinced that his enemies intended to use the Caliphate as a rallying point of resistance to his regime, and concerned regarding the prestige which the institution apparently enjoyed abroad (in November 1923 the Aga Khan and Ameer Ali, distinguished Moslem leaders, wrote to Ismet Pasha pointing out the importance of the institution to the Muslim peoples of the world), he was persuaded to change his mind. Quickly consulting with the army chiefs to secure their consent, he then instituted a major press campaign designed to point out the inadequacies and failings of the institution; and on 1 March 1924, at the opening ceremony of a new session of the assembly, he delivered a speech emphasising the need to safeguard and stabilise the republic, create a unified system of education and secure a revival of the Islamic faith, which in his view had been corrupted by its involvement in the affairs of government. What these comments meant in practice was quickly made clear. On 3 March, following a hastily convened party caucus in which the principle of abolition was agreed, motions were introduced in the assembly providing for the immediate deposition of the Caliph, the abolition of the Caliphate and the banishment of all members of the house of Osman from Turkish territory. At the same time motions were introduced providing for the abolition of the office of *Sheikh-ül-Islâm*, the suppression of the Ministries of Religious Affairs and Pious Foundations and the placing of all religious schools under the control of the Ministry of Education. Contrary to all expectations, this forthright approach proved effective. Though the abolition of the Caliphate did cause discontent, it did not provoke the violent reaction many had predicted.[6]

In the new constitution (promulgated in April 1924) Mustafa Kemal was at pains to reinforce the absolute character of the constitutional changes, accomplished in the period of the civil war and the war of independence. The form of the Turkish state, the constitution declared, was a republic, with sovereignty residing in the people. Legislative and executive authority would be vested in the Grand National Assembly, the representative of the people. Whilst some amendment of the constitution might be permitted, provided the proposed amendment received a two-thirds majority, the article declaring the Turkish state to be a republic would remain entrenched, not subject to any change. With regard to religion, however, Mustafa Kemal was obliged to insert a clause declaring Islam to be the religion of the Turkish state. Only in 1928 did he feel secure enough to have this removed.[7]

Mustafa Kemal's decision to forbid the wearing of the fez, the standard covering of the faithful and a potent symbol of Islamic orthodoxy, was according to his own later account motivated by a desire to demonstrate in the most effective manner possible the nature and extent of the changes being enacted in Turkey. Selecting a part of the country noted for its conservative attitudes, he appeared one day in Kastamonu wearing not only a European-style summer suit but also a large panama hat; and in a speech delivered at a branch of the Turkish Hearth Association, he explained that henceforth the appropriate form of headgear of a citizen of the Turkish republic would be the hat. The shock thus administered was profound, but it produced the desired effect. In every part of Turkey, mainly in the more advanced areas in the west, thousands of men rushed to emulate their leader and acquire a hat, while news of Mustafa Kemal's latest exploit was bruited throughout the world. Not that the change was accomplished without difficulty. In November, when a Bill was introduced in the assembly obliging men to wear hats, accompanied by a directive requiring civil servants to wear the type of costume 'common to the civilised nations of the world', namely the suit, riots broke out in a number of places, particularly in the east, but these were quickly put down; and in the following weeks independence courts were despatched to deal with those involved.[8]

The adoption of the Latin script was likewise imposed willy-nilly on the people. Determined to secure more effective access to the learning of the west, and to remove what he believed to be an obstacle to greater literacy, in June 1928 Mustafa Kemal had a special commission established to examine the possibility of adapting the Latin script to the needs of the Turkish language. This the commission rapidly succeeded in doing, but it suggested that between five and fifteen years might be needed to implement the proposed reform, a suggestion that Mustafa Kemal rejected out of hand. Rather, he opted for an immediate change-over, to be implemented if possible within three months. In August he personally introduced the script to an audience in the Gülhane Park in Istanbul, and in the following weeks he launched a nationwide campaign designed to promote its use. Blackboards were erected in the Dolmabahçe Palace, before which Mustafa Kemal would himself give lessons, and a so-called 'School of the Nation' was established with Mustafa Kemal as chief instructor. Finally, in November a law was passed making the use of the new script compulsory for the Turkish language.

From the purely practical point of view, the problems involved in implementing the introduction of the Latin script were by no means as great as they appeared, for the majority of the people, 90 per cent illiterate, remained largely unaffected, while many, perhaps even a majority, of the educated classes had already become acquainted with the script in the course of their studies of European languages. Moreover, in the *Tanzimat* and Young Turk periods, Ottoman scholars and others had frequently experimented with new versions of the Arabic script and adapted versions of the Latin. Indeed, in Syria in 1905–07, it is said that

Mustafa Kemal himself had taken an interest in the issue, and in the period of the First World War Enver Pasha had experimented with a reformed version of the Arabic script in the War Ministry. Yet the risks involved remained substantial, for, as many Muslims pointed out at the time, the Arabic script, the script in which the Koran was recorded, remained a potent symbol of Islamic identity. Its abandonment would entail the cutting off of the Turkish people from the great masterpieces of Islamic literature and history, their alienation from the Islamic world, and even the possible suggestion that the Turks had turned Christian; and it would almost certainly give rise to civil strife and anarchy. Nevertheless, despite these warnings, in June 1928 Mustafa Kemal decided to proceed, and in the course of the following months the operation was accomplished without undue difficulty.[9]

In the field of education in particular, secularisation went hand in hand with a vigorous programme of modernisation and reform. Following the passing of the Law for the Unification of Instruction a unified, modern, secular and egalitarian education system, based on a simplified version of the Ottoman, was rapidly created. In this the school system was divided into three horizontal tiers, *Ilk* (primary), *Orta* (secondary) and *Lise* (higher), in the first of which education was made both compulsory and free.

In order to provide teachers for these schools, crash courses were introduced, including special courses for the training of soldiers of rural origin, who might be persuaded to take up the profession. At the same time, attention was given to the promotion of adult education. In 1925 a university was opened in Ankara; and in 1931 a series of People's Houses was set up in the villages, designed to promote popular culture. As a result of these and other initiatives, in the following decade and a half school attendance all but doubled, while literacy rates rose from approximately 10 to 22 per cent.

Attempts made to modernise and control the teaching of religion and religious functionaries, on the other hand, produced no such beneficial results. Following the closure of the *medreses*, twenty-six new institutions directly controlled by the Ministry of Education were created, specifically designed to produce men of religion loyal to the republic. In these much attention was given to the teaching of the sciences and French, but little to the teaching of the Koran and the *Hadith* (the Traditions). As a result, in the following years enrolment declined rapidly, and many of the institutions were closed down for lack of students, the last in 1931. Likewise, a Faculty of Divinity, opened in Istanbul in 1924, was later closed down, again for lack of students. Yet still the authorities refused to change tack. In the 1930s, following the removal of the article defining Islam as the religion of the republic from the constitution, the teaching of religion in state schools, originally permitted, was gradually phased out.

In the field of civil law, one of the most sensitive areas in a Muslim society, the process of secularisation and reform was likewise carried through with vigour and determination. In the new civil code, enacted in 1926, a unified system of law was created based on the principles of equality before the law, freedom of contract, private property, financial responsibility and the integrity of the monogamous family. As a result the privileged position previously enjoyed by Muslims was abolished, as were the special rights previously granted to the principal non-Muslim communities – Greek, Armenian and Jewish.

In the debates which preceded the enactment of the new law, no quarter was given to those who argued that it should continue to reflect the spirit of the *Şeriat*, for as Mahmut Esat, the Minister of Justice, remarked in a preamble to the new code:

There is no fundamental difference in the needs of nations belonging to the modern family of civilization. Perpetual social and economic contacts have . . . been transforming a large civilised body of mankind into a family . . . We must never forget that the Turkish nation has decided to accept modern civilisation and its living principles without any condition or reservation . . . If there are some points of contemporary civilisation that do not seem capable of conforming to Turkish society, this is not because of the lack of capability and native capacity of the Turkish nation, but because of the medieval organisation and the religious codes and institutions which abnormally surround it . . . The

Turkish nation, which is moving with determination to seize contemporary civilisation and make it its own, is obliged not to make contemporary civilisation conform to the Turkish nation, but to adjust its steps to the requirements of contemporary civilisation at all costs ... The aim of law is not to maintain religious regulations, nor to maintain any other habitual customs, but to ensure political, social, economic and national activity at all costs.[10]

It is evident that Mustafa Kemal's authority in these years was sufficient to force through a number of highly contentious reforms, but it was not sufficient to secure all the reforms he would have wished. Though in the new civil code, introduced in 1926, he did succeed in secularising the law concerning marriage, making polygamy and divorce by repudiation illegal – Muslim men lost their right to repudiate a wife more or less at will, while Muslim women obtained for the first time the right to divorce their husbands – he dared not prohibit the wearing of the veil. Nevertheless, in his speeches and actions he invariably sought to promote the cause of equal rights for women, encouraging them to play as full a part as possible in public life. Thus he ordered that the wives of civil servants should appear unveiled at public functions, and he encouraged women to dance with men who were not their husbands, at the balls he attended. Moreover, in 1931 he enabled women to stand for election and vote in municipal elections, and in 1934 in national elections.[11] As he remarked in a speech delivered in 1926: 'If a society consisting of men and women is content to apply progress and education to one half of itself, such a society is weakened by a half. A nation aiming at progress and civilisation must not overlook this.'[12]

. . .

TURKISH NATIONALISM

Throughout these years Mustafa Kemal lost no opportunity of promoting the cause of Turkish nationalism, the essential ideological foundation of the nation state he was endeavouring to create. Arabic texts, including the Koran and the Traditions, were translated into Turkish, and school history books rewritten to emphasise the historical identity of the Turkish people. In 1931 a Turkish Historical Society was established, charged with promoting the study of Turkish, as distinct from Ottoman or Islamic history; and in 1932 a Turkish Language Association was formed, charged with promoting a purification of the Turkish language, supposedly corrupted by the admixture of Arabic and Persian words and usages. At the same time history was ransacked to find evidence of the supposed racial and cultural superiority of the Turks, and 'sun-language' theories, identifying Turkish as the original language from which both the Semitic and the Indo-European language had evolved, investigated.[13] Not that the ideology of Turkish nationalism promoted by Mustafa Kemal was necessarily racial. On the contrary, in the programme of the Republican People's Party, drawn up in the early 1930s, it was made clear that the Turkish nation should be defined not as an ethnic but as a social and political formation, comprising 'citizens linked together by the community of language, culture and ideal'.[14]

· · · · · ·

THE EFFECTIVENESS OF REFORM

The effectiveness, in terms of its primary objective – the secularisation of the Turkish state – of the reform programme introduced by Mustafa Kemal is not in doubt. Yet some qualification is required. While the constitution promulgated in 1924 proved effective in securing the survival of the republic, it failed to contain tensions created in the 1950s when, following the creation of a genuine multi-party system, the Democrat Party, a party representing a loose coalition of the commercial middle classes, the urban poor and progressive sections of the rural population, came to power. As a result, in 1960 the army, concerned regarding the effects of the increasingly illiberal and inflationary policies pursued by the Democrat Party, felt obliged to intervene, the first of a series of interventions by the military in the politics of the republic, designed, paradoxically, to secure not the overthrow of the existing democratic system but its preservation.[15] With regard to the implementation of the civil code, it is generally agreed that, while this was generally

ATATÜRK

made effective in the more advanced areas, particularly in
the towns and cities, in the more remote areas, untouched
by the hand of progress, it remained largely unobserved.
There the customs and practices traditionally associated with
the *Şeriat*, including polygamy and repudiation, continued
to apply; and there the numerous measures beneficial
to women, introduced by Mustafa Kemal, were largely
ignored.[16] Likewise, with regard to the numerous educational reforms introduced following the Law for the
Unification of Education, while these were generally implemented successfully in the more advanced areas, in the
remote areas where the peasants remained indifferent, if
not actually hostile, to secular reform, they remained largely
ineffective.[17] Nor can the language and script reforms be
considered entirely successful. With regard to the language
reform – in an attempt to simplify and purify the Turkish
language, Arabic and Persian words were frequently
replaced with words drawn from obscure Turkish dialects
– it is generally agreed that, though by no means entirely
negative in its consequences, this proved something of a
disaster, greatly impoverishing the language.[18] With regard
to the script reform, it has to be pointed out that whilst this
proved on the whole beneficial, greatly facilitating the access
of the Turkish people to European science and culture, it
had of necessity to be purchased at the cost of easy access
to Ottoman, Arabic and Persian language and culture.[19]
Finally, with regard to the attempt to modernise and control
the teaching of religion and religious functionaries, although
this was initially effective – perhaps even too effective – in
the following decades it served merely to fuel a reaction, in
the course of which a number of the secularising measures
introduced were withdrawn.

The story of Mustafa Kemal's attempt to modernise and
control the teaching of religion and religious functionaries,
and the reaction it eventually provoked, is both revealing
and instructive. As we have seen, early attempts to reform
the teaching of religious functionaries resulted merely in
the closure of the institutions concerned. Likewise, the close
supervision of religious affairs, exercised by the Department of
Religious Affairs set up under the direct control of the prime
minister, and by the Department of *Evkaf* (Pious Foundations)
set up to manage the finances of religious foundations,

resulted in a substantial decline in the popularity of public worship. The results were predictable, the opening of a vacuum in the spiritual life of the people; and in due course a marked increase in popular support for private religious practice, including, in particular, private mosque construction, pilgrimage to Mecca, private religious instruction and the observance of prayer and fasting during the month of Ramadan. Quickly responding to these developments, in 1948 Marshal Fevzi Çakmak, a hero of the war of independence, and others founded the Nation Party, calling in their programme for a return to traditional Islamic values; while the politicians of the recently founded Democrat Party made an appeal to traditional Islamic sentiment a principal feature of their campaigns. Equally quick to respond, in 1949 the government, now convinced of the need for change, decided to permit the introduction of voluntary, after-hours religious instruction in primary schools, should the parents so request; and in 1950 it permitted the reintroduction of religious instruction into the curriculum of these schools, though provision was made for the withdrawal of children from such lessons should the parents so desire. Moreover, in Ankara, a Faculty of Divinity was established along the lines of that closed down in the 1930s; and in the provinces a series of special schools was set up, designed to train religious functionaries, while restrictions earlier imposed on the use of Arabic in the call to prayer were abolished. Finally, in 1953 the government announced plans to select, train and supply *imams* (prayer leaders) for a thousand Turkish villages. In short, within a decade or so of Mustafa Kemal Atatürk's decease, a significant modification of the secularising policies of the government was under way, inspired for the most part by a marked revival of Islamic sentiment.[20] Not that the severe legal restraints imposed by the Law of Associations on the formation of political parties and associations, seeking support from particular groups, sects or orders, were in any way relaxed in these years. On the contrary, throughout the government continued rigorously to enforce them.

On two counts, in particular, criticism of Mustafa Kemal's approach to the question of reform may be considered justified: that he was inclined to adopt the élitist attitude of his predecessors in the *Tanzimat* and Young Turk

147

periods, believing that social change could be imposed from above; and that he was inclined to pay too little attention to the contribution made by religion to the spiritual and moral well-being of the individual and the community. His élitist attitudes, it has been suggested, led him to adopt a superficial approach to reform, concerned not with the underlying economic forces which ultimately determine the social order, but with its surface aspects, as expressed in systems of government, structures of law and modes of dress; while his apparent contempt for religion, and the moral codes which religion supports, led him to underestimate their significance as bonding agents of the social fabric, particularly in the rural areas. Hence, it may be supposed, the unwillingness of many of the peasants in the more remote areas to accept the reforms imposed upon them; and hence the substantial reaction which occurred in the post-Second World War period, when, following the introduction of a genuine multi-party system, an element of real choice was introduced.[21]

ECONOMIC POLICY

Mustafa Kemal's lack of interest in economic affairs, combined with the absence of a tradition of state intervention in the economy, meant that in the early years of the republic little attention was paid to the question of economic development, though some steps were taken to reduce the burden of tax on the peasantry and promote enterprise. Moreover, foreign investment, seen as a threat to national security, was discouraged, while expenditure on defence and public works was permitted to consume the greater part of the surplus capital available. As a result, though agricultural output, recovering from the collapse that had occurred in the period of the First World War and the war of independence, doubled in 1923–29, the economy as a whole remained stagnant, while imports continued to exceed exports. Faced with this unsatisfactory situation, in June 1929 Mustafa Kemal, taking advantage of the ending of restrictions imposed on Turkey's freedom of manoeuvre in the Treaty of Lausanne, introduced a new tariff law designed to protect Turkish industry and reduce imports; but he remained unconvinced of the need for radical change. Only in the early 1930s when, following the New York stock exchange crash, world trade collapsed (demand for agricultural goods and raw materials, Turkey's main exports, slumped, as did prices), was he convinced of the need to change tack. Persuaded of the advantages of a planned economy, and of the need to promote heavy industry, increasingly seen as an essential pillar of Turkish independence, he then proceeded to adopt a policy of widespread state intervention, involving further protection, state control of foreign trade and investment and the creation of a series of state-funded banks and state-managed monopoly industries; and in 1934 he introduced a fully-fledged Five Year Plan based on the Soviet model, though light industry and agriculture were for the most part permitted to remain in private hands. The results were by no means unimpressive. In the following years many new enterprises were created and the foundations of an industrial society laid, though it is generally agreed that lack of enterprise, corruption and waste remained a problem, particularly in the agricultural sector.[22]

Not that state intervention in industry was entirely lacking in the early years of the republic. On the contrary, in 1924–25, in an attempt to overcome the problems created by the elimination of the minorities, the principal agents of economic enterprise in the Ottoman Empire, an Industrial and Mineral Bank was established which in the following years invested substantial amounts of capital in state-owned enterprises and private firms, operating in the petroleum, textile, cement, glass, paper and salt industries. At the same time an Agricultural Bank was opened which endeavoured, as Berch Berberoğlu put it, to transform the countryside from a 'backward, stagnant economy to a modern, capitalist one'.[23] Later, a start was made on the distribution of state land to landless peasants; and in 1927 a Law for the Encouragement of Industry was enacted, which made provision for free land grants and subsidies to industry, exemption from tax and the granting of monopolies in certain industries for up to twenty-five years.

In the Five Year Plan introduced in 1934, plans were drawn up for the construction of twenty new factories, including a steel mill in Karabuk near Zonguldak, the coal-mining town on the Black Sea coast, a paper and cellulose factory in Izmir, a cement factory in Istanbul, six chemical plants and seven textile mills, dispersed throughout the country. Financed in part by a twenty-year, interest-free loan from the Soviet Union, the plan aimed where possible to secure a rapid increase in the output of consumer goods, an improvement in the infrastructure and a dispersal of industry throughout the country. Quickly implemented, it was generally considered a success. In 1936–37, therefore, planning was begun for a new Five Year Plan to be implemented in 1938–39. Substantially more ambitious than the first plan, this made provision for the construction of a hundred new factories and a considerable expansion in the coal, mineral, electricity, marine transport and engineering industries; but following the outbreak of the Second World War many of these projects had, of necessity, to be aborted.[24]

. . .

FOREIGN AFFAIRS

With regard to foreign affairs, on the other hand, Mustafa Kemal displayed no such uncertainty of purpose. Throughout the period of his stewardship, he made the defence of Turkey's sovereignty and independence, within the frontiers established at Lausanne, the principal objective of his policy, though in the interest of good relations with Britain he was obliged to accept a League of Nations adjudication in favour of the union of Mosul and Iraq. In 1925 he concluded a non-aggression pact with the Soviet Union, and in 1926, following the resolution of the Mosul dispute, a treaty with Britain and Iraq. In 1932 he took Turkey, now seen as a point of stability in an unstable world, into the League of Nations, and in 1936 he concluded at Montreux a new Straits convention, securing the remilitarisation of the Straits and a new Straits regime, more suitable to Turkey's needs. Only with regard to Hatay (Alexandretta) was a forward policy adopted. There, following a carefully organised manoeuvre designed to exploit French weakness in Europe, he succeeded in 1938 in securing first a period of local autonomy and then, following a Franco-Turkish condominium and elections, the return of the province to Turkish rule.[25]

The extent of Mustafa Kemal's understanding of the

forces at work in the contemporary world, and the threat they posed to the future of Turkey, was made evident in the course of a meeting he had with General Douglas MacArthur, the Chief of Staff of the United States Army, in Istanbul in 1932. The Versailles Treaty, he informed MacArthur, had been imposed irrespective of the conditions prevailing in the defeated countries. As a result it had done nothing to resolve the problems that had given rise to the First World War. On the contrary, it had merely exacerbated them. The present peace must therefore be seen as merely an armistice. In the near future, Germany, the most dynamic of the European states, capable of mastering the continent, although not Britain and Russia, would almost certainly launch a war. In the course of that war, which would, he believed, be fought in the years 1940–45, France would almost certainly be defeated, while Russia, a new power threatening civilisation, would seek to spread Bolshevik revolution throughout the world. As for Italy, whose leader Mussolini fancied himself a Caesar, she would contribute little or nothing to the preservation of peace.[26]

. . .

KEMALISM

In the early 1930s the followers of Mustafa Kemal, determined to create an ideology comparable to the ideologies of Fascism and Communism, then popular in Europe, assembled the basic principles underlying his policies, identified as republicanism, nationalism, populism, statism, secularism and reformism, in an all-embracing master doctrine known as Kemalism. In 1931 these principles were adopted by the Republican People's Party as the basis of their programme, and in 1937 they were incorporated in the constitution – though Mustafa Kemal frequently stressed that they should not be applied in a doctrinaire way, for the essence of his approach was pragmatic, based not on faith but on reason.[27]

That the individual principles underlying the ideology of Kemalism, if such it can be called, were important in shaping events in the period of the war of independence and its aftermath is not in doubt; but it is evident that it cannot, as an ideology, be compared with the dynamic and formative ideologies of Marxism–Leninism and Fascism, which in the period of the First World War and its aftermath proved so influential in shaping the course of events, for it was in effect an ideology created after the event. Only in 1929 or thereabouts was the word first coined, and only in the 1930s did it find an adequate adumbration. Nevertheless, its influence should not be underestimated, for in the following decades it was to prove a potent force, helping to shape the history of the republic. In the 1940s, 1950s and 1960s, the Republican People's Party continued to base its policies on the six principles; and even in the 1970s when it increasingly adopted class-based policies in line with its new stance as a social democratic party, it continued to assert its allegiance. Likewise, the Democrat Party and its successors were wont to refer to themselves as Kemalist parties, though their tolerance of religious reaction and their promotion of private enterprise frequently made such claims suspect. In the 1970s, however, as Turkish society became increasingly polarised between a fragmented, Marxist left and a reactionary right, and as violence escalated, the influence of Kemalism suffered a sharp decline, becoming, as Udo Steinbach put it, only one of many competing political forces in Turkish society – though the army remained throughout loyal to the cause, invariably evoking the spirit of Atatürk in justification of its numerous interventions in the politics of the republic.[28]

. . .

NOTES AND REFERENCES

1. Lewis B. 1961, *The Emergence of Modern Turkey*. Oxford University Press, Chapter 8; Berkes N. 1964, *The Development of Secularism in Turkey*. McGill University Press, Chapter 16; Ostrorog 1927, *The Angora Reform*. University of London Press; Karpat K. H. 1959, *Turkey's Politics*. Princeton University Press, Chapter 2; Yapp M. E. 1991, *The Near East since the First World War*. Longman, Chapter 5.

2. Kinross 1964, *Atatürk: The Rebirth of a Nation*. Weidenfeld and Nicolson, p. 412.

3. Mustafa Kemal 1929, *A Speech delivered by Ghazi Mustafa Kemal*. Koehler, Leipzig, p. 722.

4. Berkes N. 1964, *The Development of Secularism in Turkey*, p. 470.

5. Ibid., p. 464.
6. Mustafa Kemal 1929, *Speech*, pp. 681–5; Lewis B. 1961, *The Emergence of Modern Turkey*, pp. 256–9; Yalman A. E. 1956, *Turkey in My Time*. University of Oklahoma Press, pp. 136–43; Berkes, N. 1964, *The Development of Secularism in Turkey*, pp. 457–60.
7. *Encyclopaedia of Islam (EI)*, new edition, *Düstur*.
8. Lewis B. 1961, *The Emergence of Modern Turkey*, pp. 262–5; Berkes N. 1964, *The Development of Secularism in Turkey*, pp. 473–4.
9. Lewis B. 1961, *The Emergence of Modern Turkey*, pp. 270–4; Berkes N. 1964, *The Development of Secularism in Turkey*, pp. 474–6.
10. Ibid., p. 471.
11. Lewis B. 1961, *The Emergence of Modern Turkey*, pp. 265–6, 283; Kinross 1964, *Atatürk*, Chapter 51.
12. Akural S. M., 'Kemalist Views on Social Change' in Landau J. M. 1984, *Atatürk and the Modernisation of Turkey*. Westview Press, Boulder, Colorado, p. 139.
13. Kushner D. 1977, *The Rise of Turkish Nationalism*. Frank Cass, Chapter 6.
14. Dumont P., 'The Origins of Kemalist Ideology' in Landau J. M. 1984, *Atatürk and the Modernisation of Turkey*.
15. *EI* new edition, *Düstur*; Steinbach U. 'The Impact of Atatürk on Turkey's Political Culture Since World War II' in Landau J. M. 1984, *Atatürk and the Modernisation of Turkey*.
16. Versan V., 'The Kemalist Reform of Turkish Law and its Impact' in Landau J. M. 1984, *Atatürk and the Modernisation of Turkey*.
17. Winter M., 'The Modernisation of Education in Kemalist Turkey' in Landau J. M. 1984, *Atatürk and the Modernisation of Turkey*.
18. Lewis G. L., 'Atatürk's Language Reform as an Aspect of Modernisation in the Republic of Turkey' and Akural S. M., 'Kemalist Views on Social Change' in Landau J. M. 1984, *Atatürk and the Modernisation of Turkey*.
19. Akural S. M., 'Kemalist Views on Social Change' in Landau J. M. 1984, *Atatürk and the Modernisation of Turkey*.

20. Reed H. A. 1954, 'The Revival of Islam in Secular Turkey', *Middle East Journal*, Vol. 8.
21. Akural S. M., 'Kemalist Views on Social Change' in Landau J. M. 1984, *Atatürk and the Modernisation of Turkey*; Giritli I., 'Kemalist Ideology and its Characteristics', *Papers and Discussions*. Türkiye Iş Bankası, Ankara, 1984; Berkes N. 1964, *The Development of Secularism in Turkey*, pp. 490–5; Karpat K. H. 1959, *Turkey's Politics*, p. 271–2.
22. Lewis B. 1961, *The Emergence of Modern Turkey*, pp. 275–82; Yapp M. E. 1991, *The Near East*, pp. 159–61.
23. Berberoğlu B. 1982, *Turkey in Crisis*. Zed Press, p. 25.
24. Ibid., Chapter 3.
25. Kinross 1964, *Atatürk*, Chapter 49; Yapp M. E. 1991, *The Near East*, p. 163.
26. Volkan V. and Itzkowitz N. 1984, *The Immortal Atatürk*. University of Chicago Press, pp. 327–8; 1951 *The Caucasus*, No. 1, p. 16. I have been unable to check the original source of this extraordinary prediction.
27. Giritli I., 'Kemalism as an Ideology of Modernisation' and Dumont P., 'The Origins of Kemalist Ideology' in Landau J. M. 1984, *Atatürk and the Modernisation of Turkey*.
28. Steinbach U., 'The Impact of Atatürk on Turkey's Political Culture since World War II' in Landau J. M. 1984, *Atatürk and the Modernisation of Turkey*.

Chapter 9

POLITICS, OPPOSITION AND CONSPIRACY

OPPOSITION MOVEMENTS

In the period of rapid change that followed the abolition of the Sultanate, opposition to Mustafa Kemal grew rapidly, as Unionist elements, ambitious to recover control, liberal constitutionalists, committed to the creation of a less centralised and authoritarian system of government, and reactionary elements, opposed to secular reform, sought to exploit the widespread discontent provoked by the authoritarian attitudes of the Kemalist regime. Firstly in April 1923, former leaders of the CUP, including Dr Nazim, ex-Minister of Public Instruction, Djavid Bey, ex-Minister of Finance, Kara Kemal, the Istanbul party boss, and some fifteen or so others (including a number of notorious *fedaîs*) gathered at Djavid Bey's house in Istanbul to consider their position. At this meeting it was agreed that though they would not contest the coming elections as a political party, they might yet draw up a party programme, including measures to promote greater decentralisation, a double chamber system of government, universal suffrage, equal rights to all Turkish nationals and the preservation of Istanbul as the capital of the Turkish state.[1] Secondly in October 1924 a number of Mustafa Kemal's closest collaborators in the national struggle, including Rauf, Refet, Ali Fuat and Kiazim Karabekir, fearful that Mustafa Kemal intended to appoint himself Sultan or impose some other kind of dictatorship, agreed, with the support of a number of the army commanders, to mount a challenge to the government in the assembly. In November 1924 they formed a new party, the Progressive Republican Party, committed to the protection of individual liberty within a secure constitutional

155

framework, the promotion of a free enterprise system, and the encouragement of respect for religious opinion and belief. The president of the republic, they declared, should remain above party politics, resigning from his seat in the assembly following his election.[2] Thirdly, in February 1925, Kurdish tribes, committed to the preservation of the Caliphate and the Şeriat, led by Sheikh Said of Palu, the leader of the Nakshibandi dervishes, rose in revolt.[3] Fourthly, in June 1926 a small group of conspirators led by Ziya Hürşit, a naval officer and prominent member of the Second Group of opposition deputies formed in the first Grand National Assembly, and Abdülkadir a former governor of Ankara, initiated a plot to assassinate Mustafa Kemal during a visit to Izmir.[4]

. . . .

ORIGINS AND CHARACTER OF THE OPPOSITION MOVEMENTS

The history of the meeting of Unionist leaders, held in Istanbul in April 1923, remains obscure, but it would seem that it was inspired, in part at least, by Mustafa Kemal himself. According to later reports, Mustafa Kemal met Kara Kemal, the Unionist Party boss, at a secret meeting held in Izmit in January. At that meeting he is said to have asked Kara Kemal what the Unionists were planning to do now that the war against the Greeks had been won; and when Kara Kemal replied that he did not know, as the membership of the organisation was dispersed throughout the country and in Europe, he is said to have suggested that they meet to decide their future role. As a result, invitations to a meeting, or congress, were issued, and in April leading members of the organisation assembled in the capital. In the ensuing discussions it is said that it was agreed that the party would take no part in the coming elections as an opposition party, and that it would accept Mustafa Kemal's leadership. Moreover, it was agreed that Mustafa Kemal might be offered the leadership of a revived CUP, an offer which, it is said, he later declined.[5]

No such mystery surrounds the origins of the opposition movement, organised by the former leaders of the national movement. From the beginning they had harboured deep suspicions regarding Mustafa Kemal's ultimate intentions; and in the period of the civil war and the war of independence they had frequently endeavoured, for the most part unsuccessfully, to impose some restraint on his acquisition and exercise of power. In the period following their victory in the war of independence, a series of incidents served to confirm them in their worst suspicions. On the eve of the conference of Lausanne, Mustafa Kemal insisted, against the advice of Rauf, the prime minister, and a number of his colleagues, on appointing Ismet Pasha head of the Turkish delegation, and throughout the conference he almost invariably backed Ismet in the numerous disputes over policy which then arose. So bitter, indeed, did these disputes become that, following the conclusion of the conference, Rauf chose to resign from his post rather than suffer the indignity of having to greet Ismet following his return and congratulate him on his achievement.

In October 1923, when Mustafa Kemal engineered the proclamation of the republic and other significant constitutional changes, he neither sought the advice of the former leaders of the national movement nor informed them in advance of the proposed changes. As a result, Refet, who like Rauf and Kiazim Karabekir happened to be in Istanbul at the time of the proclamation, learned of the changes only the following morning when he was awakened by the salute of 101 guns, ordered to celebrate the occasion. So enraged was Rauf by Mustafa Kemal's duplicitous behaviour that he remarked in an interview given to a correspondent of the newspaper *Vatan* that it was a mistake to make a fetish of the word republic. After all, was not Central America full of so-called republics ruled over by power-hungry generals! In March 1924, when Mustafa Kemal abolished the Caliphate, he once again failed properly to consult the former leaders, a number of whom opposed the abolition. Finally, during the summer months, Mustafa Kemal and his colleagues Fevzi and Ismet failed properly to consult the former leaders regarding the implications of a possible occupation of Mosul, then considered a possibility.

For Kiazim Karabekir, Inspector of the First Army, in particular, the possibility that a Turkish occupation of Mosul might lead to war with Britain, and perhaps also with France and Italy, was a matter of major concern. In his view, a war fought over the Mosul question would prove a disaster for the Turkish people, already exhausted by more than a decade of continual warfare. In the west the British would, in all probability, despatch a fleet to attack the Turkish coastline in the Aegean, while in the east the British forces in Iraq, more formidable than they appeared, might well prove superior. At the same time the British might encourage the Italians to occupy Izmir and the French to reoccupy Cilicia. In any case, had not the Turkish Government agreed, in the Treaty of Lausanne, to submit the issue to League of Nations arbitration? How could they now go back on the agreement they had signed? Was this, he wondered, going to be yet another of Mustafa Kemal's heroic gestures, designed to secure not the independence and integrity of the republic but an increase in his own prestige, sufficient to transform his position into that of a Sultan?[6]

Once convinced of the need to set up an opposition party capable of imposing an element of genuine democratic control on the regime, the former leaders of the national movement acted with decision. On 26 and 30 October respectively, Kiazim Karabekir and Ali Fuat resigned from their posts as inspectors of the First and Second Armies. On 5–8 November Rauf, Refet and other opposition deputies, taking advantage of the opportunity afforded by a motion concerning the resettlement of Turkish immigrants recently arrived from Greece, under the terms of the Lausanne Treaty, then being debated in the national assembly, to raise questions regarding the competence and integrity of the government, launched a ferocious attack not only on the government but also by implication on the regime as a whole. Then on 9 November, having in the meantime resigned from the People's Party, the former leaders set up a new political party known as the Progressive Republican Party. Nor were they unsuccessful in securing support. During the following weeks, many other former leaders of the national movement, including Djafar Tayar, Adnan Adivar and Bekir Sami, resigning from the People's Party, joined the new party, while a majority of the Istanbul newspapers, including *Vatan* and *Tanin*, gave the party their backing.

In the debate held in the national assembly on 5–8 November, which proved tumultuous (in the course of the debate accusations of arbitrary action, incompetence, criminality, corruption and treason were freely exchanged), the fears of the former leaders of the national movement and their supporters regarding the autocratic attitudes adopted by the president of the republic and his government found only partial expression, for as Mustafa Kemal later remarked, in *Speech*, throughout the debate the opposition deputies concentrated their attack not on the autocratic attitudes of the regime as a whole but on individual cases of government arrogance, incompetence and corruption, in particular those concerning the resettlement of the refugees, the problem of brigandage and the policy pursued by the government with regard to the control of Istanbul, then a major cause of concern. Editorials and articles published in the Istanbul press about that time, however, convey a somewhat clearer picture of the concerns motivating the opposition. In an article entitled 'The Army and Politics' published in *Tanin* on 4 November, the editor remarked:

> The form of the Government is the Republic. But there is no advantage in only changing the name. What must really be altered are the spirit and the principles. In America today, besides the United States, there are about twenty countries bearing the name of Republic. Even Haiti, which consists exclusively of negroes, is a Republic. But the difference between a Republic and absolutism is very small in these countries. We see there a little tyrant who has become President of the Republic by force and who takes the place of a hereditary monarch. That is all. The autocrat bearing the name of President of the Republic governs according to his pleasure. As absolute sovereign, he knows no other law than that of his caprice.

Likewise, in an article published in *Vatan* on 5 November, the editor remarked that it was the intention of the government and its supporters to suppress all forms of opposition:

> Every occasion has been used to silence from the very beginning all persons who do not blindly submit to given orders, persons who seek the truth and want to speak it. Arbitrary action assumes the character of a factor which is placed above the normal state and stability.

How far, the editor of *Tanin* enquired, was the People's Party really committed to democracy, and how far was its commitment merely a matter of words?[7]

The Sheikh Said rebellion (as it became known) was the product of two interrelated, and to some extent irreconcilable, forces – Kurdish nationalism and religious reaction. In the period of the Turkish civil war and the war of independence, the Kurdish nationalists had, for the most part, proved incapable of developing either an effective nationalist ideology or an organisation capable of generating widespread support for their cause; though in November 1920 they had succeeded in raising a rebellion, known as the Koçgiri rebellion, in the Dersim region of the upper Euphrates, inspired in part by expectations that the Kurdish people might be enabled to secure thereby the creation of an independent or autonomous Kurdish state, as promised in the Treaty of Sèvres. Nevertheless, in the following months, as the Kurds became increasingly disenchanted with the 'Godless' policies being pursued by the Ankara regime, in particular those concerning the abolition of the Caliphate and the *Şeriat*, the closure of the religious schools and the compulsory use of Turkish in government institutions, they did succeed in making some progress, setting up an organisation known initially as the Society for Kurdish Freedom and later as the Society for Kurdish Independence, with branches in many of the main towns, and in the army, where many of the officers and men were of Kurdish extraction. As a result, in 1924 they were enabled to convene a congress, attended not only by army officers and intellectuals but also by a number of Sheikhs and tribal chiefs, including Sheikh Said, the redoubtable leader of the Nakshbandi order in the area. At this congress it was agreed that a rebellion aiming at the creation of an independent or autonomous Kurdistan might be attempted, and that the Soviets and the British might be approached for support.

Thereafter, events progressed rapidly. In September Kurdish nationalists organised a mutiny of Kurdish troops stationed at Beyt Şebab, a small garrison town in the neighbourhood of the Iraqi border, which resulted in a mass desertion; and in February 1925 they called on the tribes in the Dersim region once again to rise. On this occasion many of the tribes, mainly Sunni, members of the Nakshbandi order, responded. During the following weeks Sheikh Said and his followers, marching under the green banner of Islam and calling for the restoration of the Caliphate and the *Şeriat*, advanced rapidly on Elaziğ and Diyarbakir, sacking villages, looting banks and shops and occupying government offices.[8]

The origins of the plot, organised by Ziya Hurşit and Abdülkadir, to assassinate Mustafa Kemal in June 1926 remain obscure, as do the motives of the conspirators. According to their own later testimony, the conspirators originally intended to assassinate the president of the republic in Ankara, on the road down from the presidential palace in Çankaya to the centre of the town, or in front of the Anatolia Club which he frequently visited in the evening. To this end they recruited a number of professional criminals including 'Çopur' (Pock-marked)–Hilmi, 'Laz' Ismail and 'Gürcü' (Georgian) Yusuf. But security proved too tight in Ankara, so they decided to make the attempt in the course of a tour of southern and western Anatolia, undertaken by the president in the summer of 1926. A number of possible places were considered, but eventually the conspirators concluded that Izmir offered the best chance of success. In June, therefore, they assembled there, meeting up with other member of the gang including 'Sarı' (Blond) Efe Edip, a former gendarmerie officer, Unionist *fedaî* and possible police informer, and 'Giritli' Şevki, also a possible police informer. The plan was to wait for Mustafa Kemal's car at a crossing and then shoot him, if need be finishing him off with bombs hidden in flowers, before escaping to the Greek islands in a boat owned or operated by 'Giritli' Şevki. But in the event the plan went badly wrong. Mustafa Kemal, possibly forewarned, arrived a day late, 'Sari' Efe fled to Istanbul and 'Giritli' Şevki, in whose boat the conspirators had hoped to escape, informed on his colleagues, with the result that the remaining conspirators were quickly rounded up. As for the motives of the conspirators, never investigated at the trial, it would seem that they were inspired mainly by feelings of hatred for the president and a desire for revenge. Ziya Hurşit, in particular, was known as an opponent of Mustafa Kemal and a critic of the personality cult which the president's followers were busy promoting. Moreover, he had been a friend and collaborator of Ali Şükrü, the Trabzon deputy murdered by Topal Osman, Mustafa Kemal's personal bodyguard, in 1923, and of 'Deli' Halit Pasha, the Ardahan deputy murdered in 1925 by 'Kel' (Bald) Ali, another of Mustafa Kemal's henchmen, later appointed president of the independence court despatched to Izmir.[9]

. . .

MUSTAFA KEMAL'S RESPONSE TO THE OPPOSITION RAISED AGAINST HIM

Mustafa Kemal's response to the opposition ranged against him displayed his usual patience and cunning. Initially, as he struggled to consolidate his power, he chose merely to contain the threat posed to his regime. Far from arresting the former leaders of the CUP, assembled in Istanbul, he encouraged them in the expectation that they might yet be permitted to play a part in the politics of the new republic; while the opposition movement, mounted against him by the former leaders of the national movement, he countered by ordering that all serving officers sitting as deputies in the assembly resign from their posts or face dismissal, and by ordering that, following their resignation, Kiazim Karabekir and Ali Fuat be prevented from entering the national assembly building until such time as their 'successors had been appointed'. Having in this way effectively reduced the impact of the opposition campaign (all but two of the officers concerned resigned; the two remaining, Djafar Tayar and Djevad, were at once relieved of their commands), he then took energetic steps to defeat the challenge mounted by Rauf, Refet and the other opposition deputies in the national assembly. In this he proved successful. When the motion, in effect a vote of confidence in the government, was put, Ismet Pasha's government won a majority of 148 votes to 19, with one abstention.

Yet still Mustafa Kemal felt obliged to tread carefully, for his position remained uncertain. Only in 1925, when the outbreak of the Kurdish rebellion created exceptionally favourable circumstances, did he dare to proceed further. He then moved with speed and determination, enacting a draconian Law for the Maintenance of Public Order, giving the government extraordinary powers, recreating the

162

dreaded independence courts, imposing a rigorous press censorship, and closing down the Progressive Republican Party and other supposedly divisive opposition parties and organisations. At the same time he took vigorous steps to suppress the rebels, having many thousands of them imprisoned and many hundreds hanged, including Sheikh Said, their leader. Finally, following the discovery of the assassination plot, he initiated a carefully orchestrated reign of terror, arresting not only the conspirators and their immediate associates but also the former leaders of the CUP and the leaders of the Progressive Republican Party, particularly those sitting in the assembly. In the show trials which followed, held in Ankara and Izmir, no mercy was shown. Along with the conspirators and their associates four of the former Leaders of the CUP, including Dr Nazim and Djavid, and six of the twenty-nine deputies belonging to the Progressive Republican Party were hanged; Kara Kemal committed suicide in order to escape arrest; and many more, including Rauf, convicted *in absentia* (he happened to be abroad at the time of the conspiracy), were sentenced to long periods of imprisonment. As for Refet, Ali Fuat and Kiazim Karabekir, saved by their popularity as heroes of the war of independence, they were acquitted. But the message was clear: henceforth no opposition of any kind, other than that personally sanctioned by Mustafa Kemal, would be tolerated.[10]

From Mustafa Kemal's point of view, the long-expected rebellion mounted by the Kurds in eastern Anatolia posed a serious challenge, both to the integrity of the new republic and to the process of secular reform then under way. It is not surprising, therefore, that his response was both ruthless and thorough-going. Initially, he concentrated on assembling a sufficient number of troops in the area of the rebellion to encircle the rebel forces and cut off their escape routes. Then, slowly but inexorably, employing not only artillery but also air power, the effectiveness of which had been proved by the British in Iraq, he proceeded to close the circle, driving the rebels back from the major towns, capturing their strongholds in the mountains, burning their villages and destroying their crops. Meanwhile, in Diyarbakir, he had an independence court installed, which during the following months had some hundreds of the rebels hanged and some thousands imprisoned. Among those hanged on 29 June, together with some forty-six others, was Sheikh Said, who it is said died courageously, protesting the righteousness of his cause. Nor was that the end of the affair. During the next few months something approaching a reign of terror was instituted, accompanied, according to the British ambassador, by deportations on a scale reminiscent of the Armenian deportations carried out in the early months of the First World War.[11] Only in May 1928, by which time order had to some extent been restored, was a Law of Amnesty promulgated, which enabled rebels giving themselves up to escape prosecution.

Not that Mustafa Kemal's approach to the Kurdish question was merely draconian. On the contrary, throughout the period of the civil war and the war of independence he had been at pains to maintain good relations with the Kurdish tribes and their leaders, many of whom had fought with the Turkish forces against the Russians and the Armenians in the First World War and the war of independence. To this end he frequently had Kurdish chiefs and landowners, such as the Koçgiri tribal chief Alişan Beg, elected as deputies in the Grand National Assembly, or appointed to high office in the administration of the eastern provinces. In the period immediately following the outbreak of the Koçgiri rebellion he had a parliamentary commission appointed to investigate the causes of the outbreak; and in 1924, on the eve of the Sheikh Said rebellion, he had a Turkish–Kurdish congress convened in Diyarbakir, at which it was agreed that the government might consider a series of major concessions, including the creation of a special form of administration for the Kurdish provinces, the provision of generous loans, the granting of a general amnesty for Kurdish rebels, a suspension for a period of five years of conscription in the Kurdish provinces, and even a possible restoration of the Şeriat courts. As a result of these and other steps taken in the period of the Sheikh Said rebellion, many of the tribes remained loyal, as did most of the landlords, peasant farmers and craftsmen inhabiting the major towns and surrounding areas.[12]

As Robert Olson notes, it was only following the suppression of the Sheikh Said rebellion, and the passing of the draconian Law for the Maintenance of Public Order which accompanied it, that Mustafa Kemal felt secure enough to proceed with a number of his more radical reforms, including in particular the closure of the dervish orders and the banning of the fez, enacted in September–November 1925.[13] It may also be assumed that had the Law for the Maintenance of Public Order, and the instruments of its enforcement, the independence courts, not remained in place, Mustafa Kemal would not have been enabled so easily to suppress the various opposition groups in the period immediately following the attempted assassination.

The ruthless and wide-ranging nature of Mustafa Kemal's response to the discovery of the plot against him in June 1926 suggests that he had already decided to take action against the opposition groups ranged against him. In the week or so following the discovery of the plot, more than a hundred suspects were arrested, the great majority were almost certainly innocent of all charges. A number of those charged were absent abroad at the time, and according to a British Foreign Office report one, Hussein Djahid, had spent the previous fourteen months incarcerated in a Turkish fortress serving a life sentence.[14] In the show trials, which opened in Izmir on 26 June and in Ankara on 1 August, little or no attempt was made to discover the precise extent of the conspiracy. Nor was any attempt made to prove the involvement of the opposition leaders. This was simply assumed. Rather, attention was concentrated almost entirely on discrediting the CUP and its supposed heirs and successors. To this end, the opposition leaders were variously accused of acting unconstitutionally in engaging the Ottoman Empire in the First World War on the side of the Central Powers, profiteering on a massive scale in the course of the war, working to secure the return of Enver Pasha to Anatolia in the period of the war of independence, organising the so-called Second Group of opposition deputies in the first Grand National Assembly, plotting in the period immediately following the victory of the nationalist forces in the war of independence to recover their lost power, organising the Progressive Republican Party (supposedly a front organisation for the CUP), encouraging the Kurdish revolt of 1925, opposing the 'hat law', and finally, following the suppression of the Progressive Republican Party, plotting the assassination of the president. Of the accused leaders only Ahmet Şükrü, a former CUP Minister of Education, governor of Trabzon and member of the Progressive Republican Party, was in any way seriously implicated in the conspiracy, and even then some doubt remained. Kiazim Karabekir was accused simply of being acquainted with Ziya Hurşit, while Djavid and Kara Kemal were accused of having summoned the meeting of former leaders of the CUP held in Istanbul in April 1923. Nevertheless, on 11 July Ahmet Şükrü and a number of other members of the Progressive Republican Party were found guilty of conspiracy to secure the overthrow of the constitution and the government of the Grand National Assembly, based on it; and on the night of 12 July they were hanged. Similarly, on 26 August the four leading members of the CUP were condemned and hanged. On the night of the execution, Mustafa Kemal, who had signed the sentences immediately they were presented to him, attended a party organised to celebrate the founding of a model farm outside Ankara.[15]

That the principal purpose of the show trials was the suppression of the opposition is evident; but they also served another purpose. Before concluding its business, the Ankara court ordered that the ownership of all funds and property belonging to the CUP should be transferred to the state.

In March 1926, in order to justify his attack on the former leaders of the CUP, Mustafa Kemal published in *Milliyet* (a popular journal) a series of memoirs critical of their leadership in the years preceding the First World War and in the period of the war itself. Then in October 1927, in order to justify his attack on the leaders of the Progressive Republican Party, in particular the friends and colleagues with whom he had launched the national movement and fought the war of independence, he delivered, before a Congress of the Republican People's Party, a speech lasting six days, later published as *Speech (Nutuk)* in which he described in considerable detail the great drama of the national struggle, the part which he, the protagonist, had played in it, and the part, frequently discreditable, played not only by the Sultan and his ministers but also by his erstwhile colleagues Rauf, Refet, Ali Fuat and Kiazim Karabekir. As a result of these and other widely distributed accounts, a legend of epic proportions was born, on the foundation of which, in the following years, a major personality cult, of equally epic proportions, was fashioned.[16]

A graphic account of the speech delivered by Mustafa Kemal, composed by R. Hadow, a second secretary of the British Embassy, catches the spirit of the occasion.

Inasmuch as the Smyrna trials of 1926, with their consequent eradication of the only existent Opposition, and subsequent parliamentary elections, had left neither Opposition party nor independent Deputies, the congress perforce included all the 315 Deputies who will shortly take their places in the new National Assembly.

But it included also 200 of other members of the party, gathered from every part in Turkey, whose role it will be to return to their districts and there to expound to each village and township the doctrines they have learnt at the capital.

From the mouth of the great Leader of the party, *Ghazi* Mustafa Kemal Pasha himself, it was, therefore, thought politic to allow them to hear the history of the Nationalist movement from its very inception, so that Turkey's sons and daughters might, in their turn, learn their history from the desired angle.

That it was thought necessary so to instruct them in the greatest detail is an interesting proof both of Turkey's illiteracy – which makes it essential to pass on facts by word of mouth – and of the *Ghazi's* desire to have at his back at the present time the added prestige that his recital of the epic of New Turkey must surely bring to the creator and directing hand of the entire movement. With characteristic energy, the *Ghazi* has not spared himself six or more continuous days of reading for seven, eight, or even nine hours a day, from a carefully edited and prepared manuscript, which it has been the task of his inner circle of friends and advisers to revise over and over again for several months past. So careful, indeed, is the President to infuse the right spirit into his words that until 2 a.m., or later, his friends are called upon each night to put the final polish into the next day's section of the speech, which starts at 10 a.m. For the compilation of his work such actors in the story as Fethi Bey, Turkish Ambassador at Paris and former

Prime Minister, and Hikmet Bey, Minister at Belgrade and formerly secretary of the People's Party, have been called to Angora and kept in Turkey till the congress should be over; every document of any interest has been collected and exhibited – where possible in original – for the greater convincing of the audience, and no pains have been spared to make the speech a historical narrative, at all events to Turkish minds.

To an expectant audience of carefully groomed Turks, each one compulsorily clad in tail-coat, or at worst in a dark lounge suit, were added, by special invitation, the representatives of the foreign Powers or their secretaries, whose numbers – though limited to one for each Power – far exceeded the capacity of the Diplomatic Gallery.

The members of the Cabinet were grouped in front, the Public Gallery was thronged, and the President's box occupied by Fethi Bey, by the Turkish Minister from Prague, and by the Chief of Staff, Fevzi Pasha, whose presence was commented on as a proof of the solemnity of the occasion, since he rarely shows himself in public and is considered by most European observers to be the brains of the army and Mustafa Kemal's most likely successor. The heads of all Government Departments were present, and their work in the Ministries was virtually suspended for the duration of the congress, while three of the President's 'wards' smiled down upon him from his second box, having driven up in the presidential car.

The opening words of the President's oration were characteristic of the tone of the whole: –

'On the 19th May, 1919, I landed at Samsoun . . .'. Thereafter and throughout the speech care has been taken to emphasise the whole progress of events as carefully planned and thought out in advance by the *Ghazi* and his advisers, to the evident wonderment and appreciation of the audience, who, for all their uncomfortable stiff collars and European clothes, could not, in large measure, conceal their original and village mentality – a point on which the *Ghazi* is doubtless counting for the proper propagation of his words.

As already emphasised, the speech is primarily for

Turkish consumption. The great Teacher is instructing his faithful disciples, who in turn are to go out to the highways and byeways to spread the good news of Turkey's resurrection and thereby to make the villager, shopkeeper and landowner appreciate the debt he owes to the *Ghazi* and to the People's party.[17]

. . .

AN EXPERIMENT WITH DEMOCRACY

Paradoxically, though Mustafa Kemal never again relaxed the absolute control of the government of the republic that he had secured as a result of the suppression of the opposition and the show trials, he none the less remained committed, in theory at least, to the principle of representative government. Throughout his period in office, elections were regularly held; and as Frederick Frey has pointed out, he never attempted to elaborate an ideology of authoritarianism, though some of his followers came close to doing so.[18] On the contrary, in 1930 he attempted to introduce an element of genuine democracy into the political system, encouraging his old friend and colleague Ali Fethi (an admirer of the British parliamentary system) to set up a loyal opposition party, the Free Republican Party, supposedly committed to the promotion of private enterprise and greater freedom of conscience. This, it was hoped, might educate the public in the arts of political debate, and provide a useful outlet for discontent, then on the increase as a result of the world slump and the unpopularity of the government's economic policy. The results were not encouraging. When Ali Fethi arrived in Izmir in order to open the party's first branch office, he discovered, to his surprise, not the handful of adherents he had expected to greet him but a crowd of some 50,000 persons, clearly intent on expressing their support. In the ensuing chaos street fights broke out and a boy was shot by a stray police bullet, while the windows of a building housing *Anadolu*, a journal critical of the new party, were smashed. Likewise, in similar rallies held elsewhere, huge crowds seized the opportunity to gather, waving green flags, the traditional emblem of Islam, and calling for the repeal of the secular reforms, in particular those concerned with the suppression of the Caliphate, the

169

Şeriat and the Arabic script, while in the national assembly fights broke out between Ali Fethi's supporters and the supporters of the Republican People's Party. As a result, Mustafa Kemal, thus convinced of the extent of popular discontent, and of the threat which it posed to his regime, was obliged to change course, and on 17 November he had the new party quietly dissolved.[19] As Kinross has remarked, having rejected the possibility of a two-party system in 1925, when the momentum of the revolution and the calibre of the opposition leaders might have made it a success, he can hardly have expected that his experiment would succeed in a period of acute discontent.[20]

Mustafa Kemal's great fear throughout his period in office was, as we have seen, that a popular movement, seeking the restoration of the Caliphate and the *Şeriat*, might arise, inspired by the forces of reaction. The full extent of this fear was made clear in December 1930, when an ugly incident occured in Menemen, a small town near Izmir in western Anatolia. Returning from a pilgrimage to Manisa, 'bristling with arms and mad with hashish and fanaticism', as Sir George Clerk, the British ambassador, later put it, a group of dervishes belonging to the Nakshbandi order assembled in the town square, calling for the overthrow of the Ankara regime and the restoration of the veil, the fez, the Arabic script and the *Şeriat*. Moreover, when Mustafa Fehmi Kubilayi, a young officer who happened to be passing at the time, accompanied by a small band of soldiers, attempted to restrain the dervishes, firing off a few rounds of blank ammunition, Mehmet the dervish, the leader of the group, not only shot him down but, sending for a saw, cut off his head, mounted it on a pole and proceeded to parade it round the town, followed by his intoxicated followers, chanting invocations. Mustafa Kemal's response was immediate. Army units were at once despatched into the area, martial law declared, and over a hundred arrests made. As for those later condemned by the military court, established in Menemen, some for offences as simple as providing the dervishes with food on their way through the neighbouring villages, they were immediately hanged. A villager, accused of helping one of the suspects, who happened to escape, was ruthlessly hunted down. As the British ambassador later put it, it seemed that the government and the Republican People's Party (and by implication Mustafa Kemal himself) were determined to show by the severity of their sentences that they would brook no opposition.[21]

. . .

NOTES AND REFERENCES

1. Cruikshank A. A. 1968, 'The Young Turk Challenge in Postwar Turkey', *Middle East Journal*, Vol. 22; Zürcher E. J. 1984, *The Unionist Factor*. E. J. Brill, Leiden, pp. 133–5, 151.

2. Ibid., pp. 136–40; Frey F. W. 1965, *The Turkish Political Elite*. MIT Press, Cambridge, Mass., pp. 324–31.

3. Olson R. 1989, *The Emergence of Kurdish Nationalism and the Sheikh Said Rebellion*. University of Texas Press, pp. 124–6.

4. Mustafa Kemal 1929, *A Speech Delivered by Ghazi Mustafa Kemal*. Koehler, Leipzig, p. 686; Zürcher E. J. 1984, *The Unionist Factor*, pp. 143–5.

5. Ibid., pp. 133–5.

6. Ibid., pp. 136–40; Mustafa Kemal 1929, *Speech*, pp. 674–97; Mumcu U. (ed.) 1990, *Kazim Karabekir Anlatıyor*. Tekin Yayınevi, Istanbul, Chapter 16.

7. Mustafa Kemal 1929, *Speech*, pp. 686–715; Mumcu U. (ed.) 1990, *Kazim Karabekir Anlatıyor*, Chapter 17.

8. Olson R. 1989, *The Emergence of Kurdish Nationalism*, Chapter 2.

9. Zürcher E. J. 1984, *The Unionist Factor*, pp. 144–5.

10. Ibid., Chapter 6; Frey F. W. 1965, *The Turkish Political Elite*, pp. 334–5; Mustafa Kemal 1929, *Speech*, pp. 686–721.

11. Olson R. 1989, *The Emergence of Kurdish Nationalism*, p. 125.

12. Ibid., Chapter 2.

13. Ibid., pp. 158–9.

14. Foreign Office (FO) 424 265, No. 15, enclosure.

15. Zürcher E. J. 1984, *The Unionist Factor*, pp. 146–56; FO 424 265, No. 15, enclosure and No. 16, enclosure.

16. Deny J. 1927, 'Les Souvenirs du Gazi Moustafa Kemal Pacha', *Revue des Etudes Islamiques*, Vol. 1; Zürcher E. J. 1984, *The Unionist Factor*, p. 162; Mustafa Kemal 1929, *Speech*.

17. FO 424 267, No. 47.
18. Frey F. W. 1965, *The Turkish Political Elite*, p. 338.
19. Karpat K. H. 1959, *Turkey's Politics: The Transition to a Multi Party System*. Princeton University Press, pp. 64–7; Lewis B. 1961, *The Emergence of Modern Turkey*. Oxford University Press, pp. 274–5; FO 424 274, No. 18.
20. Kinross 1964, *Atatürk: The Rebirth of a Nation*. Weidenfeld and Nicolson, p. 454.
21. FO 424 274, No. 13.

Chapter 10

THE CLOSING YEARS

CONTINUED COMMITMENT TO REFORM

In the remaining years of his life Mustafa Kemal's commitment to the modernisation, westernisation and reform of Turkey remained undiminished. Travelling to every corner of the land, he continued energetically to promote the cause: making speeches, designed to spread the message, attending congresses and seminars convened to promote social and economic advancement, inspecting state-run industries and model farms, and visiting schools and colleges to check on the progress of educational reform. In Ankara, where German town-planners were employed to plan development, government buildings were erected, tree-lined boulevards and squares dominated by statues of the nation's leader constructed and marshes cleared to make way for parks; while around the city trees were planted, in the expectation that the area might once again become forested, as it is said to have been in the days of Tamhurlain. At the same time a number of prestigious cultural institutions, including an opera house and a conservatory, directed by Paul Hindemith, were opened. Elsewhere, in Anatolia, dams were constructed and roads and railways, designed as much for military as for civilian use, were built. In Istanbul, to which Mustafa Kemal returned in 1927, (after an absence of eight years) a programme of public works was initiated, designed to improve the infrastructure of the city. Finally, in order to speed up the process of modernisation, young and enthusiastic supporters of reform, such as Reşid Galib, the director of the *Halkevi* (Peope's House) movement, were appointed to high office, and foreign experts, including Jews such as Oscar Weigart (the labour law specialist, who had fled from Hitler's Germany) recruited.[1]

Proposals regarding such projects, initiated for the most part by Mustafa Kemal himself, were almost invariably considered for the first time at meetings of an inner Cabinet of senior politicians, party officials, technical experts and others, held around the dinner table of the presidential palace in Çankaya. Only when they had been thoroughly thrashed out there were they passed to the executive committee of the Republican People's Party for further consideration, and to the Cabinet and national assembly for formal approval. Membership of this inner group became, therefore, as Sir George Clerk (the British ambassador) remarked, a necessary precondition for the exercise of power and influence in the republic.[2] Not that senior Turkish politicians were invariably keen to attend such gatherings, for the hours of entertainment were long and the quantities of alcohol consumed prodigious. Ismet Inönü, a respectable married man, for one was loath to participate.

The dinner parties held by Mustafa Kemal around the 'president's table' in the presidential palace at Çankaya rapidly became famous in Turkey. In the early stages of the feast (frequently presided over not only by Mustafa Kemal but also by Afet, his adopted daughter and surrogate wife) conversation, invariably directed by the president, would usually concern one or other of the principal issues of the day, such as women's rights or the history of the Turkish people. Should a point in the argument require further elaboration, then Mustafa Kemal might make use of a blackboard and easel (supplied with chalk and duster) parked in the corner of the room, for he loved nothing better than to assume the persona of a teacher or pedagogue conducting a class or seminar. On occasion a guest might even be invited to submit an essay, in order that it might be discussed at a future meeting. Alternatively, should inspiration fail, Mustafa Kemal might pluck a thesis out of the air, and call on his guests to dispute it, in order that, having exercised his superior wit and intelligence in a display of intellectual pyrotechnics, he might eventually defeat his opponents in argument as he had once defeated his enemies in war. In such debates Mustafa Kemal would invariably out-talk and out-drink his companions, for as Yakup Kadri Karaosmanoğlu once remarked, his energy was inexhaustible: the depths of his psyche were 'turbulent with typhoons, storms and silent revolutions'.[3] Thereafter, following the departure of the less stentorian of the guests, Mustafa Kemal and his cronies might well engage in what the psychologists are wont to refer to as regressive behaviour: playing practical jokes (but never at Mustafa Kemal's expense), boasting of sexual prowess and singing the Macedonian songs of his childhood. On such occasions, noted Turkish singers and poets, guests for the evening, might be invited to perform. Not all obliged. Nazim Hikmet, a young Communist poet, is said on one occasion to have replied: 'I am not a cabaret singer.'[4] In the morning, following an all-night session, Mustafa Kemal and one or other of his friends might well change into riding gear and ride out to hunt rabbits in the countryside aroung the capital.

. . .

DEFENCE AND SECURITY

Mustafa Kemal's commitment to the defence and security of the republic remained likewise undiminished in these years. Spending on defence was maintained at some 36 per cent of the annual budget; careful attention was given to the training and modernisation of the armed forces; and secret preparations were made for a possible remilitarisation of the Straits. (This was deemed essential if, in the event of a European war, Turkey were to secure control of the area.) To this end roads were constructed and mines stored within the zone, and heavy guns and ack-ack batteries, mounted on trailers (pulled in some cases by tractors), stationed without.[5] Following the conclusion of the Montreux Convention, which permitted remilitarisation, Vickers, the British arms firm, was employed to reconstruct the defences. At the same time, in order to secure stability in the area approximate to Turkey's eastern and western borders, treaties of friendship and neutrality were either signed or renewed with Greece, Yugoslavia, Hungary, Bulgaria and the Soviet Union; and in 1934 a Balkan Pact, aimed at resisting Bulgarian and Italian expansion in the area, was concluded by Turkey, Greece, Romania and Yugoslavia. Finally, in 1937 the so-called Saadabad Pact was concluded by Turkey, Iraq, Iran and Afghanistan, committing the signatories to early consultation, in the event of an act of aggression occurring in the area, and to the prevention of subversion in their respective countries.[6]

During these years there were two possible developments that Mustafa Kemal feared most. The first was that Benito Mussolini, the Italian dictator, might attempt to realise his dreams of imperial expansion in the eastern Mediterranean and the Aegean. The second concerning Germany, was that Hitler might launch a war against the Soviet Union. In all probability this would involve not only the other great powers but also Turkey and its neighbours in the Balkans. In such a war one or other of the great powers might seek to secure control of the Straits, the sea line of communication joining the Mediterranean with the Black Sea, while the Germans and their allies might seek to extend the area of conflict to the Caucasus and the Middle East, much as they had done in the First World War. Moreover, in the event of their securing victory in the war, the Germans might seek to impose a German hegemony on the Near and Middle East, while in the event of their defeat the Russians might seek to do the same. For Mustafa Kemal, therefore, the frequently reiterated slogan 'Peace at home and peace abroad' was no idle catchword. On the contrary, in his view, it defined the essential precondition for the survival of his country as a free and independent nation–state.

Mustafa Kemal's opinion of Mussolini was less than flattering. In his view *Il Duce* was a mere caricature of a soldier, strutting about in a fancy uniform, more suited to becoming a minister of public works than the leader of a nation. One day, he predicted, he would be hanged by his own people. Stalin he respected for his profound grasp of reality and for his political acumen; though he remained sceptical regarding the effectiveness of many of his policies. He alone of the dictators, he believed, would be remembered in a hundred years time. As for Hitler, he is said to have referred to him on one occasion as a tin–pedlar, and to have expressed concern regarding the madness of his thoughts, as outlined in *Mein Kampf*.[7]

The eccentric methods occasionally employed by Mustafa Kemal in communicating his thoughts regarding the international situation to the representatives of the powers are described by Sir George Clerk (the British ambassador), in a

despatch dated 2 November 1932, concerning a dinner given
to the heads of missions at the Ankara Palace Hotel:

> The *Ghazi* arrived almost to time, but dinner was
> delayed while he discussed the events of the day with
> the two senior Turkish generals and M. de Chambrun
> and myself over several rounds of indifferent cocktails.
> In fact, the President was already fully primed before
> we sat down to dinner, and, as the accident of placing
> put me next but one to his Excellency, I observed
> with dismay that the process was being continued.
> As a rule on these occasions the President observes
> long periods of silence broken by intervals of more or
> less formal conversation with those in his immediate
> neighbourhood. This time he began to talk from the
> moment he sat down, eating nothing, smoking endless
> cigarettes, and drinking raki steadily. He began by
> saying to me, pointing to the Soviet Ambassador, who
> was on the opposite side of the table, that Comrade
> Suritz was a real and sincere friend of his and his
> oldest friend amongst the foreigners here, but that
> he had one other friend whom he put in the same
> class, namely myself. He liked the others well enough,
> but we two were in a special category. As there was
> the usual hush that occurs whenever the *Ghazi* speaks,
> everyone heard his words, which no doubt made their
> impression on my colleagues, though those of them
> who understand his Excellency will have realised, as
> I do, that this was his forcible way of saying that the
> policy of His Majesty's Government towards Turkey
> since the Mosul Treaty had convinced him of our
> sincerity.
>
> The *Ghazi* then turned to his right, where the rest
> of the Ambassadors were seated, and addressed each
> of them in turn. He was very cordial in his references
> to France and to M. de Chambrun's work which
> had culminated in the agreement that had just been
> concluded. He congratulated the Polish Ambassador
> on the regeneration of Poland, which was now once
> again a great country ready to play a worthy part in
> the progress of the world. He thanked the American
> Ambassador for his numerous public references in

glorification of Turkey, added [*sic*], with a touch of irony, that Mr. Sherrill, who has just been delivering a series of lectures on the *Ghazi* in America, was, even more than American Ambassador in Turkey, the Turkish Ambassador in the United States, and asked him to make a speech in reply. Greatly to the surprise of his colleagues, Mr. Sherrill refrained.

It then came to the turn of the new Italian Ambassador, who was making his first acquaintance with a Turkish public occasion. The *Ghazi* asked him point-blank what were his impressions of Turkey. M. Lojacono seized the opportunity to emphasise the particular intimacy of Turkey and Italy by saying that the great pleasure which he felt on coming here was enhanced by the natural and mutual attraction between two young nations, and he was considerably taken aback when the *Ghazi*, fresh from proving the antiquity of the Turkish race and the Turkish nationality of Adam, pulled him up short and observed that no one coming from Rome should dare to speak of Italy as young, while as for Turkey, it was as old as humanity. The *Ghazi* then alluded to the recent speech of M. Mussolini at Turin, and said that no doubt the representatives of England, France, Germany and Italy had been pleased at the Duce's assertion that if these four Powers collaborated they could ensure the peace and prosperity of Europe and the world. But he, the *Ghazi* was not pleased.

I tell you that he is wrong. The future of my country of 14 millions cannot be influenced or settled at the ruling or by the co-operation of any four Great Powers, nor will it be. Only the co-operation of *all* the Powers can restore peace to the world, and I, who want peace, and not war, wish this method to be followed. Let all combine to assure peace and fraternity.[8]

In the pursuit of his foreign policy objectives Mustafa Kemal never failed to make good use of the numerous visits paid by foreign dignitaries and heads of state to his country in the late 1920s and early 1930s. Visits by Amanullah Khan (the ruler of Afghanistan) in 1928 and by Riza Khan (the Shah of Iran) in 1934 were carefully managed to enhance Turkey's image in the east. Amanullah Khan, a keen horseman, was entertained at the races, and at a great banquet, held in his honour, at the Ankara Palace Hotel. Riza Khan, a straight-laced man with a limited capacity for enjoyment, was taken on a lengthy tour of the battlefields and forts of western Anatolia and the Dardanelles, military installations and industrial sites, carefully selected to show the progress made by Turkish industry. Moreover, in Ankara he was invited to a performance of a new Turkish opera entitled *Özsoy*, composed in his honour, and in Istanbul to a gala Eastern Night, featuring naked belly dancers. Visits by King Alexander of Yugoslavia in 1933 and King Carol of Romania in 1938, shortly before Mustafa Kemal's death, were likewise carefully managed to improve Turkey's image in the Balkans. In Alexander's honour, a banquet featuring the finest French cuisine was held in the Dolmabahçe Palace, while Carol (a keen sailor) was entertained by Mustafa Kemal on board his yacht, the *Ertoğrul*. Finally, relations with Britain were substantially improved by a visit to Istanbul in 1936 by Edward VIII and the American divorcee Wallis Simpson. On that occasion Edward and Mrs Simpson were entertained by a Venetian Night on the Bosphorus and a regatta on the Sea of Marmara. Observing the king's devotion to Mrs Simpson, it is said that Mustafa Kemal predicted that in due course it would cost him his throne.[9]

. . .

AN ECCENTRIC LIFESTYLE

Despite the increasingly narrow constraints imposed on his activities by ill-health in these years, Mustafa Kemal proved unwilling to alter the somewhat eccentric way of life he had fashioned for himself. Frequently rising between 2–4 p.m., he would first partake of a cup of strong Turkish coffee. Then after shaving, bathing and enjoying a body massage, he would take breakfast, usually a single slice of white Italian bread, accompanied by a glass of *ayran* (yoghurt mixed with water). In the afternoon, no longer required to engage himself in the daily business of government (this was left for the most part to Ismet Inönü and his colleagues) he might ride out to inspect the model farm he had set up near Ankara, or read some such book as H. G. Wells' *Outline of History* – a favourite work. Only in the evening, at dinner, did he eat anything substantial, and then not always very much, preferring roasted chickpeas, olives and cream cheese to the more sumptuous dishes occasionally provided by the kitchen staff. After dinner, frequently the principal event of the day, he and his friends might spend the night playing poker, a favourite pastime, at the Anatolia Club, joined on occasion by Knox Helm (a British diplomat). Whilst resident in Istanbul he might go sailing on the *Ertoğrul*, or later on the *Savarona* (a yacht he purchased from an American heiress); or visit one of the gambling casinos on the Prince's islands, frequently returning to the Dolmabahçe Palace at four or five in the morning. Increasingly, however, as his health declined, he was to find himself confined, like a superannuated sultan, in the precincts of the presidential palace in Çankaya or the Dolmabahçe Palace in Istanbul, irritable, bored and frustrated. 'I am living here like a prisoner', he is reported to have said to an official in the presidential palace on one occasion. 'During the day time I am almost always alone. Everyone else is at work. Everyone has his job, but most days I have nothing to keep me occupied even for an hour.'[10]

Deprived of the emotional comforts of family life, in the later years of his life Mustafa Kemal sought solace in the surrogate family of adopted daughters he had created for himself, accepting responsibility for their upbringing, education and marriage. Afet, who became not only his surrogate wife but also his housekeeper, secretary and companion, he had educated in Europe and trained as a historian. Sabiha, an orphan, adopted at the age of twelve, he had educated at the American College in Istanbul and trained to become Turkey's first woman pilot. Others he had educated in leading schools and colleges in Turkey and Europe, and married off to army officers, diplomats and other suitable candidates, although few of the marriages proved either long-lasting or successful. Not that Mustafa Kemal's surrogate family of adopted daughters provided the only outlet for his paternal instincts. Occasionally he would visit friends, and take an interest in the well-being of their children; and in the later years of his life, he developed an affectionate relationship with a little girl, Ülkü, the daughter of a maid in the palace, previously employed in his mother's household, with whom it is said he would spend hours playing, a slave to her every command.

. . .

LAST DAYS

In January 1938 Mustafa Kemal, whilst attending a spa at Yalova hot springs, asked Dr Nihat Reşat Belger, the resident physician there, to examine him. The disease diagnosed, cirrhosis of the liver – the consequence of a lifetime of heavy drinking – can have come as no surprise, for in recent years he had suffered from many of its symptoms, including itching, nose bleeds and a yellowing of the skin, accompanied by extreme nervous tension and bouts of depression. Thereafter, the decline was rapid. In March, following a night spent dancing *zeybek* folk dances at a ball held at the Çelik Palace Hotel in Bursa, he collapsed with pneumonia. In June, following a tour of military bases in southern Turkey (undertaken against the advice of his doctors, in order to put pressure on the French with whom he was at the time in dispute over the Hatay question), he returned to Istanbul totally exhausted and hardly able to stand, his abdomen swollen like a balloon. There he remained for some weeks, resting on board his yacht, the *Savarona*, until the heat of the sun obliged him to seek refuge in a bedroom in the Dolmabahçe Palace. Refusing to allow the use of a stretcher for the move, he was carried into the palace on an armchair, walking the final few steps to his room. On 26 September, his abdomen still swollen like a balloon, despite frequent tapping, and his body covered with vascular lesions, he fell into a coma, lasting forty-eight hours. On 9 November he fell into a second coma; and on 10 November, attended by Afet, Sabiha, and Rukiye (another adopted daughter), he died.[11]

In the closing stages of his life Mustafa Kemal made several attempts to re-establish relations with the former leaders of the national struggle, Ali Faut, Rauf, Refet and Kiazim Karabekir. Only with Ali Faut was he successful. Though supposedly reconciled with Refet and Kiazim Karabekir, relations were never re-established; while attempts to re-establish relations with Rauf failed completely. Nor were relations with Ismet Inönü, his most loyal henchman and amanuensis, of the friendliest. In 1937, following a row, in the course of which Ismet is said to have accused the president of drunkenness, Mustafa Kemal had him replaced as prime minister by Celâl Bayar, a man more in sympathy with his views on foreign policy and economic reform. Nevertheless, it was Ismet Inönü who, following Mustafa Kemal's demise, was to secure the succession. On 11 November, as a result of a prearranged plan agreed by Fevzi Çakmak, the chief of the general staff, Celâl Bayar, the new prime minister, and others, he was elected president.

In a will (signed on 5 September) Mustafa Kemal left the bulk of his estate to his sister, Makbule; and to his adopted daughters he left specific amounts of money. Surprisingly, he also left money to pay for the education of Ismet Inönü's children, possibly because he believed (erroneously) that his old friend had died. The remainder of his estate he left to the Turkish Historical Society and the Turkish Language Association. Following his death his body was embalmed and laid out in state in the throne room of the Dolmabahçe Palace for nine days, before being transferred to Ankara, where it was again laid out before the Grand National Assembly building. It was then placed in a temporary grave site in the Ethnography Museum. Only in 1953 did it find a permanent resting place in the sepulchre of a special memorial complex erected on a hill overlooking Ankara, the capital of the republic.

. . .

NOTES AND REFERENCES

1. Volkan V., Itzkowitz N. 1984, *The Immortal Atatürk*. University of Chicago Press, Chapter 26; Lewis B. 1961, *The Emergence of Modern Turkey*. Oxford University Press, pp. 282–7.
2. Foreign Office (FO) 424 266, No.45.
3. Volkan V., Itzkowitz N. 1984, *The Immortal Atatürk*, p. 317.
4. Kinross 1964, *Atatürk: The Rebirth of a Nation*. Weidenfeld and Nicolson, p. 470.
5. Macfie A. L. 1993, *The Straits Question*. Institute for Balkan Studies, p. 213.
6. Kinross 1964, *Atatürk*, Chapter 56.
7. Volkan V., Itzkowitz N. 1984, *The Immortal Atatürk*, pp. 321–2.

8. FO 424 277, No. 28.
9. Volkan V., Itzkowitz N. 1984, *The Immortal Atatürk*, pp. 322–5
10. Ibid., p. 333.
11. Ibid., Chapter 29.

CONLUSION

It is evident that Mustafa Kemal Atatürk was a man totally committed to the acquisition and use of power. In his early years, within the narrow confines of family and school, he displayed an inclination to assert control. Later, in the army (the archetypal power structure of the Ottoman empire) he found an adequate outlet for the exercise of his talent, sufficient despite numerous setbacks, to secure for him first rapid promotion, and then in the closing years of the First World War the prospect of a senior appointment in the government; though in the end his hopes in this direction were frustrated. Only following his despatch to Anatolia as Inspector of the Third Army did he secure a position of authority sufficient for him to influence the course of events; although some historians have concluded that the part he played in the Gallipoli campaign proved decisive in determining the outcome. This power he then used, with great skill and determination, to create a national movement, with well-defined aims, capable of uniting the national forces for the most part already in place and inspiring further resistance to the forces of the occupying powers and their surrogates; though his achievements in the early stages of the movement have been somewhat exaggerated.

Following the conclusion of the Congress of Sivas, which he and his colleagues had convened, Mustafa Kemal turned his attention at once to the problem of securing the convening of a new chamber of deputies in Istanbul, capable of persuading the Sultan to appoint a new government, more sympathetic to the nationalist cause. In this he proved remarkably successful, but in the weeks following the opening of the new chamber he found himself, to his chagrin, isolated in the interior, unable to influence effectively the course of events in the capital. Indeed, it is apparent that had the Allies, alarmed by recent developments and the weakness of their position, not decided to intervene, occupying Istanbul, closing down the chamber of deputies and arresting many of its members, he might well have seen his new-found career as leader of the national movement extinguished. As it was, the Allied intervention fundamentally transformed his position. Ankara, the seat of the representative committee of the Association for the Defence of the Rights of Anatolia and Rumelia (which he had set up in the interior), became the focal point of a newly-invigorated national resistance movement. As a result of this, Mustafa Kemal was enabled in the following weeks to secure not only his election as president of the Grand National Assembly (convened following the closure of the Istanbul chamber in Ankara) but also effective control, as president of the Council of Ministers, of the provisional government established there; and in the period of the war against the Greeks, which followed, his appointment as Commander-in-Chief of the national forces. Victory over the Greeks, first at Sakarya and then in the final battle, which led to the expulsion of the Greeks from Anatolia, completed the panoply of power he had assembled. Indeed, such was his power, that he was able in the weeks preceding the Conference of Lausanne to secure the abolition first of the Sultanate and then shortly after of the Caliphate, and the creation of a republic – constitutional changes designed in part at least further to enhance his own position. Moreover, in the following decade or so, he was enabled to implement a substantial series of reforms, designed to secure the secularisation of the Turkish state. Not that these revolutionary changes implied any fundamental change in the social structure of the community. As W. F. Weiker (1981, p. 21) has pointed out, in the new republic some 93 per cent of the staff officers of the Ottoman army and 85 per cent of the civil servants remained in place, supported as hitherto by a population of small peasant farmers.

Of the numerous contributions made by Mustafa Kemal to the success of the national movement, the defining of its aims and objectives, and the sustaining of these throughout the long years of struggle, were perhaps the greatest. In defining the aims and objectives of the movement Mustafa Kemal displayed a keen understanding of the problems facing the Turkish-speaking Muslim peoples of the empire, and a clear-sighted view of how these problems might be resolved. In the pursuit of his aims he displayed an extraordinary pertinacity, never for a moment bending before the pressure of events; though with regard to the question of the Straits and Mosul (both issues of substantial significance to the British) he was obliged to compromise. So far as the methods adopted to achieve these objectives were concerned, however, he showed no such consistency. On the contrary, he displayed throughout (as he himself later confessed) an extraordinary deviousness, allying with the reactionaries to defeat the Allies and their surrogates, the radicals and revolutionaries to defeat the Sultanate and the Army of the Caliphate, the reactionaries and liberal constitutionalists to defeat the revolutionaries, and finally the modernists to defeat the reactionaries.

With such an extraordinary record it is not surprising that biographers and historians have tended to laud Mustafa Kemal's achievements. Exaggerated accounts, however, suggesting that he alone conceived the idea of setting up a national resistance movement in Anatolia, organised the national forces opposing the Greeks, and foresaw from the beginning the future course of events (including the abolition of the Sultanate and the Caliphate, and the creation of a republic), must be seriously questioned. What appears to have happened in what remained of the Ottoman Empire, in the months immediately following the end of the First World War, is that, far from giving up the struggle, elements within the Ottoman élite (in particular the army, the bureaucracy and the intelligence services, mainly CUP – the precise identity of the elements concerned, and the institutions to which they belonged, is not of any great importance, for they were all interconnected), following a period of intense political debate, concluded that it was necessary to organise a movement of national resistance in Anatolia. This movement of resistance was designed to strengthen the hand of the Ottoman Government in its negotiations with the victorious Entente powers and oblige the Sultan to implement the articles of the constitution and convene a new chamber of deputies, capable of expressing the national will. To this end, in May 1919, Mustafa Kemal was despatched to Anatolia, as Inspector of the Third Army, to organise the movement and coordinate the national forces (for the most part already in place). These tasks Mustafa Kemal quickly accomplished. However, it would seem that he went somewhat further than his mentors had expected, not only going public in a manner which many believed would endanger the enterprise, but also seizing the opportunity to build up a body of support for himself in the army and the Defence of Rights Associations, sufficient for him in due course to assert his own leadership of the movement, particularly in the period following the Allied occupation of Istanbul; and ultimately, following victory in Anatolia, to secure the abolition of the Sultanate and the Caliphate, and the creation of a republic.

That Mustafa Kemal foresaw from the very beginning that the national struggle would end in the abolition of the Sultanate and Caliphate may be doubted; though it is likely that certain possibilities were from time to time discussed in private conversation. What eventually obliged him to confront seriously the question of the future of the Sultanate, it may be supposed, was the despatch by the Allies of invitations to both the Istanbul Government and the Ankara regime to send delegations to attend the London Conference of February 1921 – invitations which necessitated a response to the problems created by the existence of parallel regimes. Realising the extent of the power he had accumulated, he may well have then concluded that at some future point he might successfully attempt the abolition of the Sultanate and Caliphate.

In the context of this scenario, as Zürcher (1984, p. 118–19) has pointed out, much of the opposition to Mustafa Kemal, organised by the former leaders of the CUP, the Second Group and the Progressive Republican Party, in the national assembly and elsewhere, becomes comprehensible. In the eyes of these his opponents Mustafa Kemal had not only hijacked the leadership of the national movement in the interior, but he had also used the position of power he had acquired to build up a loyal following in the army and the assembly – a following sufficient for him to secure in due course the abolition of the Sultanate and the Caliphate, and the creation of the republic. Also explicable is the ruthlessness with which Mustafa Kemal responded to the assassination attempt of 1926, for it may be supposed that he was then seeking not only to suppress discontented elements, opposed to the policies he was pursuing, but also those elements, within the Ottoman élite, including the leadership of the CUP, *Karakol* and the army, whose power and prestige he had pre-empted, following his despatch to Anatolia.

A survey of Mustafa Kemal's early life and career reveals surprisingly little evidence to support the contention that he was from the beginning a fervent nationalist, though he did frequently emphasise the contribution made by the Turkish-speaking peoples of Anatolia to the defence of the empire. On the contrary, it would appear that until the spring of 1919 at least, he remained a loyal member of the Ottoman élite, fully committed to the defence of the empire. His later adoption of the ideology of nationalism would appear, therefore, to have been pragmatic, dictated, in the period of the national struggle, largely by the course of events; and in the period of the republic by the need to create an ideological framework, capable of supporting the new state. The speed and intelligence with which he adapted his thinking to the new situation is perhaps the principal reason why he, rather than another, emerged as the leader of the national movement and the new state.

The programme of secular reform implemented by Mustafa Kemal, in the early years of the republic, appeared at the time radical in the extreme; and to some extent it was; but it is evident that the roots of the reforms implemented lay deeply embedded in the political, constitutional, intellectual, and cultural history of the Ottoman Empire. Already, in the periods of the *Tanzimat* and the First Constitution, Ottoman statesmen had laid the foundations of a secular system of government and law; and they had created a state controlled system of education, later expanded by the governments of the Young Turk period; while writers and intellectuals (many members of the newly-formed Ottoman Scientific Society and Academy of Learning) had experimented with language reform and new versions of the Ottoman script, some involving the use of the Latin alphabet. Later, in the reign of Abdul Hamid, others had proposed even more radical changes, including the closure of the dervish orders, the banning of the fez and the introduction of equal rights for women. Mustafa Kemal's reform programme must, therefore, be seen not as a radical innovation but as the culmination of almost a century of change, remarkable for its thoroughness and consistency. As Roderick Davison (1990, p. 259) has remarked, the reform programme introduced in the period of the republic should be seen not as a radical innovation but as the 'child of the Second Constitution Period (1908–1918), the step-child of the era of Abdulhamid II (1878–1908), and the grandchild of the era of reforms (1826–1878)'.

That Mustafa Kemal's achievements owed much to his own intelligence, far-sightedness, patience and determination is not in question, but it may be doubted whether he could have succeeded in so spectacular a manner had the victorious Entente powers not made a number of crucial mistakes in the post-war period. First among these was their failure quickly to conclude an acceptable peace treaty with the Ottoman Government in Istanbul. This delay provided the nationalists with ample time to organise a powerful movement of national resistance in Anatolia. Second was their despatch of a Greek expeditionary force to occupy Izmir, a move certain to provoke resistance in the interior. Third was their occupation of Istanbul, carried out on March 1920. Far from weakening the position of the nationalists in Anatolia this served merely to strengthen it. Fourth and last was their failure throughout, particularly in the period of the so-called Chanak affair, to remain united. This failure enabled the nationalists, in the later phases of the struggle, to take full advantage of the strong negotiating position their victories in Anatolia had won for them. At the same time it may be noted that the successes of the national movement, and by implication those of Mustafa Kemal himself, were considerably facilitated by the temporary removal of Russia (traditionally a major player in the region, capable of exercising power in the eastern provinces) from the scene, and also by the resulting collapse of Allied strategic interest in the area (the elaborate partition schemes, concocted by the Allies in the course of the First World War had been drawn up on the assumption that Russia should acquire possession of the eastern provinces) though the British and the French, in particular, retained a significant strategic interest in the area of the Straits. Other factors facilitating the successes of the nationalists include the fact that Britain and France, the principal powers concerned, were preoccupied with events elsewhere (in India, Egypt, Persia, Iraq, Syria, north Africa and Europe); the fact that Anatolia and eastern Thrace (the areas inhabited by a majority of Turkish-speaking Muslims) had remained unoccupied at the end of the First World War; and the fact that the Sultanate and the Caliphate had proved so ineffective in defending the interests of Turkish Muslims.

With regard to the implementation of the reform programme, it may be assumed that this too was facilitated by the circumstances prevailing at the time, in particular the collapse of support for the concept of an Islamic state that had occured in Anatolia and eastern Thrace as a result of the failures of the Sultanate and the Caliphate, the recent defection of the Sultan's Arab subjects and the willingness of Indian Muslims to fight on the side of the Entente powers in the First World War. Also significant was the total exhaustion of Turkish Muslims, brought on by more than a decade of continuous warfare. This exhaustion made it unlikely that the reactionaries would succeed in mounting an effective opposition to secular reform.

It has frequently been argued that Mustafa Kemal, though a dictator exercising absolute power, was not one shaped in the mould of a Hitler or a Stalin: that, as Bernard Lewis puts it (1961, p. 285), though an autocrat by personal and professional bias, dominating and imperious by temperament, he 'yet showed a respect for decency and legality, for human and political standards, that is in astonishing contrast with the behaviour of lesser and more pretentious men'. It was for this reason (it is argued) that his dictatorship, though oppressive, never developed into the type of regime characterised by the 'uneasy over-the-shoulder glance', the 'Terror of the door-bell', and the 'dark menace of the concentration camp'. Volkan and Itzkowitz (1984, p. 358) Likewise conclude that though sporadically aggressive, he yet retained a 'respect of boundaries and limits', inherited perhaps from his father (a customs official), which prevented him, from indulging in the types of destructive behaviour frequently identified with narcissistic leaders of his type. No doubt, there is much truth in these assertions. Throughout his career Mustafa Kemal used the power he had accumulated with considerable skill, exercising restraint where possible in order to avoid unnecessary conflict. The fact remains, however, that in the period of the Kurdish rebellion and the show trials, when he concluded that the opposition posed a serious threat, not only to the safety of the republic and the full implementation of the reform programme but also to the preservation of his own personal power and position, he showed little or no compunction in exterminating his enemies. It may be doubted, therefore, for how long his much vaunted respect for decency and legality would have survived other, more effective challenges to his regime.

The war of independence, in which Mustafa Kemal was engaged, has frequently been portrayed as a colonial struggle, the first of a series of uprisings by the oppressed peoples of Asia and Africa against the western imperial powers (Giritli I., in *Papers and Discussions 1984*, pp. 317–18); and this is to some extent true, for in the previous century or so the imperial powers had intervened extensively in the affairs of the Ottoman Empire; but it would be misleading so to conclude, for the Ottoman Turks were themselves an imperial race, accustomed to rule. Rather, the war of independence should be seen as the last stand of the Ottoman Turks, determined to preserve, and if need be reassert, their independence; while Mustafa Kemal, their leader, should by implication be seen not as the leader of an oppressed people striving to win their independence, but rather as a member of the Ottoman élite, determined to preserve the independence his people had since time immemorial enjoyed.

FURTHER READING

Useful bibliographical guides to the history of the Near and Middle East in the late nineteenth and early twentieth centuries can be found in Yapp M.E. 1987, *The Making of the Modern Near East* (Longman) and 1991, *The Near East since the First World War* (Longman). The best of the bibliographies specifically concerned with the life of Mustafa Kemal Atatürk is Bodurgil A. 1984, *Kemal Atatürk: A Centennial Bibliography*, Library of Congress, Washington. Zürcher E.J. 1984, *The Unionist Factor* (E.J. Brill, Leiden), also contains an excellent bibliography.

Collections of documents concerning the foreign policies of the great powers in the late nineteenth and early twentieth centuries abound. Among these, official publications such as *British Documents on the Origins of the War, 1898–1914, Documents on British Foreign Policy, 1919–39, Documents Diplomatiques Français, 1871–1914* and *Die grosse Politik der Europäischen Kabinette, 1871–1914*, are generally unmanageable, because of their length; though *Documents on the Origins of the War, 1898–1914*, Vol. X, and *Documents on British Foreign Policy*, first series, Vols 4, 7, 13, 15, 17, 18 may be consulted. Much more manageable, from the student's point of view, are Hurewitz J.C. 1956, *Diplomacy in the Near and Middle East*, (D. Van Nostrand, Princeton, New Jersey); Anderson M.S. 1970, *The Great Powers and the Near East* (Edward Arnold); and Macfie A.L. 1989, *The Eastern Question* (Longman). A useful collection of British foreign office documents concerning Atatürk is published in Şimşir B.N. 1973–84, *British Documents on Atatürk*, 4 Vols (Türk Tarih Kurumu, Ankara).

Of the general histories of the Eastern Question, Anderson

M.S. 1966, *The Eastern Question* (Macmillan), is by far the best, while A.L. Macfie 1989, *The Eastern Question* (Longman), provides a somewhat shorter account. Useful studies of particular aspects of the closing phases of the Eastern Question include Kent M. 1984, *The Great Powers and the End of the Ottoman Empire* (George Allen and Unwin); Sachar H.M. 1969, *The Emergence of the Middle East* (Knopf, New York); Howard H.N. 1931, *The Partition of Turkey* (University of Oklahoma Press); Howard H.N. 1974, *Turkey, the Straits and US Policy* (Johns Hopkins University Press); Trumpener U. 1968, *Germany and the Ottoman Empire* (Princeton University Press); Nicolson H. 1937, *Curzon: the Last Phase* (Constable); Cumming H.H. 1938, *Franco – British Rivalry in the Post–War Near East* (Oxford University Press); James R.R. 1965, *Gallipoli* (Batsford); Dakin D. 1972, *The Unification of Greece* (Ernest Benn); Dakin D. 1966, *The Greek Struggle in Macedonia* (Institute for Balkan Studies, Salonika); Smith M.L. 1973, *Ionian Vision: Greece in Asia Minor* (St. Martin's Press, New York); Öke M.K. 1988, *The Armenian Question* (Rustem and Brother); Sonyel S.R. 1975, *Turkish Diplomacy* (Sage); Macfie A.L. 1993, *The Straits Question* (Institute for Balkan Studies, Salonika); Helmreich P.C. 1974, *From Paris to Sèvres: The Partition of the Ottoman Empire at the Peace Conference of 1919–1920* (Ohio State University Press); and Evans L. 1965, *United States Policy and the Partition of Turkey* (Johns Hopkins University Press).

Wide-ranging histories of the Ottoman Empire and the republic of Turkey include Shaw S. and Shaw E.K. 1977, *History of the Ottoman Empire and Modern Turkey* (Cambridge University Press); and Lewis B. 1961, *The Emergence of Modern Turkey* (Oxford University Press). This last is particularly useful as it includes not only an account of the decline of the Ottoman Empire and the numerous reform movements instituted to reverse that decline but also a valuable set of essays on Community and Nation, State and Government, Religion and Culture, and Elite and Class.

Works regarding particular aspects of the history of the Ottoman Empire and the republic of Turkey in the late nineteenth and early twentieth centuries include Mardin Ş.A. 1962, *The Genesis of Young Ottoman Thought* (Princeton University Press); Heyd U. 1979, *The Foundation of Turkish Nationalism* (Hyperion Press, Westport, Connecticut); Kushner D. 1977,

The Rise of Turkish Nationalism (Frank Cass); Karpat K. 1975, 'The Memoirs of Nicolae Batzaria: the Young Turks and Nationalism', *International Journal of Middle Eastern Studies*, Vol. 6; Ramsaur E.E. 1970, *The Young Turks* (Princeton University Press); Ahmad F. 1969, *The Young Turks* (Oxford University Press); Kedourie E. 1971, 'Young Turks, Freemasons and Jews', *Middle Eastern Studies*, Vol. 7; Mango A. 1972, 'The Young Turks', *Middle Eastern Studies*, Vol. 8; Swanson V.R. 1970, 'The Military Rising in Istanbul, 1909', *Journal of Contemporary History*, Vol. 5; Selek S. 1966, *Anadolu Ihtilâli* (Burçak Yayınevi, Istanbul); Landau J.M. 1981, *Pan-Turkism* (C. Hurst); Berkes N. 1964, *The Development of Secularism in Turkey* (McGill University Press); Rustow D.A. 1958–59, 'The Army and the Founding of the Turkish Republic', *World Politics*, Vol. 11; Harris G.S. 1967, *The Origins of Communism in Turkey* (Stanford University Press); Tunçay M. 1967, *Türkiye'de Sol Akımlar* (Ankara University Press); Dyer G. 1972, 'The Turkish Armistice of 1918', *Middle Eastern Studies*, Vol. 8; Olson R. 1989, *The Emergence of Kurdish Nationalism and the Sheikh Said Rebellion* (University of Texas Press); Berberoğlu B. 1982, *Turkey in Crisis* (Zed Press); Keyder C. 1987, *The Missing Bourgeoisie* (Reed); Karpat K. 1959, *Turkey's Politics: The Transition to a Multi-Party System* (Princeton University Press); Frey F.W. 1965, *The Turkish Political Elite* (MIT Press, Cambridge, Mass.); and Weiker W.F. 1981, *The Modernisation of Turkey* (Holmes and Meier). Davison R.H. 1990, *Essays on Ottoman and Turkish History* (Saqi Books), contains, as the title suggests, a useful and perceptive set of essays on aspects of Ottoman and Turkish history. An article outlining the development of the Ottoman constitution is published, under *Düstur*, in *Encyclopaedia of Islam*, new edition.

Original material regarding the early life of Atatürk, by no means as plentiful as might be supposed, is contained in Yalman A.E. 1922, 'Büyük Millet Meclisi Reisi Başkumandan Mustafa Kemal Paşa ile bir mülâkat', *Vakit*, 10 January; Deny J. 1926, 'La Biographie de Moustafa Kemal', *Revue du Monde Musulman*, Vol. 63 and Deny J. 1927, 'Les Souvenirs du Gazi Moustafa Kemal Pacha', *Revue des Etudes Islamiques*, Vol. 1. In addition to these, Ayşe Afetinan (Atatürk's adopted daughter) has published a number of articles containing information provided by Atatürk, including 'Le Revolver

Sacré', and 'La Société "Patrie et Liberté"', *Belleten*, Vol. 1, 1937. For the history of the national movement, and the part played in it by Atatürk, the most important source remains *Nutuk* (Speech), 1927. An authorised English translation of this, not considered entirely reliable, has been published, under the title *A Speech Delivered by Ghazi Mustafa Kemal*, by Koehler (Leipzig, 1929). This version has been quoted here as it is the only one generally available. Atatürk's speeches and writings are published in Nimet Arsan et al. (eds) 1961–72, *Söylev ve Demeçler*, 5 Vols.

Of the numerous biographies of Atatürk published, Kinross 1964, *Atatürk: The Rebirth of a Nation* (Weidenfeld and Nicolson), is generally considered the best, thought like most biographies it emphasises the heroic element. The orthodox Kemalist version is best exemplified by *Ghazi Mustafa Kemal Atatürk, Founder of the Turkish Republic*, published in 1961 by the Turkish Ministry of Press, Broadcasting and Tourism. This is an English translation of an article, written by a commission of Turkish historians, first published in 1946. Other biographies published in English include Wortham H.E. 1930, *Mustafa Kemal* (Home Press), a short but lively account; Armstrong H. 1932, *The Grey Wolf* (Arthur Barker), one of the first to reveal details of Atatürk's scandalous private life; and Volkan V., Itzkowitz N. 1984, *The Immortal Atatürk* (University of Chicago Press), an interesting psychobiography, containing much original material. A German perspective may be obtained in Mikusch, Dagobert von 1931, *Gasi Mustafa Kemal* (P. List, Leipzig); Melzig H. 1937, *Kemal Atatürk* (Frankfurt); and Froembgen H. 1937, *Kemal Atatürk* (Stuttgart). A French perspective may be obtained in Benoist-Méchin J. 1954, *Le Loup et le Léopard* (Albin Michel, Paris), and Jevakhoff A. 1989, *Kemal Atatürk* (Tallandier, Paris); and a Spanish – Argentinian perspective in Villalta J.B. 1979, *Atatürk* (Türk Tarih Kurumu, Ankara). Of the Turkish biographies, Aydemir Ş.S. 1969, *Tek Adam* (Ankara), is generally considered the best. Orga I. 1958, *Pheonix Ascendant: The Rise of Modern Turkey* (R. Hale) a dramatic and colourful account, is not considered completely reliable.

Among the works associated with particular aspects of Atatürk's life and work, Zürcher E.J. 1984, *The Unionist Factor* (E.J. Brill, Leiden), must be considered outstanding.

This analyses the relationship between Mustafa Kemal and the CUP in both the Young Turk period and the period following the victory of the nationalists in the war of independence. Simon R. 1980, 'Beginnings of Leadership: Mustafa Kemal's First Visit to Libya', *Belleten*, Vol. 44 and Simon R. 1984, 'Prelude to Reforms: Mustafa Kemal in Libya', in Landau J.M. 1984, contain original material regarding Mustafa Kemal's visits to Libya. Jäschke G. has written numerous articles on aspects of Mustafa Kemal's career, published for the most part in *Welt des Islams* and *Belleten*. Among these, 1957–58, 'Beiträge zur Geschichte des Kampfes der Türkei um ihre Unabhängigkeit', *Welt des Islams*, new series, Vol. 5, and 1958, 'Auf dem Wege zur Türkischen Republik', *Welt des Islams*, new series, Vol. 5, are particularly useful. Goloğlu M. 1968, *Milli Mücadele Tarihi, Erzurum Kongresi* (Nüve Matbaasi, Ankara), and 1969, *Milli Mücadele Tarihi, Sivas Kongresi* (Başnur Matbaası, Ankara), contain much useful information on the part played by Mustafa Kemal in the Erzurum and Sivas Congresses. Dumont P. 1978, 'La Révolution Impossible', *Cahiers du Monde Russe et Soviétique*, Vol. 19, analyses aspects of the opposition posed to the nationalists in Anatolia in the period 1920–21; while Tachau F. 1962–63, 'The Search for National Identity among the Turks', *Welt des Islams*, new series, Vol. 8, provides interesting material on ideological developments in that period. Bayur H. 1966, 'Birinci Genel Savaştan Sonra Yapilan Bariş Antlaşmalarımız', *Belleten*, Vol. 30, is particularly useful on Turco–Russian relations. With regard to the reforms implemented by Atatürk, Landau J.M. 1984, *Atatürk and the Modernisation of Turkey* (Westview Press, Boulder, Colorado), is essential reading, as is Kazancigil A. and Ozbudun E. 1981, *Atatürk: Founder of a Modern State* (C. Hurst). A collection of papers discussed in an international symposium held in Ankara in May 1981 is published in *Papers and Discussions* (Türkiye Iş Bankasi) 1984. More recent studies include Gökay B. 1993, 'The Turkish Communist Party: the Fate of the Founders', *Middle Eastern Studies*, Vol. 29; and Deringil S. 1993, 'The Ottoman Origins of Kemalist Nationalism: Namik Kemal to Mustafa Kemal', *European History Quarterly*, Vol. 23.

Memoirs composed by Atatürk's contemporaries include Edib H. 1928, *The Turkish Ordeal* (John Murray); Ryan A.

1961, *The Last of the Dragomans* (Geoffrey Bles); Cebesoy A.F. 1953, *Milli Mücadele Hatıraları* (Istanbul); Yalman A.E. 1956, *Turkey in my Time* (University of Oklahoma Press); Ertürk H. 1964, *Iki Devrim Perde Arkası* (Pinar Yayınevi, Istanbul); Bayar, Celâl 1965, *Ben de Yazdim* (Istanbul); Karabekir K.K. 1960, *Istiklâl Harbımız* (Istanbul); and Inönü I. 1985, *Hatıraları* (Istanbul). Of these Halide Edib's *The Turkish Ordeal* is perhaps the most accessible and readable for the English–speaking student.

CHRONOLOGY

1839

3 November — Hatt-i Şerif of Gülhane inaugurates the period of reform in the Ottoman Empire known as the *Tanzimat*.

1853

October — Outbreak of the Crimean War.

1856

18 February — Hatt-i Humayun reaffirms principle of reform set out in the Hatt-i Şerif of Gülhane.

30 March — Treaty of Paris.

1875

October — Suspension of payment on the Ottoman Public Debt.

1876–78

Eastern Crisis.

1876

23 December — Proclamation of the First Ottoman Constitution.

1880–81

Mustafa Kemal Atatürk is born.

1881

December — Creation of a Council of the Ottoman Debt.

1883

German military mission to
Ottoman Empire.

1889

Foundation of Society of
Ottoman Union.

1893

Mustafa Kemal Atatürk enters
Military Secondary School at
Salonika, where he is given the
name Kemal.

1895

Enters Military High School at
Monastir.

1896
August

Society of Ottoman Union
attempts a *coup d'état*.

1897

War with Greece.

1898

State visit of Kaiser William II
to the Ottoman Empire.

1899
March

Mustafa Kemal enters War
College in Istanbul.

1902

Enters Staff College in
Istanbul.

1905
February

Posted to Fifth Army in
Damascus.

March–April

Participates in campaign
against Druze insurgents.
Joins Fatherland and Freedom
Society.

1906
February–March

Leaves Syria for Salonika.

| September | Foundation of Ottoman Freedom Society (later known as the Committee of Union and Progress) in Salonika. |

1907

| September | Transferred to Third Army in Macedonia. |

1908

July	Young Turk Revolution in Salonika.
24 July	Restoration of Ottoman Constitution.
5 October	Bulgaria proclaims independence.
7 October	Austria–Hungary annexes Bosnia and Herzegovina.
12 October	Crete votes for union with Greece. Mustafa Kemal sent to Tripolitania.

1909

| 13 April | Mutiny or counter-revolution in Istanbul. |
| April | Mustafa Kemal joins the Action Army sent to suppress the outbreak. |

1910

| | Takes part in operations in Albania. |

1911

| 5 October | Italy invades Tripolitania. Mustafa Kemal joins forces defending Tobruk and Derna. |

1912

| 8 October | Outbreak of First Balkan War. |

1913

| 23 January | *Coup d'état* in which CUP seize power. |

	Mustafa Kemal participates in campaigns against forces of Balkan powers.
30 June	Outbreak of Second Balkan War.
27 October	Appointed Military Attaché in Sofia.

1914

| July–August | Outbreak of First World War. |
| October–November | Ottoman Empire enters war on side of Central Powers. |

1915

2 February	Mustafa Kemal appointed to Command of Nineteenth Division.
19 February	First Allied assault on Dardanelles.
25 April	Allied landings at Ariburnu. Mustafa Kemal's forces immediately engaged.
March–May	Allied agreement promises Istanbul to Russia.
26 April	Treaty of London promises Italy a share in the partition of the Ottoman Empire.

1916

3 January	Sykes–Picot Agreement.
9 January	Allied forces evacuate Gallipoli peninsula.
14 January	Mustafa Kemal appointed Commander of the Sixteenth Army Corps.
May	Allied agreements promise parts of eastern Anatolia to Russia.
June	Arab revolt.
August	Mustafa Kemal recovers Bitlis and Muş.

1917

11 March	British forces capture Baghdad.
5 July	Mustafa Kemal appointed Commander of the Seventh Army Corps in Syria.
December	Visits Germany with Crown Prince Vahideddin.

1918

7 August	Reappointed Commander of the Seventh Army Corps.
September–October	Defends frontier north of Aleppo.
30 October	Armistice concluded at Mudros.
November	Allied occupation of Istanbul.
21 November	Dissolution of Parliament.

1919

18 January	Opening of Peace Conference at Versailles.
30 April	Mustafa Kemal appointed Inspector of Ninth Army, later renamed Third Army.
15 May	Greek expeditionary force occupies Izmir.
19 May	Mustafa Kemal lands at Samsun.
22 June	Amasya Declaration.
23 July–6 August	Congress of Erzurum.
4–13 September	Congress of Sivas.
4 October	Fall of Ottoman Government.
November–December	Election of a new parliament.
27 December	Representative Committee moves to Ankara.

1920

12 January	Parliament opens in Istanbul.
28 January	National Pact adopted.
9 February	Evacuation of French garrison from Maraş.
16 March	Allied occupation of Istanbul.

11 April	Dissolution of Ottoman Parliament.
23 April	Grand National Assembly convened in Ankara.
10 June	Treaty of Sèvres presented by Allies to Ottoman Government.
22 June–9 July	Greek army advances on western Anatolia.
10 August	Conclusion of Treaty of Sèvres.
September–October	Nationalist forces invade Armenia.
3 December	Treaty of Gümrü concluded.

1921

6–10 January	First Battle of Inönü.
20 January	Law of Fundamental Organisation passed.
23 February–12 March	London Conference.
16 March	Treaty of Moscow concluded.
23 March–1 April	Second Battle of Inönü.
July	Greeks capture Eskişehir.
5 August	Mustafa Kemal appointed Commander-in-Chief.
23 August–13 September	Battle of Sakarya.

1922

26 August–10 September	Expulsion of the Greek expeditionary force from western Anatolia.
September–October	Chanak affair.
11 October	Mudanya Armistice.
19 October	Resignation of Lloyd George and his government.
1 November	Abolition of Sultanate.
20 November	Opening of peace conference at Lausanne.

1923

29 January	Mustafa Kemal marries Latife in Izmir.
24 July	Treaty of Lausanne concluded.

9 August	Foundation of the People's Party.
11 August	Second Grand National Assembly.
2 October	Allied forces evacuate Istanbul.
9 October	Ankara proclaimed capital.
29 October	Turkish Republic proclaimed. Mustafa Kemal elected president.

1924

3 March	Abolition of Caliphate.
8 April	Abolition of religious courts.
17 November	Foundation of Progressive Republican Party.

1925

11 February–12 April	Revolt in Kurdistan.
4 March	Law for the Maintenance of Public Order.
3 June	Suppression of Progressive Republican Party.
5 August	Mustafa Kemal divorces Latife.
August–September	Abolition of the fez. Suppression of religious brotherhoods. Closure of sacred tombs.

1926

17 February	Adoption of new Civil Law code.
5 June	Mosul Agreement.
15 June–13 July	Plot against the life of Mustafa Kemal.
July–August	Trial and execution of ringleaders followed by trial and execution of CUP leaders and others.

1927

1 July	Mustafa Kemal revisits Istanbul.

15–20 October	Mustafa Kemal delivers great speech at Congress of Republican People's Party.
1928	
3 November	Introduction of Latin alphabet.
1930	
12 August	Foundation of Free Republican Party.
1932	
12 August	Turkey becomes a member of League of Nations.
1934	
9 January	First Five Year Plan for industrial development.
1936	
20 July	Montreux Convention concluded.
1938	
July–September	Franco-Turkish agreement regarding Hatay concluded.
10 November	Death of Kemal Atatürk.

MAPS

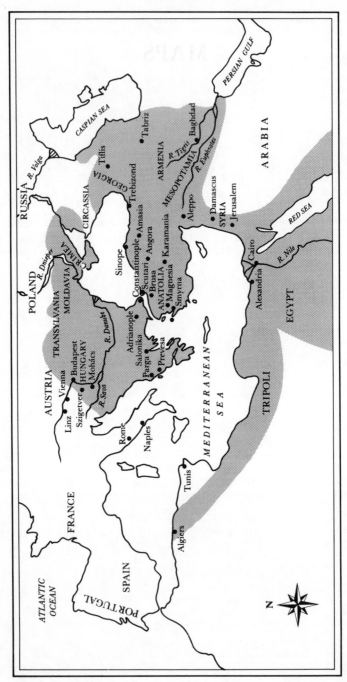

The Ottoman Empire under Suleiman

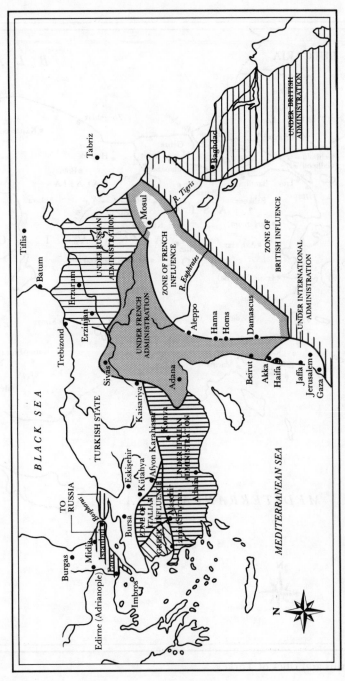

The partitioning of Turkey according to the secret agreements of 1915–17

Towns and cities of Turkey

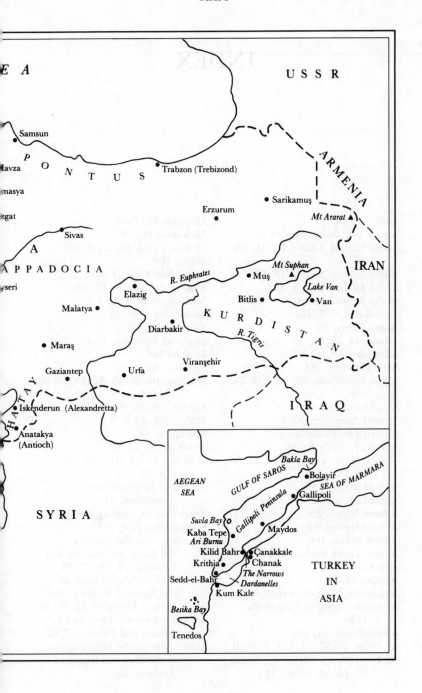

INDEX

212

INDEX